D1728389

Power IC Design

From the Ground up

Power IC Design

From the Ground up

5th Edition

By

Gabriel Alfonso Rincón-Mora

School of Electrical and Computer Engineering
Georgia Institute of Technology

www.Rincon-Mora.com

Discovering the universe through the art of design

Contents

Preface

I. Intended Audience

Integrated circuit (IC) design, system design, product, and market engineers, managers, and undergraduate and graduate students engaged and/or interested in expanding their knowledge on how to design, evaluate, specify, develop, and test power ICs.

II. Description and Objectives

This slide book introduces the demands of emerging high-performance power-management ICs and discusses up-to-date circuit-design techniques aimed at addressing them, especially within the context of portable microelectronics. The material starts with a top-down design perspective, much like in an industry setting, and discusses the system "*from the ground up*" (from basic analog IC concepts and voltage references to low-dropout regulators and switched-inductor supplies) with an educational mindset, rigorously surveying, analyzing, and evaluating basic concepts and the state of the art. The driving objective of the book is to enable the reader to model, analyze, and design power-conditioning ICs using bipolar and CMOS transistors. The material places emphasis on basic understanding and critical thinking, that is, on intuitive grasp of concepts, which is the foundation for innovative IC design.

G.A.R.M.

Shenzhen, China

Power IC Design

From the Ground up

Power IC Design

– From the Ground Up –

Gabriel Alfonso Rincón-Mora

Georgia Institute of Technology

www.Rincon-Mora.com

Chapters

1. Microelectronic Systems

2. Analog IC Design

3. Bias Currents

4. Voltage References

5. Linear-Regulator ICs

6. Linear-Regulator Systems

7. Switched-Inductor Supplies

8. Switched-Inductor Systems

Final Notes on Design

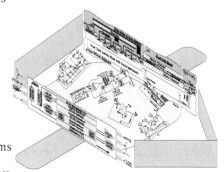

Chapter 1. Microelectronic Systems

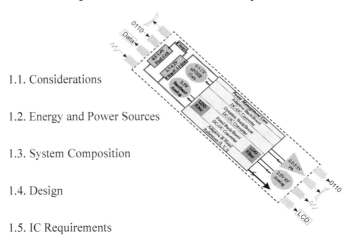

1.1. Considerations

1.2. Energy and Power Sources

1.3. System Composition

1.4. Design

1.5. IC Requirements

1.1. Emerging Markets

Applications: Bio-monitors, micro-sensors, pacemakers, cochlear processors,
10–200 µW

defibrillators, hearing aids, reconnaissance, micro-robots, remote meters,
Peak to 5–10 W   0.2–2 mW   1–10 mW

neural recorders/stimulators, retinal implants, and others.
1–100 mW   40–250 mW

Requirements: Useful, nonintrusive, and low cost.

Smart (e.g., low-power sensor, processor, transmitter)

Portable (i.e., small and compact)

Lightweight

Self-powered (i.e., includes power source)

Self-sustained (i.e., harnesses ambient energy)

Silicon microchip (i.e., on-chip, in-package,

and on-package integration)

Micro-sensor

Micro-robot

Bio-monitor

1.1. Technological Constraints

Portable and Nonintrusive	→ Small Footprint: 1 Microchip
Low Breakdown Voltages	→ Low Supply Voltages: 1–1.8 V
High Integration	→ Diverse Power Levels: nW's to W's
	→ Diverse Supply Voltages: 0.5–2 V
Low Filter Density	→ Low $C_{MAX}/\mu m^2 \leq 15$ fF/μm^2
	E.g.: 1 nF requires 260×260 μm^2
	→ $L_{MAX} \leq 40$–100 nH

Noise-Sensitive (analog) Blocks → Accurate and Fast Supplies:

$$\Delta v_{SUPPLY(DC-AC-TRAN)} \leq 10\text{–}100 \text{ mV}$$

High Silicon (wafer) Density → Digital VLSI (CMOS) and

Mixed-Signal (BiCMOS) ICs

1.1. Typical Power Profile

Load: Mixed signal → Steady and switching power components.

Typical state → Lightly loaded → Low P_{AVG}.

Highly functional   → Diverse i_{LOAD}–v_O profiles.

→ High P_{PEAK}.

Supply: Draw maximum input energy and power → Condition source.

Reduce losses → Manage on-demand modes with nA's.

P_{AVG} is low, P_{PEAK} is high, and low- and high-power efficiencies are both critical.

1.2. Energy and Power Sources

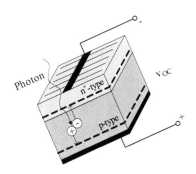

1.2. Energy and Power Sources

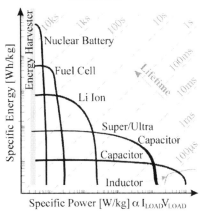

Harvester:	Very Low Power
	Virtually Infinite Energy
	Intermittent

Inductor:	High Power
	Very Low Energy
	Quasi Lossless
	Cumbersome
Capacitor:	High Power
	Very Low Energy
	Quasi Lossless
	Very Fast
Li Ion & Super Capacitor:	Moderate Power
	Moderate Energy
	Moderate Speed
Fuel Cell:	Low Power
	High Energy
	Slow
Nuclear Battery:	Very Low Power
	Very High Energy
	Unsafe and Costly

Li Ion: Low leakage with moderate cycle life. Super C: Long cycle life but high leakage.

1.2. Power-Assisted Energy Sources

Microsystems cannot afford to over-size: Energy-dense source for power.

Power-dense source for energy.

∴ Power-assist an energy-dense source and match source to load level.

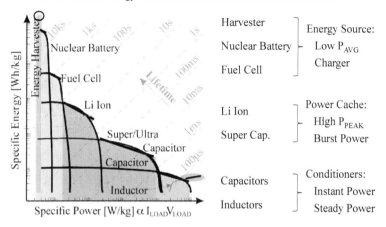

		Energy Source:
Harvester		
Nuclear Battery	}	Low P_{AVG}
Fuel Cell		Charger

		Power Cache:
Li Ion	}	High P_{PEAK}
Super Cap.		Burst Power

		Conditioners:
Capacitors	}	Instant Power
Inductors		Steady Power

Specific Power [W/kg] $\alpha\ I_{LOAD}V_{LOAD}$

1.2. Terminology

Battery: Energy-constrained source.

Primary: Non-rechargeable battery.

Secondary: Rechargeable battery.

Parameters: Capacity in mA.Hr → Energy-storage capacity.

Cycle Life → Number of recharge cycles possible.

Internal (Equivalent Series) Resistance R_{ESR}

→ Series voltage drop and power lost.

Self-Discharge → Leakage.

Size and Weight → Energy density and power density.

1.2. Energy Sources: Carbon Fuels

Fuel Cell: Electrochemical energy-conversion device (i.e., ion filter):

Carbon Fuel + Oxidant → Water + Carbon Byproduct + H⁺ + e⁻

Basic Advantage: 10× Li Ion's energy density.

Miniaturization: Eliminate fuel reformer.

∴ Direct-methanol (DM)

    proton-exchange membrane (PEM)

    Glucose battery

Challenges:

    Manage water and carbon byproducts.

    Low current levels (i.e., low power density).

    Slow to respond.

    Fuel leaks across filters and membranes (e.g., methanol crossover).

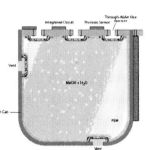

1.2. Energy Sources: Light, Temperature, and EM Radiation

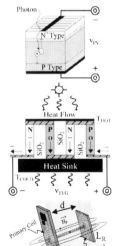

Photovoltaic Cell: Photons separate electron–hole pairs.	+ 15 mW/cm² for solar light. + SoC. − 5 µW/cm² for artificial light.
Thermoelectric Piles: Thermal gradient induces e⁻'s in N and h⁺'s in P to flow to cold plate.	+ MEMS compatible. − 200 µV/°K per pile pair. ∴ 10–200 mV with 3°–5°. − 5–30 µW/cm³ with 3°–5°.
Electromagnetic Transponder: Couples magnetic-flux energy from L to L.	+ mW/cm³ across mm's. − µW/cm³ across cm's. − Small coils capture little EM energy. − AC–DC conversion. − Rich Source.

1.2. Energy Sources: Motion

Vibrations and shocks are abundant and usually steady at 1–300 Hz.

Electromagnetic

Transducer:

Changes in magnetic flux

induce charge flow.

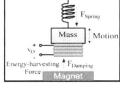

+ Simple structure.

− Low voltage.

− 1 μW/cm³.

− AC–DC conversion.

− Bulky magnet and coil.

Piezoelectric Transducer:

Mechanical stress

re-arranges/polarizes

ions to produce charge.

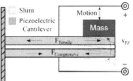

+ 200–300 μW/cm³.

+ Mature technology.

− AC–DC conversion.

− SoP and SiP.

Electrostatic Transducer:

Motion loses energy to

field across plates when

pulling the plates apart.

+ 50–100 μW/cm³.

+ MEMS compatible.

− Synchronization.

− C_{VAR} conditioning.

1.2. Power Sources: Rechargeable Batteries

Lead Acid: Bulky, low cycle life, but high power → Good for cars.

Alkaline: Low power density, low cycle life, but long shelf life.

→ Good for electronics that are used infrequently like flashlights.

Nickel Cadmium (NiCd): Contains toxic metals, suffers from

cyclic memory effects (non-recoverable crystalline formations that

induce higher self-discharge rates), but higher energy density.

Nickel–Metal Hydride (NiMH): Less memory effects, less toxic,

and even higher energy density, but poorer electronic performance.

Lithium Ion (Li Ion): No memory effect, not toxic, and better electronic

performance, but costly and sensitive chemistry (explosive).

Super/Ultra Capacitor: Long cycle life, but leaky.

1.2. Power Sources: Nickel-Based Batteries

Nickel-Based Chemistries:

Periodic discharge cycles mitigate

cyclic memory effects on

degraded discharge rates.

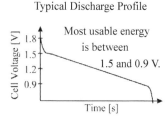

Typical Discharge Profile

Most usable energy

is between

1.5 and 0.9 V.

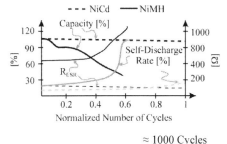

Nickel Cadmium:

Higher cycle life.

Lower R_{ESR}.

Lower self-discharge.

≈ 1000 Cycles

1.2. Power Sources: Li-Ion Batteries

Li Ions: Higher capacity, lower R_{ESR},

lower self-discharge, and

more consistent across cycle life.

Charge Sequence:

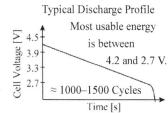

Typical Discharge Profile

Most usable energy

is between

4.2 and 2.7 V.

$\approx 1000-1500$ Cycles

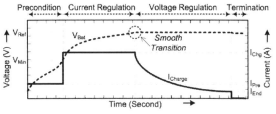

Precondition: With constant low trickle current.

Current Regulation: Charge with constant current.

Voltage Regulation: Regulate v_{BAT} so i_{CHG} drops as v_{BAT} nears target.

Termination: Stop when i_{CHG} reaches I_{MIN}.

1.3. System Composition

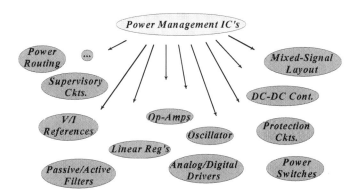

1.3. Complete Microelectronic System

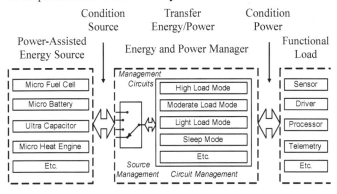

	Condition Source	Transfer Energy/Power	Condition Power	

Power-Assisted Energy Source   Energy and Power Manager   Functional Load

Energy Source: Switched-Inductor Charger–Supply

Harvester or Fuel Cell   Maximum Power-Point Tracker   Low P_{AVG}

Power Source: Fast Multiple-Output Supply   High P_{PEAK}

Li Ion or Super Capacitor   Fast Low-Voltage Starter

1.3. Typical Components

Bias Currents: Supply and process independent.

Voltage References: Temperature, supply, and process independent.

Power Supplies (i.e., Voltage Regulators):

Fast and temperature, supply, process, and load independent.

Difference between voltage references and regulators: Load.

Regulators *supply* heavy loads and references *bias* light loads.

Battery Chargers

Protection: Electrostatic discharges (ESD), thermal, over-current,

under-voltage lockout (UVLO), safe-operating area (SOA), etc.

1.3. Regulating Power Supplies

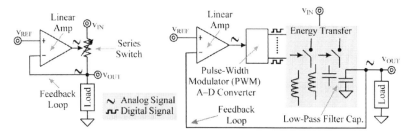

Linear: Modulates the conductance of a series switch

linearly and continuously to regulate v_{OUT} → Analog.

Switched: Energize and drain inductors or capacitors into a load

in alternate phases of a switching cycle to regulate v_{OUT}.

→ Switched feedback network incorporates analog and digital.

1.3. Regulating Power Supplies

Linear Regulators	Switched Regulators
Limited output range: $v_{OUT} < v_{IN}$	√ Flexible: $v_{OUT} \leq$ or $\geq v_{IN}$
√ Low cost: Less PCB and Si area	Expensive: More PCB and Si area
√ Low noise	Switching noise
√ Quick to respond	Slow to respond
Limited efficiency: $\eta_C \leq v_{OUT}/v_{IN}$	√ High efficiency: $\eta_C \approx 80\text{–}95\%$
Low-noise/-power applications	Boosting and high-efficiency systems

Check mark √ highlights features → Advantages.

1.3. Regulating Power Supplies

Point-of-Load (PoL) Regulation: Regulate at the load.

To shunt supply noise → Less noise.

To regulate v_{OUT} at the load → More accurate.

To accommodate specific load → Better performance.

Classify supplies according to voltage, power, accuracy, speed, etc.

High power and poor accuracy → Switched Inductor.

High power and good accuracy → Switched Inductor + Linear Regulator.

Low power and good accuracy → Linear Regulator.

Boost, low power, and poor accuracy → Switched Capacitor.

Example:

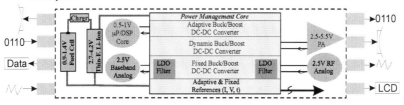

1.3. Sample Wireless Power-Supply System

Objectives: Draw, condition, and supply power to the loads.

Point-of-load (PoL)

  regulation for accuracy.

Multiple outputs for

  better PoL performance.

Dynamically adaptive

  for better efficiency.

Harvester-assisted for

  longer operational life.

One inductor

  for SiP/SoC integration.

Harvester-Assisted Li-Ion Power-Supply System

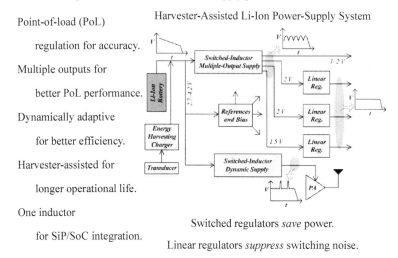

Switched regulators *save* power.

Linear regulators *suppress* switching noise.

1.4. Design

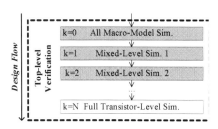

1.4. Design Flow

Top–Down Design/Down–Top Assembly

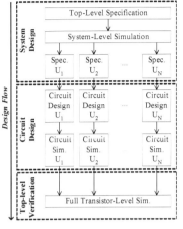

Fabricate IC

System Design:

Design architecture.

Verify (simulate) functionality.

Determine system/block specifications.

Integrated-Circuit Design:

Design architecture.

Verify with simulations.

Design physical layout.

Top-Level Assembly:

Assemble top-level circuit and layout.

Ensure (compare) circuit matches layout.

Verify (simulate) functionality.

Extract circuit from layout and simulate.

Tape-out Submission and Fabrication

* Iterate and Re-design (at every level)

1.4. Top-Level Simulations

Transistor-level simulations can be computationally intensive (and long) ∴

Start with behavioral-based simulation.

Then, substitute one block at a time.

Gradually build transistor-level

system by sequentially

substituting most-to-least

computationally intensive blocks.

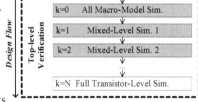

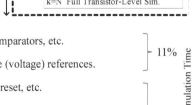

1ˢᵗ Analog/linear blocks: Op amps, comparators, etc.

2ⁿᵈ Analog/nonlinear blocks: Bi-stable (voltage) references.

3ʳᵈ Slow-switching blocks: Power-on-reset, etc.

4ᵗʰ At-speed digital gates: Drivers, etc.

5ᵗʰ At-speed/high transistor-count blocks: Oscillator (ramp generator).

11%

60%

Simulation Time

1.5. IC Requirements

Parameter	Specifications			Simulated Perf.			Meas. Perf.		Un
	Min.	Typ.	Max.	Min.	Typ.	Max.	Mean	Sigma	
Linear Regulator									
Vout (overall accuracy)	2.85	3	3.15	2.87		3.1	3.05	0.1	V
Line Regulation			10	3		7	10	2	m
Load Regulation			50			42	45	5	m
Short Ckt. Current				190		250	225	30	m
Reference									

1.5. Market Demand

Nonintrusive → Compact and battery powered.

On-chip, in-package, and on-package integration.

Tiny battery

Wide input-voltage range: E.g., 0.9–1.8 V or 2.7–4.2 V.

→ Low headroom (minimum supply) $v_{IN(MIN)}$

Limited energy and power

→ Low quiescent power: Low quiescent current i_Q.

→ Low conduction power: Low-resistance switches R_{SW}.

→ Low gate-drive power: Low switching frequency f_{SW}.

→ Duty-cycled operation

∴ Disable blocks: Short wake-up time t_{WAKE}.

Low leakage current i_{LEAK}.

Power modes: Adjust supply voltages.

1.5. Market Demand

Parameter	Specifications			Simulated Perf.			Meas. Perf.		Un
	Min.	Typ.	Max.	Min.	Typ.	Max.	Mean	Sigma	
Linear Regulator									
Vout (overall accuracy)	2.85	3	3.15	2.87		3.1	3.05	0.1	V
Line Regulation			10	3		7	10	2	m
Load Regulation			50			42	45	5	m
Short Ckt. Current				190		250	225	30	m
Reference									

High functionality

Multiple outputs

Wide-range power supplies: E.g., 0.5–4 V.

Wireless telemetry

Power-hungry power amplifier (PA)

→ Dynamic power supply ∴ High bandwidth f_{BW}.

Extreme power-performance modes: E.g., Idle–high performance.

Wide load dumps: E.g., From nA's to A's.

Fast load dumps: E.g., In ns's.

→ Fast power supplies ∴ High switching frequency f_{SW}.

Highly integrated

Noisy supplies: High power-supply rejection PSR.

Noisy ground: Design common-mode circuits.

High common-mode rejection ratio CMRR.

1.5. Designs

Noise-sensitive loads

Accurate power supplies: E.g., Within 1% to 2%.

Fast power supplies: E.g., Variation within 2% to 5%.

Reliable and low cost (for higher profit).

Simple circuit because fewer transistors

Occupy less silicon area → Higher yield: More chips per wafer.

∴ Exhibit less parasitic capacitance → Higher-frequency poles.

Incorporate fewer nodes.

∴ Introduce fewer poles   → Faster response.

→ Feedback loops are more stable.

I.e.: Highly functional: complex, fast, accurate, low cost: CMOS and few components, small: SoC/SiP/SoP, long life: low power, reliable: few transistors, etc.

Chapter 2. Analog IC Design

2.1. Two-Port Models

2.2. Frequency Response

2.3. Analog Circuits

2.4. Analog Building Blocks

2.5. Negative Feedback

2.6. Simulations

Norton Equivalent Thevenin Equivalent

2.1. Two-Port Models: Philosophy and Extraction

Purpose: Model input and/or output of a device or complicated circuit with simple two-component networks.

Philosophy: Avoid model redundancies, so use orthogonal components.

Extraction: In deriving a parameter, nullify the effects of the other.

Two-Port Models

Norton Equivalent Thevenin Equivalent

Norton Equivalent: Derive R_P when control signal $s_C = 0$.

Derive A_{NI} when $i_R = 0 \rightarrow v_N = 0$: Short circuit.

Thevenin Equivalent: Derive R_S when control signal $s_C = 0$.

Derive A_{TV} when $v_R = 0 \rightarrow i_R = 0$: Open circuit.

2.1. Two-Port Models: Examples

Sample Model   Popular Model

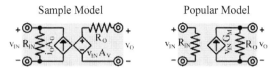

Sample Model: Derive R_{IN} when $i_O = 0$ → Remove load.

Derive A_G when $i_{RIN} = 0$ → $v_{IN} = 0$: Short input.

Derive R_O when $v_{IN} = 0$ → Short input.

Derive A_V when $v_{RO} = 0$ → $i_O = 0$: Remove load.

Popular Model: Derive R_{IN} as is → No redundancies to consider.

Derive G_M when $i_{RO} = 0$ → $v_O = 0$: Short output.

Derive R_O when $v_{IN} = 0$ → Short input.

2.2. Frequency Response

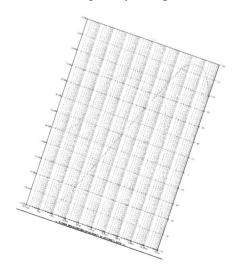

2.2. Poles and Feed-Forward Zeros

Shunt capacitors steer signal energy away from nodes, so

a shunt C_{EQ} sets a pole p_C when $1/sC_{EQ}$ falls below parallel R_{EQ}.

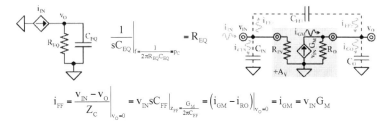

$$\frac{1}{sC_{EQ}}\Bigg|_{f=\frac{1}{2\pi R_{EQ}C_{EQ}} \,\equiv\, p_C} = R_{EQ}$$

$$i_{FF} = \frac{v_{IN} - v_O}{Z_C}\Bigg|_{v_O=0} = v_{IN}sC_{FF}\Bigg|_{z_{FF}=\frac{G_M}{2\pi C_{FF}}} = \left(i_{GM} - i_{RO}\right)\Big|_{v_O=0} = i_{GM} = v_{IN}G_M$$

Feed-forward capacitors Steer energy away from v_{IN} → Input pole p_{IN}.

Add energy to v_O → Zero z_{FF} when $i_{FF} \geq i_{GM}$.

An in-phase capacitor reverses the effects of a pole → Recovers 0°–90°.

An out-of-phase capacitor opposes circuit → Subtracts 0°–90°.

2.2. Current-Limiting Zeros

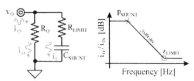

At Low Frequency: C_{SHUNT} is open, so $i_O = i_{IN}$ → Flat response.

At Higher Frequency: C_{SHUNT} shunts current energy away from R_O,

so i_O drops past pole p_{SHUNT} when $1/sC_{SHUNT} \leq R_O + R_{LIMIT}$.

At High Frequency: Series R_{LIMIT} limits C_{SHUNT}'s shunting current,

so R_{LIMIT} arrests (i.e., removes) the effects of p_{SHUNT} past LFP zero z_{LIMIT}

when $1/sC_{SHUNT} \leq R_{LIMIT}$ → Response flattens to $i_O = i_{IN}(R_O \| R_{LIMIT})/R_O$.

$$\frac{1}{sC_{SHUNT}}\Bigg|_{f=\frac{1}{2\pi R_{LIMIT}C_{SHUNT}} \,\equiv\, z_{LIMIT}} = R_{LIMIT}$$

2.2. Miller Split

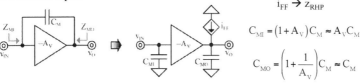

$$i_{FF} \rightarrow z_{RHP}$$

$$C_{MI} = (1 + A_V)C_M \approx A_V C_M$$

$$C_{MO} = \left(1 + \frac{1}{A_V}\right)C_M \approx C_M$$

When v_{IN} rises, v_O falls more, so $v_{IN} - v_O$ rises more than v_{IN}.

$\therefore$ $(v_{IN} - v_O)C_M$ demands more current than $v_{IN}C_M$, like higher capacitance would.

$$Z_{MI} \equiv \frac{v_{IN}}{i_C} = \frac{v_{IN}}{(v_{IN} - v_O)sC_M} = \frac{v_{IN}}{(v_{IN} + v_{IN}A_V)sC_M} = \frac{1}{s(1 + A_V)C_M} \equiv \frac{1}{sC_{MI}}$$

When v_O rises, v_{IN} hardly fell, so $v_O - v_{IN}$ rises nearly as much as v_O.

$\therefore$ $(v_O - v_{IN})C_M$ demands nearly as much current as $v_{IN}C_M$.

$$Z_{MO} \equiv \frac{v_O}{i_C} = \frac{v_O}{(v_O - v_{IN})sC_M} = \frac{v_O}{\left(v_O + \dfrac{v_O}{A_V}\right)sC_M} = \frac{1}{s\left(1 + \dfrac{1}{A_V}\right)C_M} \equiv \frac{1}{sC_{MO}}$$

2.2. Capacitors Shunt Resistors

Capacitors open at low frequencies: Capacitors are absent at low frequencies.

Capacitors shunt resistors to establish $1/2\pi R_{EQ}C_{EQ}$ poles.

Capacitors replace resistors above the poles they establish.

The highest $R_{EQ}C_{EQ}$ product corresponds to the lowest pole.

→ Intentional, load, and C_{GS} and C_π capacitors normally shunt first.

Frequency-Response Analysis

Low-frequency gain A_0: Exclude all capacitors to determine A_0.

p_1: Determine which capacitor shunts its parallel resistance first.

→ Largest $R_{EQ}C_{EQ}$ when all other capacitors are still open.

p_2: Replace R_{EQ1} with C_{EQ1} and find the next highest $R_{EQ}C_{EQ}$.

f_p: If N $R_{EQ}C_{EQ}$'s are close, N poles are near $f_P \approx \dfrac{1}{2\pi\left[Avg\left(R_{EQ}C_{EQ}\right)\right]}$.

2.3. Analog Circuits

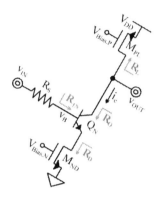

2.3. Signal Composition and Flow

Signal Composition:

Bias (i.e., dc, steady state): All upper-case variable → I_C, V_{DS}, etc.

Small-Signal Variations: All lower-case variable → i_d, v_{be}, etc.

Entire Signal: Lower-case variable with

upper-case subscript → i_S, v_D, etc.

Signal Flow in Transistors:

Bases and gates carry little to no current → Bad outputs.

Collectors (drains) and emitters (sources) carry

output current: $i_C \approx i_E$ and $i_D = i_S$ → Good outputs.

i_C and i_D change *considerably* with v_{BE} and v_{GS}.

→ Bases, emitters, gates, and sources are good inputs.

i_C and i_D change *little* with v_C and v_D.

→ Collectors and drains are bad inputs.

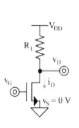

2.3. Signal Flow

Collector/drain and emitter/source carry output current i_C and i_D ∴ Good outputs.

i_C and i_D are sensitive to v_{BE} and v_{GS} ∴ Base/gate and emitter/source are good inputs.

Possible Signal-Flow Paths

First Input: Higher v_B (+) raises v_{BE} ∴ i_C rises (+) → i_C lowers v_C (−) and raises v_E (+).

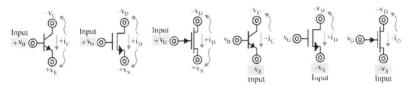

Second Input: Lower v_E (−) raises v_{BE} ∴ i_C rises (+) → i_C lowers v_C (−).

Polarity: Base/gate to emitter/source → In phase.

           Emitter/source to collector/drain → In phase.

           Base/gate to collector/drain → Out of phase → Only one that inverts.

2.3. Possible Transistor Configurations

Note common terminal is unused small-signal terminal.

Common Emitter/Source:	Common Collector/Drain:
Transconductor	Voltage Follower

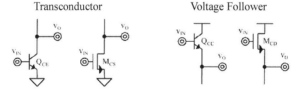

Base and gate are bad outputs ∴ When used, they should be inputs.

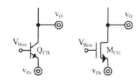

Common Base/Gate: Current Buffer

Collector and drain are bad inputs ∴ When used, they should be outputs.

2.3. Key Relationships

BJT: A_E refers to emitter area.

$i_C = i_B \beta_0 = I_S \{\exp(v_{BE}/V_t) - 1\} (1 + v_{CE}/V_A) \propto A_E,$

$v_{BE} \approx 0.6\text{–}0.7\,V, \quad V_{CE} \geq 200\text{–}300\,mV \equiv V_{CE(MIN)},$

$g_m \approx I_C/V_t, \quad r_\pi = \beta_0/g_m, \quad \text{and} \quad r_o \approx V_A/I_C.$

MOS: For ease, S_i refers to $(W/L)_i$.

$i_{D(SUB)} = (W/L)\,I_{ST}\,\exp(v_{GS}/nV_t)\,[1 - \exp(-v_{DS}/V_t] \propto W/L,$

$V_{DS} \geq 4V_t \equiv V_{DS(MIN)}, \quad g_m \approx I_D/nV_t, \quad r_{ds} \approx V_A/I_D.$

$i_{D(SAT)} = 0.5\,K'\,(W/L)\,(v_{GS} - v_T)^2\,(1 + \lambda v_{DS}) \propto W/L,$

$v_{GS} = v_T + V_{DS(SAT)}, \quad V_{DS(SAT)} = \mathrm{sqrt}\{2I_D/K'(W/L)\},$

$g_m \approx \mathrm{sqrt}\{2I_D K'(W/L)\}, \quad \text{and} \quad r_{ds} \approx 1/\lambda I_D.$

Notes: $g_m \quad \gg \quad 1/r_\pi, g_{mb} \quad \gg \quad g_{ds} \quad \therefore$

$1/g_m \quad \ll \quad r_\pi, 1/g_{mb} \quad \ll \quad r_o, r_{ds} \quad \ll \quad g_m r_\pi r_o = \beta_0 r_o, g_m r_{ds}^2.$

And $C_\mu, C_{GD} \ll C_\pi, C_{GS(SAT)} \ll C_{INTENTIONAL}.$

Low $\ll$ Moderate $\ll$ High $\ll$ Very High.

2.3. Resistances and Currents

R_{DEG} degenerates base's $g_m \therefore g_m$ is lower.

R_B degenerates emitter's g_m.

$\therefore g_m'$ is lower and $R_{E(EQ)}$ is higher.

$R_{C/D}$ loads emitter's $1/g_m \therefore R_{E/S(EQ)}$ is higher.

→ Loaded $1/g_m$. $\quad g_m' = \dfrac{g_m r_\pi}{r_\pi + R_B}$

R_{DEG} in series with $R_{B(EQ)}$ and $R_{C/D(EQ)}$.

$\therefore R_{B(EQ)}$ and $R_{C/D(EQ)}$ are higher.

$1/g_{mb}$ loads v_s and $v_s g_{mb}$ reinforces $v_s g_m$ degeneration.

i_e's v_{be}/r_π reinforces $v_{be} g_m$ → $1/r_\pi + g_m.$

$$R_{E/S(EQ)} = \left[\frac{r_o + R_{C/D}}{1 + (g_m' + g_{mb})r_o}\right] \| (r_\pi + R_B)$$

$$R_{C/D(EQ)} = r_o + (g_m' + g_{mb})r_o R_{DEG}' + R_{DEG}'$$

$$R_{B(EQ)} = r_\pi + (1 + g_m r_\pi)R_{DEG} = r_\pi + (1 + \beta_0)R_{DEG}$$

$$i_{c/d/s}\Big|_{v_{c/d}=0} = v_{be/gs}G_{M(EQ)} = \frac{v_{b/g}g_m}{1 + \left(g_m + g_{mb} + \dfrac{1}{r_o}\right)R_{DEG}} = v_{e/s}\left(g_m' + g_{mb} + \frac{1}{r_o}\right)$$

$$R_{DEG}' = R_{DEG} \| (r_\pi + R_B)$$

2.3. Analytical Approach

Analysis: Trace small-signal path and track voltage–current conversions.

Insightful Approach: Use direct translations.

Example: $i_{in} \rightarrow v_{g(CS)} \rightarrow v_{e(CB)} \rightarrow i_{c(CB)} \rightarrow v_{o1} \rightarrow i_{e(CC)} \rightarrow v_o$

$$\frac{v_{o1}}{i_{in}} = \left(R_S\right)\left(-g_{m(CS)}\right)\left(r_{ds(CS)} \| r_{\pi(CB)} \| R_{I(CB)}\right)\left(\frac{1}{R_{I(CB)}}\right)\left(r_{ds(PL)} \| R_{IN(CC)}\right) \approx -R_S g_{m(CS)} r_{ds(PL)}$$

$$\frac{v_o}{v_{o1}} = \left[\frac{\dfrac{1}{r_{\pi(CC)}} + g_{m(CC)}}{1 + \left(\dfrac{1}{r_{\pi(CC)}} + g_{m(CC)} + \dfrac{1}{r_{o(CC)}}\right) r_{ds(NL)}}\right] r_{ds(NL)} \approx 1$$

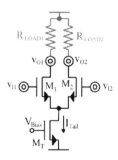

Where:

$$R_{I(CB)} = \frac{r_{o(CB)} + r_{ds(PL)}}{1 + g_{m(CB)} r_{o(CB)}} \approx \frac{2}{g_{m(CB)}}$$

$$R_{IN(CC)} = r_{\pi(CC)} + \left(1 + \beta_{0(CC)}\right)\left(r_{ds(NL)} \| r_{o(CC)}\right)$$

2.4. Analog Building Blocks

2.4. Current Mirror

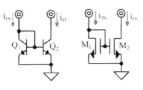

Basic Operation

i_C and i_D are sensitive to v_{BE} and v_{GS}.

i_C and i_D are insensitive to v_{CE} and v_{DS}.

v_{BE}'s and v_{GS}'s equal $\therefore$ $i_O \approx i_{IN}$.

$$i_C = I_S\left[\exp\left(\frac{v_{BE}}{V_t}\right) - 1\right]\left(1 + \frac{v_{CE}}{V_A}\right) \approx I_S\left[\exp\left(\frac{v_{BE}}{V_t}\right) - 1\right] \approx i_{IN} \approx i_O$$

$$i_D = \left(\frac{W}{L}\right)K'\left(v_{GS} - v_T\right)^2\left(1 + \lambda v_{DS}\right) \approx \left(\frac{W}{L}\right)K'\left(v_{GS} - v_T\right)^2 \approx i_{IN} \approx i_O$$

Since $v_{IN} = v_{BE} = v_{DIODE}$, Q_1 is a diode-connected transistor.

And by translation, M_1 is also a diode-connected transistor.

Voltage Limits: $v_{IN} = v_{BE}$ or v_{GS} $\quad$ and $\quad$ $v_O \geq V_{CE(MIN)}$ or $V_{DS(SAT)}$.

2.4. Differential Pair

Small-Signal Transformation: Steady-state signals and v_{IC} are 0.

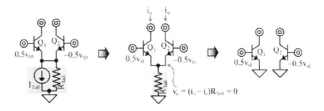

Small-Signal Model: Equal, but opposite i_o's drop zero volts across R_{Tail}.

$\rightarrow$ Circuit reduces to two CE/CS transistors.

$$R_{ID} \equiv \frac{v_{id}}{i_{id}} = \frac{v_{id}}{\left(\dfrac{0.5v_{id}}{r_\pi}\right)} = 2r_\pi \qquad\qquad R_{OD} \equiv \frac{v_{od}}{i_{od}} = \frac{v_{od}}{\left(\dfrac{0.5v_{od}}{r_o}\right)} = 2r_o$$

$$G_D \equiv \frac{i_{o1} - i_{o2}}{v_{id}} = \frac{i_{o1}}{v_{id}} - \frac{i_{o2}}{v_{id}} = \frac{\left(-0.5v_{id}g_m\right)}{v_{id}} - \frac{0.5v_{id}g_m}{v_{id}} = -g_m$$

2.4. Differential Pair: Voltage Summer

Matched differential pairs project voltages into currents in the same way.

$$\rightarrow i_{OD} = (v_P - v_N)g_m + (v_{AP} - v_{AN})g_{mA} \rightarrow i_{OD} = v_{ID}g_m + v_Ag_{mA}.$$

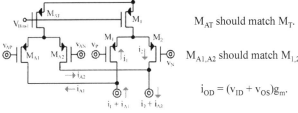

M_{AT} should match M_T.

$M_{A1,A2}$ should match $M_{1,2}$.

$$i_{OD} = (v_{ID} + v_{OS})g_m.$$

$M_{A1,2}$ produces a programmable offset that M_1–M_2 refers to v_{ID} as $v_{OS} = v_A\left(\dfrac{g_{mA}}{g_m}\right)$.

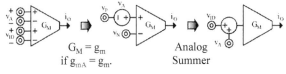

$$G_M = g_m$$
if $g_{mA} = g_m$.

Analog
Summer

2.5. Negative Feedback

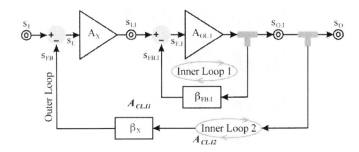

2.5. Loop Composition and Action

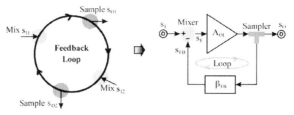

Definition: Loop Gain $A_{LG} \equiv A_{OL}\beta_{FB}$.

Negative feedback opposes the effects of external forces on s_O.

Loop gain reduces s_E to nearly 0 when stable, or s_E oscillates.

$$s_E = s_I - s_{FB} = s_I - s_E A_{OL}\beta_{FB} = s_I - s_E A_{LG} = \frac{s_I}{1+A_{LG}} \approx \frac{s_I}{A_{LG}} \to 0$$

$$\therefore \ s_{FB} \approx s_I \to s_{FB} \text{ "mirrors" } s_I \to \text{Loop regulates } s_{FB} \text{ to } s_I.$$

$$s_{FB} = s_E A_{OL}\beta_{FB} = s_E A_{LG} = \left(s_I - s_{FB}\right)A_{LG} = \frac{s_I A_{LG}}{1+A_{LG}} \approx s_I$$

2.5. Important Concepts

Mixers: Sum (mix) voltages in series.

Sum (mix) currents in parallel (shunt).

Samplers: Monitor (sample) voltages in parallel (shunt like a voltmeter).

Monitor (sample) currents in series (like an ammeter).

Impedance: Series feedback raises open-loop impedance.

$$Z_{CL} = Z_{OL} + Z_{SERIES} = Z_{OL} + Z_{OL}\left(A_{OL}\beta_{FB}\right) = Z_{OL}\left(1+A_{OL}\beta_{FB}\right)$$

Shunt feedback shunts open-loop impedance.

$$Z_{CL} = Z_{OL} \| Z_{SHUNT} = Z_{OL} \| \frac{Z_{OL}}{A_{OL}\beta_{FB}} = \frac{Z_{OL}}{1+A_{OL}\beta_{FB}}$$

Gain Relationships: $A_{OL} \equiv s_O/s_E$ and $\beta_{FB} \equiv s_{FB}/s_O$.

2.5. Embedded Loops

Trace and identify outer loop and determine if it is negative feedback.

Trace and identify inner loops and determine if they are negative feedback.

Analyze inner loops one at a time with outer loop open.

Analyze outer loop using inner loop's closed-loop model.

Analyze overall gain using outer loop's closed-loop model.

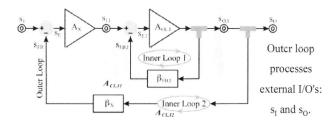

Outer loop processes external I/O's: s_I and s_O.

$A_{CL.I}$ changes with frequency → Designers normally ensure $f_{-3dB.INNER} \gg f_{0dB.OUTTER}$.

2.5. Stability Criterion

With two poles below f_{0dB}, phase shift is 180° at f_{0dB}.

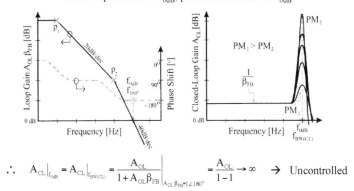

$$\therefore \quad A_{CL}\big|_{f_{0dB}} = A_{CL}\big|_{f_{BW(CL)}} = \frac{A_{OL}}{1+A_{OL}\beta_{FB}}\bigg|_{A_{OL}\beta_{FB}=1\angle 180°} = \frac{A_{OL}}{1-1} \to \infty \quad \to \quad \text{Uncontrolled}$$

Stability Criterion: A_{LG} should reach f_{0dB} with less than 180° of phase shift.

Phase Margin PM: Margin of phase at f_{0dB} to 180° before system becomes unstable.

Gain Margin GM: Margin of gain below 0 dB at $f_{180°}$.

2.5. Compensation

Objective:

Establish dominant low-frequency pole p_1.

Approach:

Keep second pole p_2 at or above f_{0dB}

for 45° or more of phase margin.

Use in-phase zeros to offset poles.

Keep parasitic poles above $10f_{0dB}$

to keep phase margin from

avalanching near f_{0dB}.

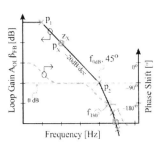

Since out-of-phase zeros invert signals

to close a non-inverting loop

at higher frequency, keep them above $10f_{0dB}$.

2.5. Frequency Response

$$A_{CL} = \frac{A_{OL}}{1 + A_{OL}\beta_{FB}} = A_{OL} \parallel \frac{1}{\beta_{FB}} \quad \therefore \quad A_{CL} \approx \text{Whichever is lower.}$$

When $1/\beta_{FB}$ dominates, negative feedback reduces A_{OL} by $1 + A_{LG}$ and

zeros and poles in A_{OL} do not affect A_{CL} → $p_{OL1,2,3}$ and z_{OL2}.

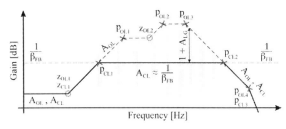

When A_{OL} dominates, zeros and poles in A_{OL} appear in A_{CL} → z_{OL1} and p_{OL4}.

$1/\beta_{FB}$–A_{OL} crossings establish poles and zeros in A_{CL} → p_{CL1} and p_{CL2}.

2.5. Frequency Response

$$A_{CL} = \frac{A_{OL}}{1 + A_{OL}\beta_{FB}} = A_{OL} \| \frac{1}{\beta_{FB}} \qquad \therefore \quad A_{CL} \approx \text{Whichever is lower.}$$

Poles in β_{FB} are zeros in $1/\beta_{FB}$ and zeros are poles $\rightarrow$ $p_{FB1,2}$ and z_{FB1}.
When $1/\beta_{FB}$ dominates, zeros and poles in $1/\beta_{FB}$ appear in A_{CL} $\rightarrow$ p_{FB1} and p_{FB2}.

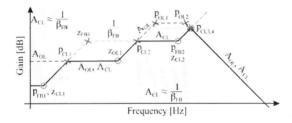

$1/\beta_{FB}$–A_{OL} crossings establish poles and zeros in A_{CL} $\rightarrow$ p_{CL1}, p_{CL2}, and $p_{CL3,4}$.
A_{CL}'s phase follows whichever dominates $\rightarrow$ A_{CL}'s phase after $p_{CL3,4}$ is A_{OL}'s $-90°$.

2.6. Simulations

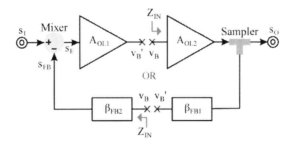

2.6. Differential Amplifiers: Static Parameters

Bias

Bias in unity-gain configuration when $v_{in} \equiv 0$ and V_{IN} is within its ICMR.

Monitor all node voltages and currents.

Ensure all transistors are in the

desired region of operation.

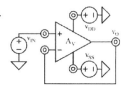

Static Parameters

Quiescent Power P_Q: Bias in unity-gain configuration when

$v_{in} \equiv 0$ and V_{IN} is within its ICMR and monitor $i_{VDD}(v_{DD} - v_{SS})$.

Input-Referred Offset V_{OS}: Bias the same way and monitor

$v_{IN} - v_O$ → Valid if gain error is negligible.

Output Swing $\Delta v_{O(MAX)}$: Fix v_{IC} within its ICMR,

sweep v_{IN} below and above v_{IC}, and monitor v_O.

2.6. Differential Amplifiers: Static and Dynamic Parameters

Static Parameters

Input Common-Mode Range ICMR

Bias in unity-gain configuration

when $v_{in} \equiv 0$, sweep V_{IN}, and

monitor v_O *and* I_{Tail}.

ICMR when $v_O \approx v_{IN}$ and

I_{Tail} is unchanged.

Valid only when Δv_O is within $\Delta v_{O(MAX)}$.

Dynamic Parameters

Open-Loop Gain A_V: Bias in unity-gain

configuration when $V_{IN} \equiv 0$, nil high-frequency feedback with $L_{DC} \approx 1$ kH

and $C_{AC} \approx 1$ kF, inject ac signal with $v_{in} \equiv 1$, and monitor $v_o = v_o/v_{in}$.

2.6. Feedback Loops: Small-Signal Response

Open the loop at a convenient location v_B'–v_B.

Reconnect bias without closing the loop: With high L_{DC}.

Reconstruct the load without altering the bias: With Z_{IN} through high C_{ACO}.

Inject distinguishable small signals: Through high C_{ACI}.

Simulate: $A_{LG} = v_b'/v_b$.

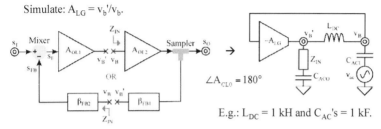

$\angle A_{CLO} = 180°$

E.g.: L_{DC} = 1 kH and C_{AC}'s = 1 kF.

Convenient Location: At a gate because Z_{IN} is C_G and C_{ACO} can be a short.

Ultimate Stability Test: When disturbed with sudden wide-step changes

in the supply or load, loaded closed-loop system settles after a delay.

Chapter 3. Bias Currents

3.1. Voltage Primitives

3.2. PTAT and CTAT Currents

3.3. Temperature Compensation

3.4. Startup

3.5. Frequency Compensation and Noise

3.6. Bandgap Current References

3.7. Precision

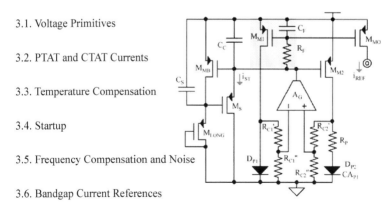

3.1. Voltage Primitives

Extract voltages and currents from predictable voltages.

Diode Voltage v_D

$$i_D = I_s \left(e^{\frac{v_D}{V_t}} - 1 \right) \approx I_s e^{\frac{v_D}{V_t}} \qquad \rightarrow \qquad v_D \approx V_t \ln\left(\frac{i_D}{I_s}\right) = \frac{KT}{q}\ln\left(\frac{i_D}{I_s}\right)$$

Logarithm suppresses variations in diode current Δi_D.

$v_D \approx 0.6\text{–}0.7$ V $\pm 2\%$ at T_{ROOM} and falls -2.2 mV/°C.

$\rightarrow v_D$ is accurate and consistent across close to five decades of current.

Breakdown Voltage v_{BD}

Logarithm-like response suppresses variations in current Δi_D.

$v_{BD(ZENER)} < 5$ V $\pm 2\%$ to 4% at T_{ROOM} and *falls* with temperature.

$v_{BD(AVALANCHE)} > 5$ V $\pm 2\%$ to 4% at T_{ROOM} and *rises* with temperature.

Typically, $v_{BD} \approx 5\text{–}7$ V and rises $+2\text{–}+4$ mV/°C $\rightarrow v_{BD}$ is high.

3.1. Voltage Primitives

Gate–Source Voltage v_{GS} in Strong Inversion

$$i_{DS} \approx 0.5\left(\frac{W}{L}\right)K'\left(v_{GS} - v_T\right)^2 \qquad \rightarrow \qquad v_{GS} = v_T + \sqrt{\frac{2i_{DS}}{K'(W/L)}} \equiv v_T + V_{DS(SAT)}$$

Square root suppresses variations in drain–source current Δi_{DS}.

$\Delta v_T \approx \pm 100\text{–}150$ mV, $\Delta K' \approx \pm 20\%$, and both fall with temperature.

$\therefore \Delta v_{GS} \approx \pm 5\%$ to 10% at T_{ROOM} $\rightarrow$ Less accurate than diode.

Gate–Source Voltage v_{GS} in Subthreshold

$$i_{DS(SUB)} \approx \left(\frac{W}{L}\right)I_{ST}e^{\frac{v_{GS}}{nV_t}} \qquad \text{Where } n = 1.5\text{–}3.$$

Logarithm suppresses variations in drain–source current $\Delta i_{DS(SUB)}$.

v_{GS} is sensitive to noise energy in subthreshold.

Behavior of v_{GS} is consistent across one or two decades of currents.

3.2. Proportional-to-Absolute-Temperature Currents

Definition: Rises with temperature $\rightarrow$ v_{PTAT} and $i_{PTAT} \propto T$

Popular Example: Thermal voltage $V_t = \dfrac{KT}{q}$

Features of V_t: Predictable, linear across temperature, consistent,

and good to cancel V_t effects $\rightarrow$ $g_{m.BJT} = i_{PTAT}/V_t \propto T/T$

v_{PTAT} Generation: Difference of two matched, but ratioed

diode or gate–source voltages in subthreshold is PTAT.

$$\Delta v_D = v_{D1} - v_{D2} \approx V_t \ln\left(\frac{i_{D1}I_{S2}}{I_{S1}i_{D2}}\right) = V_t \ln\left(\frac{i_{D1}A_{D2}}{A_{D1}i_{D2}}\right) = v_{PTAT}$$

Where $I_S \propto A_D$.

$$\Delta v_{GS} = v_{GS1} - v_{GS2} \approx nV_t \ln\left[\frac{i_{DS1}\left(\frac{W}{L}\right)_2}{\left(\frac{W}{L}\right)_1 i_{DS2}}\right] = v_{PTAT}$$

Where $I_{ST} \propto W/L$.

If currents, areas, and width–length ratios match, ln term is constant.

$i_{PTAT} = v_{PTAT}/R_P$ $\rightarrow$ R_P should drift little across temperature.

Poly-silicon resistances vary $\pm 20\%$ $\rightarrow$ R_P requires adjustment $\rightarrow$ Trimming.

3.2. PTAT Currents: Cross-Coupled Quad

Difference of four matched base–emitter voltages.

$$i_R = \frac{\Delta v_{BE}}{R_P} = \frac{v_{BE1} + v_{BE4} - v_{BE3} - v_{BE2}}{R_P} = \frac{V_t}{R_P}\ln\left(\frac{i_1 i_4 A_3 A_2}{A_1 A_4 i_3 i_2}\right) \approx \frac{V_t}{R_P}\ln\left(C_2 D_3\right) = i_{PTAT}$$

$$i_{RB} \approx (v_{IN} - 2v_{BE})/R_B$$

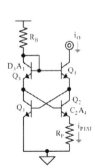

$v_{IN(MIN)} \approx v_{RB} + 2v_{BE}$ (High)

Base-current error:

$$i_{B4} \neq i_{B1} \therefore i_O = i_{C4} \neq i_{C2}$$

$$i_{C2} = i_{PTAT} - i_{B2} < i_{PTAT}$$

Voltage error: $v_{CE1} \approx v_{CE2} + v_{RP}$ and $v_{CE3} \neq v_{CE4}$

PTAT for close to five decades of current.

3.2. PTAT Currents: Latched Cell

Latched BJT Cell: Difference of two matched base–emitter voltages.

Current mirror matches currents and positive feedback latches cell into PTAT state.

$$i_R = \frac{\Delta v_{BE}}{R_P} = \frac{V_t}{R_P}\ln\left(\frac{i_{P1}A_{P2}}{A_{P1}i_{P2}}\right) \approx \frac{V_t}{R_P}\ln\left(C\right) = i_{PTAT}$$

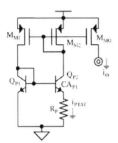

$$v_{IN(MIN)} \approx V_{SD(SAT)} + v_{BE}$$

Base-current error:

$$i_{C1} \neq i_{C2} \text{ and } i_{C2} = i_{PTAT} - i_{B2} < i_{PTAT}$$

Voltage error: $v_{C1} \neq v_{C2}$

PTAT for close to five decades of current.

Circuit is stable when: $\quad i_{C1} \approx i_{C2} \approx \Delta v_{BE}/R_P = i_{PTAT}$

$$i_{C1} \approx i_{C2} = 0 \rightarrow \text{Bi-stable}$$

$\therefore$ Requires a startup circuit.

3.2. PTAT Currents: Latched Cell

Latched MOS Cell: Difference of two matched gate–source voltages.

Current mirror matches currents and positive feedback latches cell into PTAT state.

In Subthreshold

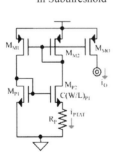

$$i_R = \frac{\Delta v_{GS}}{R_P} \approx \frac{nV_t}{R_P}\ln\left[\frac{i_{P1}\left(\frac{W}{L}\right)_{P2}}{\left(\frac{W}{L}\right)_{P1}i_{P2}}\right] = \frac{nV_t}{R_P}\ln\left(C\right) = i_{PTAT}$$

$$v_{IN(MIN)} \approx V_{SD(SAT)} + v_{GS}$$

No base-current error.

Voltage error: $v_{D1} \neq v_{D2}$

PTAT for maybe two decades of current.

Bi-stable $\rightarrow$ Requires a startup circuit.

To operate in subthreshold:

$$V_{DS(SAT)\text{ STRONG INV}} \leq 50 \text{ mV}$$

Less linear across temperature than BJT.

3.2. PTAT Currents: Latched Cell

Error-Compensated BJT Cell

Replace diode connection with voltage-matching feedback loop.

$$v_{IN(MIN)} \approx Max\{v_{SG} + V_{CE(MIN)}, V_{SD(SAT)} + v_{BE}\}$$

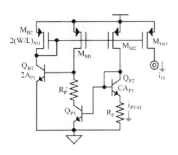

Low base-current error:

$$i_{CB1} \approx 2i_{CP} \therefore i_{BB1} \approx 2i_{BP} \text{ and } i_{CP1} \approx i_{CP2},$$

But $i_{M2} = i_{PTAT} + i_{BP1} > i_{PTAT}$

Low voltage error: $R_p' = R_p$, so

$$v_{SD1} \approx v_{SD2} \text{ and } v_{CE1} \approx v_{CE2} \approx v_{BEP1} - v_R$$

PTAT for close to five decades of current.

Bi-stable → Requires a startup circuit.

Ensure + and – feedback loops are stable.

3.2. PTAT Currents: Latched Cell

Latched Diode Cell: Difference of two matched diode voltages.

Current mirror matches currents and gate-coupled pair matches voltages.

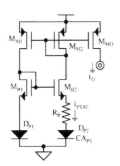

$$v_{IN(MIN)} \approx V_{SD(SAT)} + v_{GS} + v_D \quad \text{(High)}$$

No base-current error.

Voltage error: $v_{DM1} \neq v_{DM2}$

PTAT for close to five decades of current.

Bi-stable → Requires a startup circuit.

3.2. PTAT Currents: Latched Cell

Error-Compensated Diode Cell: Difference of two matched diode voltages.

Amplifier diode-connects M_{M2} $\therefore$

Mirror matches currents and feedback matches voltages.

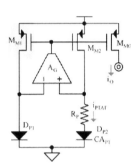

$v_{IN(MIN)} \approx$

$\text{Max}\{V_{SD(SAT)} + v_D, v_{SG} + v_{OA(MIN)}\}$

No base-current error.

Low voltage error: $v_{DM1} \approx v_{DM2}$

PTAT for close to five decades of current.

Bi-stable $\rightarrow$ Requires a startup circuit.

Ensure $+$ and $-$ feedback loops are stable.

3.2. Complementary-to-Absolute-Temperature Currents

CTAT is the complement and counterpart to PTAT.

Definition: v_{CTAT} and i_{CTAT} fall with rising temperatures.

Popular Examples:

Diode voltage falls -2.2 mV/°C.

Threshold voltage v_T falls with temperature.

Transconductance parameter K' falls with temperature.

Feature of v_{CTAT}: Good to cancel PTAT effects

For temperature independence $\rightarrow$ $s_{REF} = s_{PTAT} + s_{CTAT} \neq f(\text{Temperature})$

Benefit of Temperature-Independent Current:

Good to bias blocks, so quiescent power does not rise with temperature.

i_{CTAT} Generation: Impress diode voltage v_D across a resistor.

$$i_R = \frac{v_D}{R_C} = \frac{V_t}{R_C}\ln\left(\frac{i_D}{I_S}\right) = i_{CTAT}$$

v_D is not perfectly linear with temperature $\rightarrow$ i_{CTAT} is not perfectly linear.

3.2. CTAT Currents: BJT and Diode Derived

Use negative feedback to sample and convert a diode voltage v_D into a CTAT current.

Current-Sampled BJT	Voltage-Sampled Diode

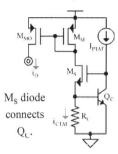 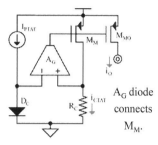

M_S diode connects Q_C.	A_G diode connects M_M.

"T" mixes/mirrors i_{CTAT} and i_S.

M_S series-samples i_{CTAT}.

M_M–M_{MO} mirrors i_{CTAT} to i_O.

$v_{IN(MIN)} \approx v_{SG} + V_{DS(SAT)} + v_{BE}$ (High)

A_G mixes/mirrors v_D and v_R.

M_M series-samples/mirrors i_{CTAT} to i_O.

$v_{IN(MIN)} =$

$\quad Max\{V_{SD(SAT)} + v_D, v_{SG} + v_{OA(MIN)}\}$

3.3. Temperature Compensation

Approach: Use PTAT behavior to cancel CTAT component.

PTAT Primitive: Thermal voltage V_t is zero at 0 K and linear with temperature.

CTAT Primitive: Diode voltage v_D is $V_{BG} \approx 1.2$ V at 0 K and 0.6–0.7 V at 27°C.

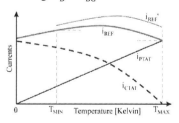

Taylor-series expansion of v_D when $i_D = K_X T^X$:

$$v_D \approx V_{BG} - \left(\frac{V_{BG} - v_{D(ROOM)}}{T_{ROOM}}\right) T^1 - (\eta - x) V_t \ln\left(\frac{T}{T_{ROOM}}\right)$$

Where $\eta \approx 4$ and x is from $i_D = K_A T^X$.

$\therefore$ v_D has T^0-, T^1-, and T ln T terms $\rightarrow$ v_D is nonlinear with temperature.

3.3. Temperature Compensation

Compensated v_D leaves bandgap voltage $V_{BG} \approx 1.2$ V.

$$\therefore \text{At } T_{ROOM}, v_D + v_{PTAT} \equiv V_{BG} \quad \rightarrow \quad v_{PTAT} \approx 1.2 \text{ V} - v_{D(ROOM)} \approx 0.5\text{--}0.6 \text{ V}.$$

Compensated reference current i_{REF}: v_{PTAT} cancels v_D's $K_1 T^1$ term.

$$i_{REF} = i_{CTAT} + i_{PTAT} = \frac{v_D}{R_C} + \frac{\Delta v_D}{R_P} = \frac{v_D}{R_C} + \frac{V_t}{R_P}\ln(C) \equiv \frac{V_{BG}}{R_C} - \underbrace{\left[\frac{(\eta-1)V_t}{R_C}\right]\ln\left(\frac{T}{T_{ROOM}}\right)}_{\text{Nonlinearity}} \approx \frac{V_{BG}}{R_C}$$

$$\text{If} \quad i_{PTAT(ROOM)} = \frac{V_{t(ROOM)}}{R_P}\ln(C) \approx \frac{V_{BG}}{R_C} - \frac{v_{D(ROOM)}}{R_C} \quad \rightarrow \quad \frac{R_C}{R_P} \approx \frac{V_{BG} - v_{D(ROOM)}}{V_{t(ROOM)}\ln(C)}$$

$i_D = i_{PTAT}$ reduces v_D's nonlinearity $\rightarrow$ 1 in T^1 corresponds to 1 in $\eta - 1$.

T ln T term causes curvature.

When T_{MIN} is higher, optimal i_{REF}' requires more i_{PTAT} $\therefore$ $i_{REF}' > i_{REF}$.

3.3. Temperature Compensation

Example: What resistances produce a temperature-compensated 5-µA

reference current when the diode voltage at room temperature is 0.62 V

and the area ratio of the matched diodes is eight?

Solution:

$$\frac{R_C}{R_P} \approx \frac{V_{BG} - v_{D(ROOM)}}{V_{t(ROOM)}\ln(C)} \approx \frac{1.2 - 0.62}{(26m)\ln(8)} = 10.73$$

$$R_C \approx \frac{V_{BG}}{i_{REF}} = \frac{1.2}{5\mu} = 240 \text{ k}\Omega$$

$$R_P \equiv R_C\left(\frac{R_P}{R_C}\right) = (240k)\left(\frac{1}{10.73}\right) = 22.4 \text{ k}\Omega$$

After, simulate and adjust R_P or R_C until i_{REF} flattens across temperature.

3.3. Temperature Compensation: BJT Derived

PTAT-to-Reference Conversion

Use resistors across matching and mirrored v_D's or v_{BE}'s

to pull matched and compensating i_{CTAT}'s from mirror.

Error-Compensated BJT Current Reference

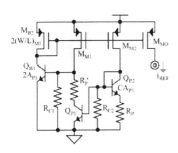

Q_{P1}–Q_{P2}–R_P establishes i_{PTAT} and

R_{C1} and R_{C2} pull matched i_{CTAT}'s

from mirror $\therefore$

$$i_{REF} \approx \frac{v_{BE}}{R_C} + \frac{\Delta v_{BE}}{R_P} = i_{CTAT} + i_{PTAT}$$

Base currents and transistor

voltages still match: $i_{BB} \approx 2i_{BP}$,

$v_{SD1} \approx v_{SD2}$, and $v_{CE1} \approx v_{CE2}$

3.3. Temperature Compensation: Diode Derived

Diode-Derived Current Reference

Error-Compensated Diode-Derived
Current Reference

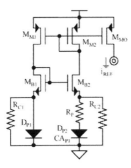

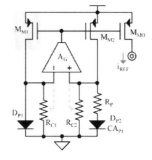

D_{P1}–D_{P2}–R_P establishes i_{PTAT} and
R_{C1}–R_{C2} pulls matched i_{CTAT}'s $\therefore$

$$i_{REF} \approx \frac{v_D}{R_C} + \frac{\Delta v_D}{R_P} = i_{CTAT} + i_{PTAT}$$

To relax $v_{IN(MIN)}$ and A_G's ICMR, A_G can mix fraction of v_D across R_C's.

3.4. Startup

Challenge: Latched positive-feedback cells are bi-stable: $i_{OUT} = 0$ or i_{BIAS}.

Fix: Ensure positive-feedback currents are not 0, so i_{OUT} can latch to i_{BIAS}.

Continuous: Source/sink $I_{TRICKLE}$ continuously from/to positive-feedback node.

→ $I_{TRICKLE}$ is independent of circuit's state.

→ $I_{TRICKLE}$ dissipates power and can produce error ∴ $i_{ST} \ll i_{PTAT}$

Use narrow- and long-channel JFETs or PFETs to generate $I_{TRICKLE}$.

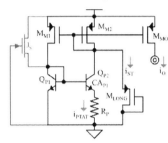
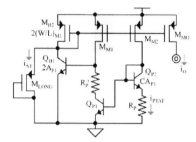

$i_{C1} \approx i_{C2} + i_{ST}$ → Error $i_{C1} \approx i_{C2}$ → Low Error when i_{CB} nears i_{C1}.

3.4. Startup

Example: What PMOS width–length dimensions for a diode-connected

PFET can generate 250 nA at room temperature when impressing

2.5 V across the device and $|v_{TP}| = 0.5$ V, $K_P' = 25$ µA/V^2,

$L_{MIN} = 0.5$ µm, and $W_{MIN} = 2$ µm?

Solution:

$I_{TRICKLE}$ is low, so use minimum width → $W = W_{MIN} = 2$ µm

PMOS is in saturation ∴.

$$i_{SD} \approx 0.5 \left(\frac{W}{L} \right) K_P' \left(v_{SG} - |v_{TP}| \right)^2$$

$$L \approx \left(\frac{0.5W}{i_{SD}} \right) K_P' \left(v_{SG} - |v_{TP}| \right)^2 = \left[\frac{0.5(2\mu)}{(250n)} \right] (25\mu) \left[(2.5) - (0.5) \right]^2 = 400 \text{ µm}$$

3.4. Startup: On Demand – Voltage Mode

On Demand: Source/sink $I_{TRICKLE}$ only when i_{PTAT} nears zero.

→ Must sense the state of the circuit.

Voltage Mode: Engage $I_{TRICKLE}$ when v_{BE} or v_{GS} drops.

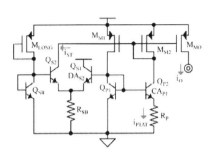

Example:

Differential pair Q_{S1}–Q_{S2} senses

and compares v_{BEP1} with v_{BESR}.

$A_{S1} > A_{S2}$ ∴ Q_{S1}–Q_{S2} favors v_{BEP1}

→ Q_{S2} is off when $v_{BEP1} \approx v_{BESR}$

→ Q_{S2} sinks i_{ST} when $v_{BEP1} \ll v_{BESR}$

In practice, i_{ST} is low, but not zero.

3.4. Startup: On Demand – Current Mode

On Demand

Current Mode: Engage $I_{TRICKLE}$ when i_{BIAS} drops.

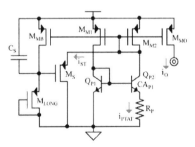

Example:

Mirror M_{M2}–M_{MB} senses

and compares i_{PTAT} with i_{LONG}.

M_S is off when $i_{PTAT} > i_{LONG}$

M_S sinks i_{ST} when $i_{PTAT} < i_{LONG}$

C_S keeps noise from triggering i_{ST}.

Design Notes: $i_{LONG} \ll i_{PTAT}$ across temperature and process.

Connect C_S to the positive supply v_{DD} to

keep noise from affecting M_S's v_{SG} and i_{ST}.

3.5. Frequency Compensation

Latching cells employ positive feedback to latch i_O to i_{BIAS}.

and negative feedback to diode-connect the mirroring transistor.

Design: $A_{LG+} > A_{LG-}$ when circuit is off.

→ Use i_{ST} to raise A_{LG+}.

$A_{LG-} > A_{LG+}$ when circuit is on.

→ Attenuate A_{LG+} with a

low-pass filter R_F–C_F.

→ Use R_P to degenerate A_{LG+}

or boost A_{LG-}.

Stabilize A_{LG-} with C_C's.

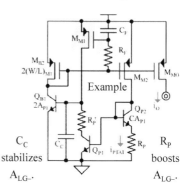

C_C
stabilizes
A_{LG-}.

R_P
boosts
A_{LG-}.

Notes: More feedback loops raises the number of stable states → Difficult to start.

Startup is often cumbersome and empirical → Involves some trial and error.

3.5. Suppressing Supply Noise

Modern ICs integrate sensor-interface circuits, power amplifiers (PA), receivers,

analog/digital (A/D) and digital/analog (D/A) converters, power supplies,

digital-signal processors (DSP), regulators, bias circuits, and more.

Switching power supplies produce supply noise.

Time-variant components pull power from the supply to produce supply

and ground noise.

Power-Supply Rejection (PSR): Ability to suppress noise.

Noise Rejectors

Negative feedback opposes the effects of noise disturbances up to f_{0dB}.

Differential pairs reject common-mode noise

in inputs because $i_O = (v_P - v_N)G_M$.

Transistors reject common-mode noise in inputs because $i_o = (v_{g/b} - v_{s/e})g_m$.

Common-mode capacitors couple source/emitter noise to/from

gate/base terminals for transistors to reject noise.

3.5. Compensation and Noise: Example

R_P boosts A_{LG-}.

$$A_{LG-} \equiv \frac{i_{p1}}{i_i} \approx \left[r_{\pi B1} \parallel \left(r_{oP1} + R_P' \right) \parallel r_{dsM1} \parallel \left(\frac{1}{sC_C} \right) \right] g_{mB1} \left(\frac{1}{g_{mB2}} \right) g_{mM2} \left(\frac{1}{g_{mP2}} + R_P \right) g_{mP1}$$

$$A_{LG+} \equiv \frac{i_{m1}}{i_i} \approx \left[r_{\pi B1} \parallel \left(r_{oP1} + R_P' \right) \parallel r_{dsM1} \parallel \left(\frac{1}{sC_C} \right) \right] g_{mB1} \left(\frac{1}{g_{mB2}} \right) \left(\frac{1}{1 + R_F C_F s} \right) g_{mM1}$$

R_F–C_F filters A_{LG+}.

How much circuit favors A_{LG-} over A_{LG+}.

$$\frac{A_{LG-}}{A_{LG+}} \approx \frac{g_{mM2}}{g_{mM1}} \left(\frac{1}{g_{mP2}} + R_P \right) g_{mP1} \left(1 + R_F C_F s \right)$$

$$= \left(\frac{1}{g_{mP2}} + R_P \right) g_{mP1} \left(1 + R_F C_F s \right)$$

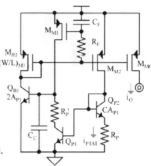

C_C couples emitter ground noise to Q_{B1}'s base.

C_F couples source supply noise to M_{M1}'s gate.

Negative feedback opposes the effects of noise.

3.6. Bandgap Current References: BJT Derived

Integrate base–emitter-derived CTAT currents into PTAT-current generators.

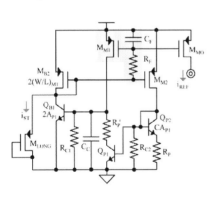

$$i_{REF} = i_{CTAT} + i_{PTAT} = \frac{v_D}{R_C} + \frac{\Delta v_D}{R_P}$$

Q_{P2}–Q_{P1}–Q_{B1}–M_{B2}
    diode-connects M_{M2}, so
M_{M2}–M_{M1}–M_{B2}–M_{MO}
    mirrors currents and
    sources both i_{PTAT} and i_{CTAT}.
R_{C1} and R_{C2} pull matched i_{CTAT}'s.
Q_{P1}–Q_{P2}–R_P generates i_{PTAT}.
Q_{B1} and Q_{P1}–Q_{P2} pull
    similar base currents.
R_F–C_F filters the + feedback loop.
C_C stabilizes the – feedback loop.
M_{LONG} starts the circuit.

3.6. Bandgap Current References: Diode Derived

Integrate diode-derived CTAT currents into PTAT-current generators.

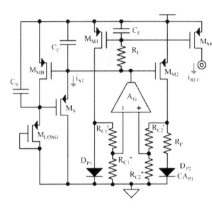

A_G mixes fraction of M_{M1}–M_{M2}'s

  drain voltages, so

R_{C1} and R_{C2} pull matched i_{CTAT}'s.

A_G diode-connects M_{M2}, so

M_{M2}–M_{M1}–M_{MB}–M_{MO}

  mirrors currents and

  sources both i_{PTAT} and i_{CTAT}.

D_{P1}–D_{P2}–R_P generates i_{PTAT}.

R_F–C_F filters the + feedback loop.

C_C stabilizes the – feedback loop.

M_{MB}–M_{LONG}–M_S starts the circuit.

$$i_{REF} = i_{CTAT} + i_{PTAT} = \frac{v_D}{R_C} + \frac{\Delta v_D}{R_P}$$

3.7. Precision: Tolerance and Drift

$$i_{REF} = i_{CTAT} + i_{PTAT} = \frac{v_D}{R_C} + \frac{\Delta v_D}{R_P} = \frac{V_{BG}}{R_{EQ}}$$

If R_C and R_P match, v_{CTAT} and v_{PTAT} shift proportionately

 with R_C and R_P's ±20% tolerance.

  $\therefore$ i_{REF}'s temperature drift is nearly independent of tolerance.

But since $i_{REF} \propto 1/\text{Resistance}$,

 i_{REF} drifts with R_C and R_P's temperature drift.

  $\rightarrow$ Choose low-drift resistors.

 Absolute value of i_{REF} shifts with R_C and R_P's ±20% tolerance.

  $\rightarrow$ Bias current shifts ±20% across fabrication corners.

  $\rightarrow$ If more precision is necessary,

   adjust R_C and R_P after fabrication (i.e., trim).

3.7. Precision: Layout

Mismatch between non-degenerated transistors offset i_{REF}.

∴ Match   PTAT-generating pair $D_{P1}-D_{P2}$, $Q_{P1}-Q_{P2}$, or $M_{P1}-M_{P2}$,

PTAT Resistors R_P and R_{PTAT},

Mirroring Devices $Q_{M1}-Q_{M2}$, $M_{M1}-M_{M2}$, or $R_{L1}-R_{L2}$, and

Non-degenerated transistors in diode-connecting loop.

The effect of mismatch between degenerated transistors is low in i_{REF}.

∴ Cascode transistors need not match as well.

Best-Matched Layout ≡ Cross-coupled, common centroid, same orientation,

compact, low spread, and

dummy devices.

Typical Layout Strategies

for the PTAT-generating pair:

A) 8 around 1 → Compact.

B) 1 or 2 on either side of 1.

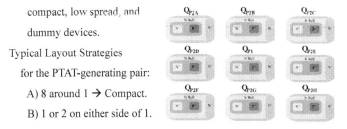

Chapter 4. Voltage References

4.1. Bandgap References

4.2. Power-Supply Rejection

4.3. Precision

4.4. Trim

4.5. Curvature Correction

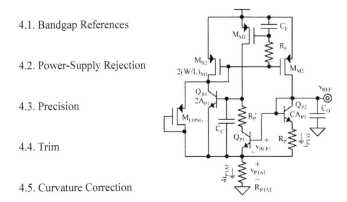

4.1. Current-Mode Bandgap

Balanced PTAT and CTAT currents flow into a resistor.

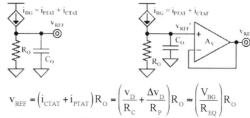

$$v_{REF} = \left(i_{CTAT} + i_{PTAT}\right)R_O = \left(\frac{v_D}{R_C} + \frac{\Delta v_D}{R_P}\right)R_O \approx \left(\frac{V_{BG}}{R_{EQ}}\right)R_O$$

R_O should match R_C and R_P.

C_O shunts noise coupled and injected.

v_{REF} can be a fraction of the bandgap voltage V_{BG}.

Regulating current mode's i_{BG} helps reject supply noise,

    but does not help shunt coupled noise.

Buffering v_{REF} with unity-gain amplifier helps shunt noise,

    except amplifier's input-referred offset V_{OS} degrades accuracy.

4.1. Current-Mode Bandgap: BJT Implementation

Q_{P1}, Q_{B1}, and M_{B2} diode-connect M_{M2}, so

M_{M1}, M_{M2}, and M_{MO}

    mirror i_{REF}'s $i_{PTAT} + i_{CTAT}$.

Q_{P1}, Q_{P2}, and R_P

    generate i_{PTAT}.

R_{C1} and R_{C2} establish i_{CTAT}.

R_P' keeps $v_{CEP1} \approx v_{CEP2}$.

R_O converts i_{REF} to v_{REF}.

M_{LONG}'s i_{ST} ensures $i_{PTAT} \neq 0$.

C_O shunts noise coupled and injected.

R_F and C_F filter the positive feedback path.

Note $i_{ST} + i_{CB1} \approx 2i_{PTAT}$ and mirror voltages and base currents match.

$$i_{PTAT} = \frac{v_{BEP1} - v_{BEP2}}{R_P} = \frac{V_t}{R_P}\ln C$$

$$i_{CTAT} = \frac{v_{BEB1}}{R_{C1}} - \frac{v_{BEP1}}{R_{C2}}$$

4.1. Voltage-Mode Bandgap

Stack PTAT and diode voltages.

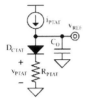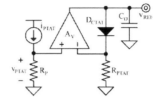

$v_{REF} = i_{PTAT}R_P + v_D \approx i_{PTAT}R_{PTAT} + v_D = v_{PTAT} + v_{CTAT} \approx V_{BG}.$

R_{PTAT} should match i_{PTAT}'s R_P.

C_O shunts noise coupled and injected.

v_{REF} is roughly 1.2 V.

Regulating v_{REF} or v_{PTAT} helps shunt noise without degrading accuracy,

if v_{REF} accounts for amplifier A_V's offset V_{OS} drift $\rightarrow$ A_V is in v_{REF}.

4.1. Voltage-Mode Bandgap: BJT Implementation

Q_{P1}, Q_{B1}, and M_{B2} diode-connect M_{M2}, so

M_{M1}, M_{M2}, and M_{B2} mirror i_{PTAT}.

Q_{P1}, Q_{P2}, and R_p generate i_{PTAT}.

R_p' matches v_{CEP1} and v_{CEP2}.

M_{LONG} ensures $i_{PTAT} \neq 0$.

C_O shunts noise coupled and injected.

M_{B2}, M_{M1}, and M_{M2}'s $4i_{PTAT}$

    into R_{PTAT} establishes v_{PTAT}.

Q_{P1}'s v_{BEP1} establishes v_D.

R_F and C_F filter A_{LG+}.

Notes: $i_{ST} + i_{CB1} \approx 2i_{PTAT}$.

    Mirror voltages and base currents match.

    Reacting to noise in v_{REF} alters i_{PTAT}.

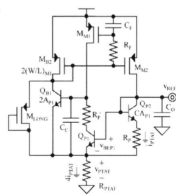

$$i_{PTAT} = \frac{v_{BEP1} - v_{BEP2}}{R_P} = \frac{V_t}{R_P}\ln C$$

$$v_{REF} = 4i_{PTAT}R_{PTAT} + v_{BEP1}$$

4.1. Voltage-Mode Bandgap: Diode Implementation

A_G diode-connects M_{M2}, so

M_{M1} and M_{M2} mirror i_{PTAT}.

A_G impresses v_{DP1} on R_P and D_{P2}, so

Mirror voltages match and

D_{P1}, D_{P2}, and R_P generate i_{PTAT}.

$2i_{PTAT}$ into R_{PTAT} establishes v_{PTAT}.

D_{P1} establishes v_D.

A_G shunt-samples v_{REF}.

$R_F C_F$ filters A_{LG+}.

C_O shunts noise coupled and injected.

Reacting to noise in v_{REF} alters i_{PTAT}.

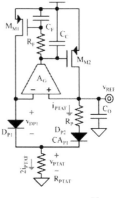

$$i_{PTAT} = \frac{v_{DP1} - v_{DP2}}{R_P} = \frac{V_t}{R_P} \ln C$$

$$v_{REF} = 2i_{PTAT} R_{PTAT} + v_{DP1}$$

4.1. Voltage-Mode Bandgap: Shunt Feedback

To incorporate shunt feedback, modify diode-connecting loop to drive v_{REF} with a source or an emitter $\therefore$ i_{PTAT} is less sensitive to loop reactions.

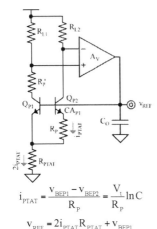

$$i_{PTAT} = \frac{v_{BEP1} - v_{BEP2}}{R_P} = \frac{V_t}{R_P} \ln C$$

$$v_{REF} = 2i_{PTAT} R_{PTAT} + v_{BEP1}$$

A_V impresses v_{RL2} on v_{RL1}, so

R_{L1} and R_{L2} mirror i_{PTAT}.

Q_{P1}, Q_{P2}, and R_P generate i_{PTAT}.

Q_{P1} shunt-samples v_{REF}.

$2i_{PTAT}$ into R_{PTAT} establishes v_{PTAT}.

Q_{P1}'s v_{BEP1} establishes v_D.

R_P' matches v_{CEP1} and v_{CEP2}.

A_V sources base currents, so

no base-current error.

C_O shunts noise coupled and injected.

4.1. Voltage-Mode Bandgap: Shunt-Feedback Implementation

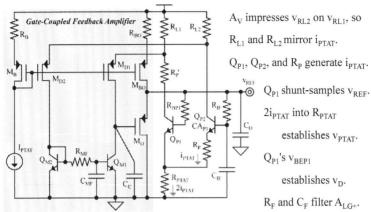

A_V impresses v_{RL2} on v_{RL1}, so

R_{L1} and R_{L2} mirror i_{PTAT}.

Q_{P1}, Q_{P2}, and R_p generate i_{PTAT}.

Q_{P1} shunt-samples v_{REF}.

$2i_{PTAT}$ into R_{PTAT}

establishes v_{PTAT}.

Q_{P1}'s v_{BEP1}

establishes v_D.

R_F and C_F filter A_{LG+}.

R_p' matches v_{CEP1} and v_{CEP2}. R_{BP1} matches R_{IF}'s v_{RIF}.

A_V sources base currents. R_p degenerates A_{LG+} and $M_{D1,2}$ series-mixes v_{RL}'s.

$R_{MF}C_{MF}$ and $R_{IF}C_{IF}$ filter A_{LG+}. C_O shunts noise coupled and injected.

4.1. Voltage-Mode Bandgap: Shunt-Feedback Implementation

A differential pair Q_{P1}–Q_{P2} can also implement a loop that

impresses Δv_{BE} across an external R_p to generate i_{PTAT}.

Q_{P1}, Q_{P2}, and R_p generate i_{PTAT}.

R_F and C_F filter A_{LG+}.

R_B matches R_F's v_{RF}.

C_O shunts noise coupled and injected.

R_p's i_{PTAT} through R_p and R_{PTAT}

establishes v_{PTAT}.

D_C's v_{DC} establishes v_D.

i_{BIAS} ensures currents are not $0 \rightarrow$ Starts v_{REF}.

i_{PTAT} is less sensitive to loop reactions.

$\therefore$ Loop shunts coupled noise.

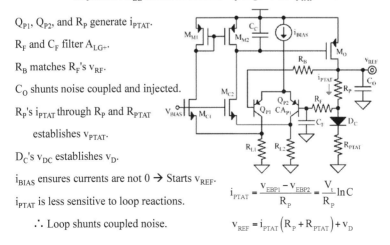

$$i_{PTAT} = \frac{v_{EBP1} - v_{EBP2}}{R_p} = \frac{V_t}{R_p}\ln C$$

$$v_{REF} = i_{PTAT}\left(R_p + R_{PTAT}\right) + v_D$$

4.1. Voltage-Mode Sub-Bandgap: Shunt-Feedback Implementation

Since a voltage divider reduces v_D, $v_{CTAT} + v_{PTAT}$ can be a fraction of V_{BG}.

Feedback loop ensures R_P conducts i_{PTAT}, so R_P is like a current source.

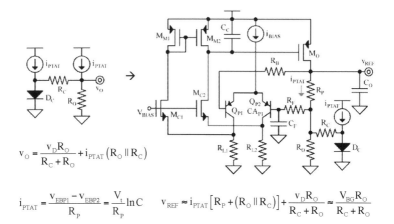

$$v_O = \frac{v_D R_O}{R_C + R_O} + i_{PTAT}\left(R_O \| R_C\right)$$

$$i_{PTAT} = \frac{v_{EBP1} - v_{EBP2}}{R_P} = \frac{V_t}{R_P}\ln C \qquad v_{REF} \approx i_{PTAT}\left[R_P + \left(R_O \| R_C\right)\right] + \frac{v_D R_O}{R_C + R_O} \approx \frac{V_{BG} R_O}{R_C + R_O}$$

4.2. Power-Supply Rejection

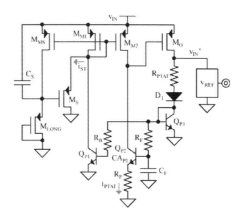

4.2. Power-Supply Rejection

Power-Supply Rejection (PSR) is the ability to suppress power-supply noise.

→ Inability to amplify power-supply noise.

∴ PSR is the complement of supply gain A_{IN}.

Line Regulation (LNR) is how v_O varies with steady-state changes in v_{IN}.

$$PSR \equiv \frac{1}{A_{IN}} = \frac{\partial v_{IN}}{\partial v_O} \equiv \frac{v_{in}}{v_o} \qquad LNR \equiv \frac{\Delta V_O}{\Delta V_{IN}} \approx \frac{\partial v_O}{\partial v_{IN}}\bigg|_{Low.Freq.} = A_{IN0} = \frac{1}{PSR_0}$$

PSR Model → Voltage Divider

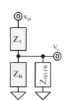

Supply impedance Z_T couples noise.

Ground impedance Z_B shunts noise.

Shunt feedback $Z_{SH.FB}$ opposes the effects of noise.

∴ Raise Z_T, lower Z_B, and raise the gain and bandwidth of the feedback loop.

4.2. Power-Supply Rejection

Current-mode bandgaps: Regulate i_{REF} → Raise Z_T.

Voltage-mode bandgaps: Shunt-feedback loops that do not alter i_{PTAT}

shunt noise and reduce Z_B.

Cascode supply-connected current-sourcing transistors.

Filter the input supply v_{IN}:

RC shunts high-frequency ripples.

Linear pre-regulator rejects low-frequency ripples.

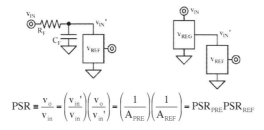

$$PSR \equiv \frac{v_o}{v_{in}} = \left(\frac{v_{in}'}{v_{in}}\right)\left(\frac{v_o}{v_{in}'}\right) = \left(\frac{1}{A_{PRE}}\right)\left(\frac{1}{A_{REF}}\right) = PSR_{PRE}PSR_{REF}$$

4.2. Pre-Regulators

Pre-regulated supply v_{IN}' should accommodate v_{REF}'s headroom $v_{IN(MIN)}$ across process and temperature.

Uncompensated and Unregulated

Temperature-Compensated and Regulated

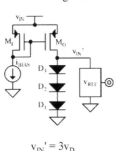

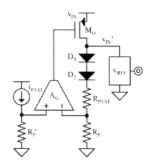

$v_{IN}' = 3v_D$

Falls with temperature.

$v_{IN}' = i_{PTAT}(R_P + R_{PTAT}) + 2v_D$

Can rise or fall with temperature.

4.2. Pre-Regulators

Self-contained, temperature-compensated, and regulated pre-regulator.

Q_{P1}, Q_{P2}, and R_P generate i_{PTAT}.

R_F and C_F filter A_{LG+}.

R_B matches R_F's v_{RF}.

Startup: M_S pulls i_{ST} when

M_{MS}'s $i_{MS} < M_{LONG}$'s i_{LONG}.

C_S couples supply noise to

reduce noise in M_S's v_{SG}.

Q_{P3} mirrors Q_{P1}'s i_{PTAT}, so

$v_{IN}' = 2v_D + i_{PTAT}R_{PTAT}$.

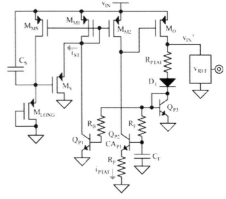

Remove or insert diodes and adjust R_{PTAT}

$$i_{PTAT} = \frac{v_{BEP1} - v_{BEP2}}{R_P} = \frac{V_t}{R_P}\ln C$$

to define voltage level and temperature drift.

4.3. Precision

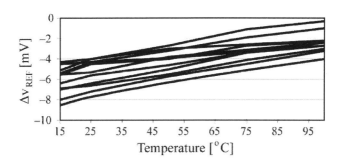

4.3. Sources of Errors

First-Order Core: PTAT Generator → Δv_{BE} loop.

Current Mirror → With or without feedback amplifier.

Summer → Current mode or voltage mode.

Error Sources:

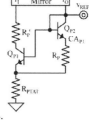

Mismatch of resistors, transistors, and mirror.

Tolerance of v_{BE} and resistors.

Error Analysis: Deviations from ideal produce Δv_{REF}.

Mismatched currents $\Delta i_{C/D}$ appear as $\Delta v_{BE/GS}$ in v_{REF}.

Q_{P1}–Q_{P2} impresses $\Delta v_{BE/GS}$ across R_P to produce Δv_{PTAT} in v_{REF}.

→ $\Delta v_{REF} = v_{REF(IDEAL)} - v_{REF(ERR)} = \Delta v_{BE} + \Delta v_{PTAT}$.

4.3. Sources of Errors

$$v_{REF} = v_{BE} + v_{PTAT} = V_t \ln\left(\frac{i_{PTAT}}{I_S}\right) + 2V_t\left(\ln C\right)\left(\frac{R_{PTAT}}{R_P}\right)$$

1% Resistor Mismatch $\Delta(R/R)$:

No effect in i_{PTAT} $\therefore$ No effect in v_{BE}.

$\Delta v_{PTAT} = 2V_t\ln(C)\Delta(R/R) \propto T^1$ and small $\rightarrow$ Trimmable with R_{PTAT}.

20% Resistor Tolerance ΔR:

No effect in R/R $\therefore$ No effect in v_{PTAT}.

$\Delta v_{BE} = V_t\ln(R_{ERR}/R) \propto T^1$ and small $\rightarrow$ Trimmable with R_{PTAT}.

Resistor's Drift over Temperature:

No effect in R/R $\therefore$ No effect in v_{PTAT}.

$\Delta v_{BE} = V_t\ln(R_{TC}/R) =$ Nonlinear, but small $\rightarrow$ Not trimmable.

4.3. Sources of Errors

5% Current Mismatch $\Delta i_{P/M}$ between PTAT and Mirror Transistors.

Effect in v_{BE} and i_{PTAT}.

$\Delta v_{BE/GS} = \Delta i_{C/D}/g_m = (\Delta i_{C/D}/i_C)V_t$ for BJT pair $Q_{P1,2}$.

$= (\Delta i_{C/D}/i_C)nV_t$ for MOSFET pair $M_{P1,2}$.

$\Delta v_{PTAT} = \Delta v_{BE/GS}(R_1/R_P) = (\Delta i_{C/D}/i_C)V_t(R_1/R_P)$ for BJT pair $Q_{P1,2}$.

$= (\Delta i_{C/D}/i_C)nV_t(R_1/R_P)$ for MOSFET pair $M_{P1,2}$.

$\therefore \Delta v_{BE/GS} + \Delta v_{PTAT} \propto T^1$ and high $\rightarrow$ Trimmable with R_{PTAT}.

0.5-V Mirror-Voltage Mismatch $\Delta v_{C/D}$ $\rightarrow$ $\Delta v_{C/D}$ and V_A *can vary with temp.*:

$\Delta i_{C/D} = \Delta v_{C/D}/r_{ds/o} = i_{C/D}\Delta v_{C/D}/V_A$ $\therefore$ $\Delta v_{BE/GS} = (\Delta i_{C/D}/i_C)V_t$ and

$\Delta v_{PTAT} = (\Delta i_{C/D}/i_C)V_t(R_1/R_P)$ $\rightarrow$ Nonlinear, but small $\rightarrow$ Not trimmable.

4.3. Sources of Errors

Package-Induced Offset:

Thermal Coefficient of Expansion (TCoE): $TCoE_{Packagae} \gg TCoE_{Silicon \, Die}$.

Plastic melts at 170 °C and undisturbed die remains relatively flat.

As temperature T rises, plastic contracts and bends die.

∴ Add fillers to reduce $TCoE_{Package}$ and avoid cracking die.

∴ Die's electrical properties change with T → Piezo effects.

Die-wide stress bends die and produces a variable systemic offset $\Delta V_{OS(S)}$.

Die is unstressed at 170 °C → Die un-stresses with T.

→ $\Delta V_{OS(S)} \approx 2\text{–}6$ mV $\propto T^1$ and small → Trimmable.

Fillers produce localized random stress fields → ΔV_{OS}^*.

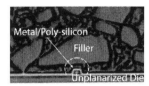 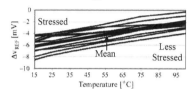

4.3. Typical Error Profile

Error Source	Untrimmed Error	Δv_{REF}
Resistor Mismatch	1%	6 mV
Resistor Tolerance	20%	–5 mV
Drift of Poly-silicon Resistors	$TC_1 = 500/°C$ $TC_2 = 200/°C^2$	0.0 mV
PTAT-Pair I Mismatch	5%	15 mV
Voltage Mismatch ($V_A = 50$ V)	0.5 V	3 mV
Current-Mirror I Mismatch	5%	15 mV
v_{BE} Tolerance	2%	24 mV
Total $\pm\Delta v_{REF}$ (RMS Sum)		±33 mV
Package Shift		±12 mV
Total $\pm\Delta v_{REF}$ (RMS Sum)		±35 mV

Full-scale trim range should cover 60–70 mV → 5%–6% of V_{BG}.

Wafer adjustments cannot cancel package effects.

Post-package adjustments require more silicon area and additional test time.

4.3. Mismatch-Error Reduction

Dynamic Element Matching:

Circulate pair or bank of transistors.

→ All transistors occupy all positions.

∴ Average offset between positions is zero.

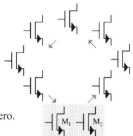

Drawbacks:

Changing positions generates switching noise.

Switching network occupies silicon area.

∴ Apply only to critical match-sensitive transistors.

4.3. Mismatch-Error Reduction

Startup Calibration: "Survivor" Scheme

Sample and compare the offsets of two transistor pairs.

Discard loser and replace loser with another pair.

Repeat and ripple winner until all pairs are tested.

∴ The winner is the best-matched pair.

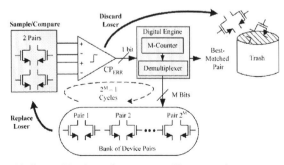

Challenge: Untrimmed comparator CP_{ERR} must be accurate.

4.3. Mismatch-Error Reduction: Startup Comparator

Reduce V_{OS} with dynamic element matching.

→ Generates noise only during startup,

when the system is off.

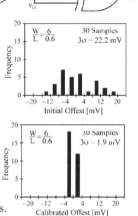

Short the inputs of a summing comparator CP_{SUM}.

Use latch to store CP_{SUM}'s output v_O.

Flip one differential pair:

If v_O trips, flipped pair's V_{OS} dominates.

→ XOR transitions ∴ Discard flipped pair.

If v_O does not trip, flipped pair's V_{OS} is lower.

→ XOR does not transition.

∴ Discard un-flipped pair.

Results: Can select a ±2-mV pair from ±22-mV pairs.

Drawback: Controller and transistor bank can occupy substantial silicon area.

4.3. Package-Shift Reduction

Systemic Offset: Model in simulations and include in design → Lower v_{PTAT}.

Random Offset: Buffer the effect of fillers with mechanically compliant layers.

Examples: Nitride layer, uniform metal planes, and

post-fabrication layers, which add cost.

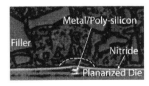

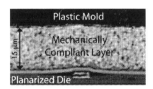

Planarized Die:

16%–18% lower Δv_{REF}^{*}.

Planarized Die and

15-μm Copper Layer:

35% lower Δv_{REF}^{*}.

Ceramic packages stress dies substantially less, but they cost more.

4.4. Trim

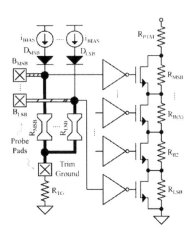

4.4. Trim Basics

$v_{REF} = v_{PTAT} + v_D \approx K_{PTAT}T + (V_{BG} - K_{CTAT}T) \approx V_{BG}$ if $K_{PTAT} = K_{CTAT}$.

Since $V_{BG} \approx 1.2$ V and $v_{D(ROOM)} \approx 0.65$ V $\therefore v_{PTAT} \approx 0.55$ V.

Since $v_{PTAT} = 0$ at 0 °K, only one more point sets correcting slope.

$\therefore$ All T^1 errors can be trimmed at one temperature $\rightarrow$ At T_{ROOM}.

First-order PTAT compensation cancels the first-order T^1 term only.

$\therefore$ Higher-order terms in T ln T produces curvature in v_{REF}.

$\rightarrow v_{REF}$'s fractional temperature coefficient TC at T_{MID} is zero.

$\rightarrow$ Note T_{ROOM} is not always T_{MID}.

$$TC \equiv \left(\frac{1}{v_{REF}}\right)\left(\frac{\Delta v_{REF}}{\Delta T}\right)$$

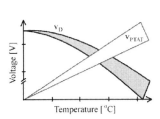

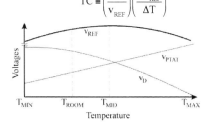

4.4. Trim Process

Adjust v_{PTAT} by trimming R_{PTAT}.

v_{REF}'s TC at T_{MID} rises with R_{PTAT}.

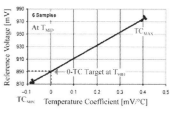

$\therefore$ TC at $R_{PTAT(MAX)}$ is TC_{MAX}.

TC at $R_{PTAT(MIN)}$ is TC_{MIN}.

TC rises linearly with trimmed v_{REF}.

$\therefore$ 0-TC $v_{REF(MID)}$ setting is a linear extrapolation of TC_{MIN} and TC_{MAX}.

Extrapolate $v_{RFF(ROOM)}$ target from $v_{RFF(MID)}$ setting.

Typical commercial range is 0 to 85°C.

Extended commercial range can be –40 to 125°C.

$\therefore T_{MID} = 42.5°C > T_{ROOM}$ and $V_{MID(0TC)} > V_{TARGET(ROOM)}$.

Typical 3σ TC is 20–100 ppm/°C $\rightarrow$ 3–15 mV across 125°C at 1.2 V.

4.4. Trim Methods

Zener Zap: Zener diodes short with high reverse voltages.

Fusible Links: Poly-silicon strips break with high currents.

Laser Trim: A laser beam cuts poly-silicon strips into desired shape.

E-EP-ROM: Floating gates receive/lose charge with high on-chip voltages.

Trimming Methods		Normally Open	Normally Closed	Resolution	Stress on IC	Cost
At Wafer	Zener Zap	√		Bit Defined	High	Low
	Fusible Link		√	Bit Defined	Moderate	Low
	Laser Trim		√	Laser Defined	Low	Highest
Post-Package	Fusible Link		√	Bit Defined	Highest	Moderate
	EEPROM	√	√	Bit Defined	Low	High

On-chip EEPROM and fusible poly-silicon links are popular.

Zapping packaged fusible links is not as reliable $\rightarrow$ Possible fuse re-growth.

4.4. Fusible-Link Circuit

Poly-Silicon Fuses: 200-Ω fuses break to MΩ's with 5 V and 25 mA.

200-Ω fuses and 1–5-kΩ R_{TG} drop mV's, so FETs short trim resistors.

Bias currents raise bit lines

    after fuses open.

Trim ground and R_{TG} steer fuse

    current away from the substrate.

Wide traces carry

    breakdown current.

Diodes block reverse currents into bias

    currents when $v_{TRIM} > v_{IN}$ and $v_{IN} = 0$ V.

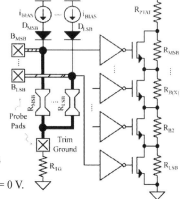

$R_{DS.LSB(HOT)} \ll R_{LSB}$, so keep ladder near ground for maximum gate drive.

4.4. Design Process

Conceptualize circuit.

Simulate functionality: Steady state, startup, stability, response time, etc.

Simulate temperature drift:

    Monte-Carlo simulations under nominal conditions.

    Trim every corner when using Monte-Carlo simulations

        because untrimmed cases are unrealistic worst cases.

Determine worst-case trim range and expand for characterization.

Temperature models are imperfect, so measure and characterize drift.

Determine optimum v_{TARGET} (i.e., $v_{REF(ROOM)}$ setting with lowest temperature drift)

    before packaging die for low cost, or after if test time allows it for high accuracy.

Incorporate results into next design cycle: Re-center trim and reduce trim range.

Trim to v_{TARGET} at T_{ROOM}.

4.4. Measurements

Temperature Considerations

Soak Time t_{SOAK}: Variations Δv_{REF} have a slow time constant.

∴ Allow sufficient soak time t_{SOAK} for v_{REF} to settle to its final value.

Thermal Hysteresis Δv_{HYS}:

Δv_{REF} for ΔT_{RISE} may not match Δv_{REF} for ΔT_{FALL}.

∴ Raise soak time t_{SOAK} to ensure t_{SOAK} is not the problem.

Temperature Coefficient TC: Include all statistical effects.

→ Box Method:

$$TC_{REF} \approx \frac{1}{v_{REF(MEAN)}} \left(\frac{v_{REF(3\sigma MAX)} - v_{REF(3\sigma MIN)}}{T_{MAX} - T_{MIN}} \right)$$

Thermal Stability: Thermal feedback loop may exist.

E.g.: High power → Temperature rises → System shuts → Die cools.

→ System restarts → Power again rises → Cycle repeats.

4.5. Curvature Correction

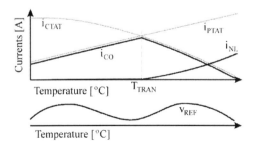

4.5. Correction

First-Order Reference: v_{PTAT} cancels v_D's T^1 term.

∴ T ln T produces a curvature in v_{REF}.

Second-Order Reference: Parabolic v_{PTAT}^2 cancels v_D's T^2 term.

→ At low temperatures, T^2 term disappears ∴ v_{REF} is first order.

→ At higher temperatures, T^2 term over-compensates ∴ v_{REF} curves up.

Curvature Correction: v_{PTAT}^2 and/or other components offset v_D's T ln T term.

$$v_D \approx V_{BG}$$

$$-\left(\frac{V_{BG} - v_{D(ROOM)}}{T_{ROOM}}\right)T^1$$

$$-(\eta - x)V_t \ln\left(\frac{T}{T_{ROOM}}\right)$$

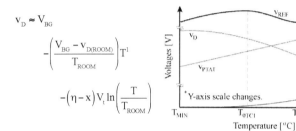

4.5. Parabolic Correction

Current Mode:

Generate a nonlinear current i_{NL}.

Superimpose i_{NL} on PTAT resistor stack.

∴ $i_{PTAT}(R_{PTAT} + R_{PTAT2}) + i_{NL}R_{PTAT2} = v_{PTAT} + v_{NL}$.

Parabolic Correction:

$$V_{BE1} + V_{BE2} = V_t \ln\left(\frac{i_{Q1}i_{Q2}}{I_s I_s}\right)$$

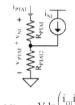

Q_P mirrors Q_1's i_{PTAT}.

R_C's i_{CTAT} compensates Q_{P2}'s $0.5i_{PTAT}$.

∴ $i_{Q3} \approx i_{CTAT} + 0.5i_{PTAT} \approx i_{OTC}$.

→ $i_{OTC} \approx i_{PTAT}$ near T_{ROOM}.

Q_1, Q_2, Q_3, and Q_4 close a v_{BE} loop.

∴ $i_{Q1}i_{Q2} = i_{PTAT}^2 \approx i_{Q3}i_{Q4} \approx i_{OTC}i_{Q4}$ → $i_{Q4} \approx i_{PTAT}^2$.

Since $i_{OTC} \approx i_{PTAT}$ near T_{ROOM}, Q_{1-4}'s current densities are similar.

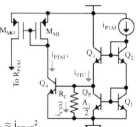

4.5. Parabolic Correction

M_S, M_{MB}, and M_{LONG} start the circuit and C_S keeps noise from engaging i_{ST}.

M_{M1}, M_{M2}, M_{M3}, and M_{MO} mirror M_{NL}'s i_{NL}.

M_{P1} and M_{P2} are in

  sub-threshold.

M_{P1} and M_{P2} impress Δv_{GS}

  across M_{NL}'s $R_{DS.NL}$.

M_{NL} is in triode $\therefore$.

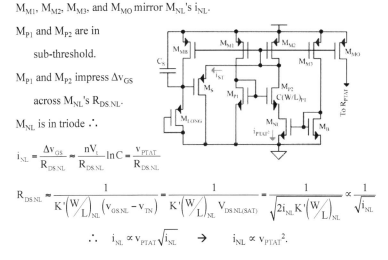

$$i_{NL} = \frac{\Delta v_{GS}}{R_{DS.NL}} \approx \frac{nV_t}{R_{DS.NL}} \ln C = \frac{v_{PTAT}}{R_{DS.NL}}$$

$$R_{DS.NL} \approx \frac{1}{K'\left(\frac{W}{L}\right)_{NL}\left(v_{GS.NL} - v_{TN}\right)} = \frac{1}{K'\left(\frac{W}{L}\right)_{NL} V_{DS.NL(SAT)}} = \frac{1}{\sqrt{2i_{NL}K'\left(\frac{W}{L}\right)_{NL}}} \propto \frac{1}{\sqrt{i_{NL}}}$$

$$\therefore \quad i_{NL} \propto v_{PTAT}\sqrt{i_{NL}} \qquad \rightarrow \qquad i_{NL} \propto v_{PTAT}{}^2.$$

4.5. Piecewise-Linear Correction

At low temperatures, below transitional point T_{TRAN}, i_{CTAT} overwhelms i_{PTAT}.

$\therefore$ M_{CO} pulls v_{NL} toward v_{DD}, M_{MO}'s $i_{NL} \approx 0$, and v_{REF} is first order to T_{TRAN}.

At high temperatures, above T_{TRAN}, M_{CO}'s $i_{CTAT} < i_{PTAT}$.

$\therefore$ M_{NL} sources $i_{NL} = i_{PTAT} - i_{CTAT} \approx$ PTAT, so v_{REF} is first order after T_{TRAN}.

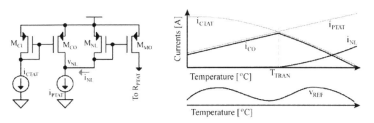

More i_{NL} segments with staggered T_{TRAN}'s can reduce Δv_{REF} further.

4.5. T ln T Correction

Q_P and Q_{0TC} impress diode difference Δv_{BE} across R_{NL}.

Δv_{BE} with PTAT and 0-TC currents I_{PTAT} and I_{0TC} generate T ln T behavior.

$$i_{NL} = \frac{\Delta v_{BE}}{R_{NL}} = \frac{v_{BEP} - v_{BE0TC}}{R_{NL}} \approx \frac{V_t}{R_{NL}} \ln\left(\frac{I_{PTAT}}{I_{0TC}}\right) \propto T \ln T$$

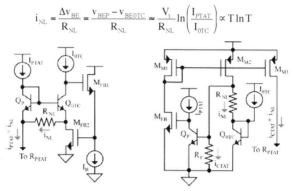

M_{FB1}–M_{FB2} and M_{FB}–M_{M1}–M_{M2} implement inverting feedback loops

that ensure i_{NL} flows through R_{NL}.

4.5. Higher-Order Correction

T ln T^X Voltage: Δv_{BE} offsets v_{BG1}'s T ln T term:

$$v_{REF} = v_{BG1} - v_{BEC} + v_{BEP} \text{ where}$$

$$\Delta v_{BE} = V_t \ln\left(\frac{I_{PTAT}}{I_{CTAT} - I_{PTAT}}\right) \propto T \ln\left(\frac{I_{PTAT}}{K_X I_{CTAT}}\right) \rightarrow T \ln\left(+TC\right)$$

Quasi-Exact Correction:

Since "1" in v_D's "$\eta - 1$" corresponds

to i_D's PTAT dependence T^1,

$\therefore A v_{D(iPTAT)} - B v_{D(i0TC)}$ removes

T ln T term when $\dfrac{A}{A - B} \equiv \eta$.

E.g.: If $\eta = 4$, $A \equiv 4$, and $B \equiv 3$.

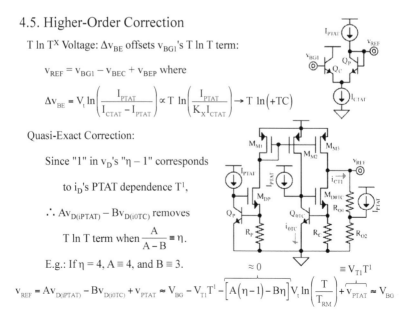

$$v_{REF} = A v_{D(iPTAT)} - B v_{D(i0TC)} + v_{PTAT} \approx V_{BG} - \overbrace{V_{T1} T^1}^{\approx 0} - \left[A\left(\eta - 1\right) - B\eta\right] V_t \ln\left(\frac{T}{T_{RM}}\right) + \overbrace{v_{PTAT}}^{\equiv V_{T1} T^1} \approx V_{BG}$$

4.5. Parasitic Correction

Use "parasitic" effects to correct nonlinearity.

Base Current: Add $i_{BP1}R_B$ to v_{BG1}.

Base-Width Modulation: Adjust $i_{PTAT}R_P{}'$

to mismatch collector–emitter voltages v_{CE}'s.

High-TC Resistor R_{HTC}: Add $i_{PTAT}R_{HTC}$ to v_{BG1}.

$$i_{PTAT}R_{HTC} = V_t\left(\frac{R_{HTC}}{R_P}\right)\ln\left(C\right) \propto T^2$$

Trimming at more than one temperature is too costly.

∴ Do not trim curvature-correcting component.

Systemic correction reduces 20–100-ppm/°C 3σ first-order variation.

But randomness limits improvement to 5–40 ppm/°C.

Parasitic correction requires less power and silicon area.

BJT PTAT pair suppresses offsets more than MOSFETs.

Chapter 5. Linear-Regulator ICs

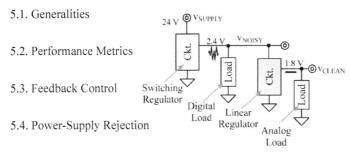

5.1. Generalities

5.2. Performance Metrics

5.3. Feedback Control

5.4. Power-Supply Rejection

5.5. Integrated Circuits

5.1. Generalities

Purpose: Establish accurate supply voltage.

            Regulate output v_{OUT} against

                supply, load, and temperature variations and noise.

Input: Unregulated dc source: Battery → E.g.: 2.7–4.2 V.

            Switched ac–dc or dc–dc regulator → Rippling voltage.

Important Parameters

    Accuracy: Steady State

                         Transient → Response Time → Speed

    Conversion Efficiency: Power Losses

    Operating Requirements: v_{IN}, v_{OUT}, i_{OUT}, and C_O.

    Footprint: Silicon area and board space.

5.1. Regions of Operation

Linear Region: Feedback loop regulates v_{OUT} (with high loop gain).

Dropout Region: One or several nodes rails, so loop gain drops.

    → Circuit still operates, but it no longer regulates v_{OUT} well.

    → Dropout voltage V_{DO} is the voltage dropped in dropout.

Off: Circuit loses headroom, so it no longer senses or regulates v_{OUT}.

Conduction Power Lost: $P_C = i_O(v_{IN} - v_{OUT})$.

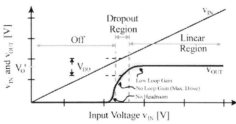

Linear Region:

    Most accurate.

Dropout Region:

    $P_C = i_O V_{DO}$.

    → Least lossy.

Optimum Point:

    Just above dropout.

5.1. Typical Application

Linear Regulators: Low-noise supplies for A/D's, D/A's, PLL's, VCO's, etc.

Bridge wide voltage gaps with switched regulators for low losses.

Suppress noise in rippling supplies with linear regulators.

Desktop-Computer Example:

120 V → AC–DC → 24 V → DC–DC → 2.4 V → Lin. Reg. → 1.8 V.

Cellular-Phone Example: 3.6 V → DC–DC → 2.0 V → Lin. Reg → 1.8 V

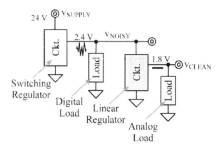

5.1. Operating Environment

Components, board, and package incorporate parasitic devices.

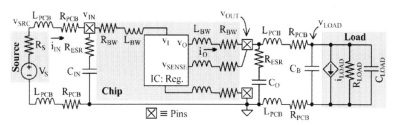

Loop regulates feedback point v_{OUT} → Effective load is at v_{OUT} (not v_{LOAD}).

Feedback sense path carries no current → No voltage drops ∴ Accurate.

R_{LOAD} is not always V_{OUT}/I_{OUT} → E.g.: For a 2.5-V, 100-μA op amp,

$$R_{LOAD} \text{ is not } 2.5V/100\mu A.$$

5.1. Operating Environment

Simplified ⎤ Lump R_{PCB}'s to R_{PCB}' and C_{LOAD}–C_B to C_B'.

Load ⎦ Neglect impedances in low-current paths → Sense and IC ground.

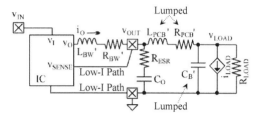

C_O is usually a tantalum or ceramic multi-layer chip CMC capacitor in nF's–μF's.

C_O's Equivalent Series Resistance R_{ESR} is 50 mΩ–5 Ω and Inductance L_{ESL} in nH's.

C_B is usually a high-frequency (i.e., low-ESR) bypass capacitor in nF's–μF.

1-m" bond wire's R_{BW} ≈ 150 mΩ and L_{BW} ≈ 5 nH and lower with multiple bond wires.

5.1. Classification

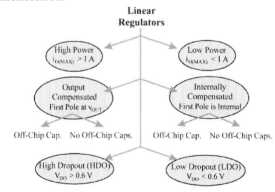

Output Compensated	Internally Compensated
High C_O ∴ Low $\Delta v_{OUT(LD\_DUMP)}$	Low C_O ∴ High $\Delta v_{OUT(LD\_DUMP)}$
$C_{OFF-CHIP}$ ∴ More PCB area	High $C_{ON-CHIP}$ ∴ More Si area
High-Power Applications	Low-Power Applications

5.1. Typical Block-Level Composition

Power Pass Transistor:

Draws power from v_{IN} to supply load.

Control Loop:

Regulates v_{OUT} to v_{REF}.

Voltage Reference

Feedback Error Amplifier

Feedback Network

Output Filter

Housekeeping:

Current Limiter

Thermal Shutdown

Electrostatic-Discharge (ESD) Protection

…

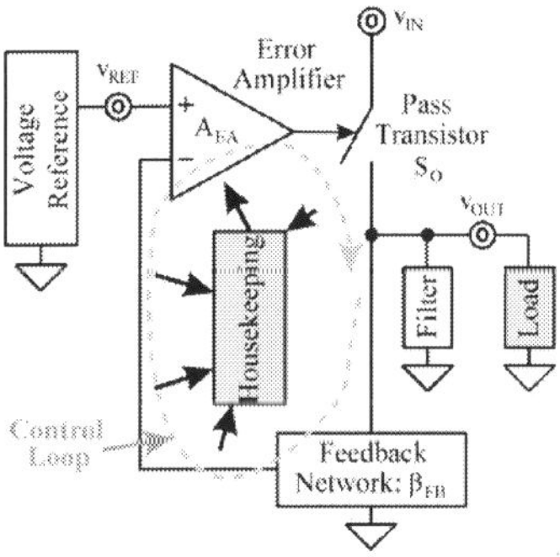

5.2. Performance Metrics

Circuit Parameter	Specification	Process Parameter	Value
v_{IN}	1.1–1.6 V	$|V_{TP0}|$ & V_{TN0}	0.6 ± 0.15 V
v_O	1 V	$V_{TN0.NAT}$	0 ± 0.15 V
v_{REF}	0.9 V	K_P'	$40\ \mu A/V^2 \pm 20\%$
A_E	≈ 40 dB	K_N'	$100\ \mu A/V^2 \pm 20\%$
i_Q	$\leq 6\ \mu A$	L	$\geq 0.35\ \mu m$
$v_{OE(MAX)}$	$v_{IN} - 0.3$ V	C_{OX}''	$5\ fF/\mu m^2$
$v_{OE(MIN)}$	0.2 V	$\lambda_{L(MIN)}$	$500\ mV^{-1}$
f_{0dB}	1 MHz	$\lambda_{3L(MIN)}$	$10\ mV^{-1}$
V_{OS}^*	≤ 25 mV	β_{P0}	50–150 A/A
$\Delta v_{O(LD)}$	≤ 10 mV	V_A	15 V

5.2. Accuracy

Simplified Feedback Circuit

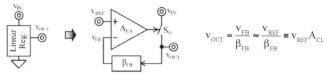

$$v_{OUT} = \frac{v_{FB}}{\beta_{FB}} \approx \frac{v_{REF}}{\beta_{FB}} \equiv v_{REF} A_{CL}$$

Tolerance: Feedback amplifies v_{REF}'s random steady-state error ΔV_{REF}^{*}.

A_{EA}'s random input-referred offset $V_{EA.OS}^{*}$.

$$V_{OS}^{*} = \left[\sqrt{\left(\Delta V_{REF}^{*}\right)^2 + \left(V_{EA.OS}^{*}\right)^2} \right] A_{CL} \approx \frac{\sqrt{\left(\Delta V_{REF}^{*}\right)^2 + \left(V_{EA.OS}^{*}\right)^2}}{\beta_{FB}}$$

Gain Error: Finite loop gain $A_{OL}\beta_{FB}$ limits closed-loop gain A_{CL}.

$$v_{OUT} = \frac{v_{FB}}{\beta_{FB}} = v_{REF}\left(\frac{A_{OL}\beta_{FB}}{1+A_{OL}\beta_{FB}}\right)\left(\frac{1}{\beta_{FB}}\right) = v_{REF}\left(\frac{A_{OL}}{1+A_{OL}\beta_{FB}}\right) \equiv v_{REF} A_{CL}$$

$$\Delta V_{GE} = v_{OUT} - V_{OUT(IDEAL)} = v_{REF}\left(\frac{A_{OL}}{1+A_{OL}\beta_{FB}} - \frac{1}{\beta_{FB}}\right) = \frac{v_{REF}}{\beta_{FB}}\left(\frac{-1}{1+A_{OL}\beta_{FB}}\right)$$

5.2. Accuracy

Temperature Drift: v_{REF} and A_{EA}'s $V_{EA.OS}$ drift across temperature.

→ Fractional Temperature Coefficient

$$TC_O \equiv \frac{1}{V_{OUT}}\left(\frac{dV_{OUT}}{dT_J}\right) \approx \frac{1}{V_{OUT}}\left(\frac{\Delta V_{TD}}{\Delta T_J}\right) \approx \frac{1}{V_{REF}A_{CL}}\left(\frac{\Delta V_{OS}^{*}A_{CL}}{\Delta T_J}\right) = \frac{\Delta V_{OS}^{*}}{V_{REF}}\left(\frac{1}{\Delta T_J}\right)$$

Line Regulation: Regulator and v_{REF} are sensitive to slow v_{IN} variations.

→ Low-Frequency Supply Gain: $A_{IN0} \equiv \frac{\Delta v_{OUT}}{\Delta v_{IN}}$.

$$\Delta V_{LN} = \Delta V_{IN}\left(A_{IN0.REG} + A_{IN0.REF}A_{CL}\right) = \Delta V_{IN}\left[\left.\frac{\Delta V_{OUT}}{\Delta V_{IN}}\right|_{\Delta V_{REF}=0} + \left(\frac{\Delta V_{REF}}{\Delta V_{IN}}\right)A_{CL}\right]$$

Power-Supply Rejection: Power switch and v_{REF} feed supply noise to v_{OUT}.

→ Rejection is the inability (reciprocal) to amplify supply noise.

$$PSR \equiv \frac{1}{A_{IN}} = \frac{\partial v_{IN}}{\partial v_{OUT}} \qquad A_{IN} = \frac{1}{PSR} = \frac{A_{CL}}{PSR_{REF}} + \frac{1}{PSR_{REG}} \qquad \Delta v_{PSR} = \Delta v_{IN}A_{IN} = \frac{\Delta v_{IN}}{PSR}$$

5.2. Accuracy

Load Regulation: Finite loop gain partially counters slow load variations.

→ Shunt-feedback resistance R_{CL} drops voltage.

$$\Delta V_{LD} = \Delta I_{LOAD} R_{CL} = \Delta I_{LOAD} \left(R_{OL} \parallel \frac{R_{OL}}{A_{OL0}\beta_{FB0}} \right) = \Delta I_{LOAD} \left(\frac{R_{OL}}{1 + A_{OL0}\beta_{FB0}} \right)$$

Load-Dump Response:

→ Response to wide and sudden load dumps Δi_{LOAD}.

→ Bandwidth delays response.

$$t_{BW} \approx 2.3\tau_{RC} = \frac{2.3}{2\pi f_{-3dB}}$$

→ Current-starved capacitors further delay response.

$$\Delta t_R = t_{BW} + t_{SO.SR} = t_{BW} + C_{PAR} \left(\frac{\Delta v_{PAR}}{i_{O.EA(MAX)}} \right) = \frac{2.3}{2\pi f_{-3dB}} + C_{PAR} \left(\frac{\Delta i_{LOAD}}{G_{M.SO} I_{SR}} \right)$$

5.2. Accuracy

Load-Dump Response:

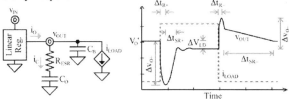

→ During delay, C_O and C_B supply what i_O cannot: Δi_{LOAD}.

→ C_O supplies fraction of load variation Δi_{LOAD}.

→ C_O's current i_{CO} drops voltage Δv_{ESR} across R_{ESR} instantaneously.

$$\Delta v_{ESR} \approx \left(\frac{C_O}{C_O + C_B} \right) \Delta i_{LOAD} R_{ESR}$$

→ i_{CO} slews C_O.

$$\Delta v_C \approx \left(\frac{\Delta i_{LOAD}}{C_O + C_B} \right) \Delta t_R$$

5.2. Accuracy

Load-Dump Response:

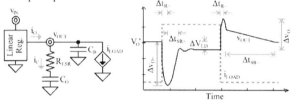

→ Slew-rate current $i_{O.EA(MAX)}$ is usually not symmetrical, so $\Delta t_{R+} \neq \Delta t_{R-}$.

→ After rising load dump, i_O momentarily surpasses i_{LOAD} (overshoots),

so v_{OUT} rises quickly and settles to loaded state: $V_O' - \Delta V_{LD}$.

∴ $\Delta v_{DUMP} = \Delta v_O - \Delta V_{LD} = \Delta v_{ESR} + \Delta v_C - \Delta V_{LD}$

→ After falling load dump, i_O drops momentarily below i_{LOAD},

so resistive feedback network β_{FB} slews C_O and

v_{OUT} falls (usually slowly) to unloaded state: V_O'.

5.2. Accuracy

Example: Determine ΔV_{LD} and Δv_{DUMP} for $\Delta i_{LOAD} = 100$ mA in 1 ns when

$v_{REF} = 1.5$ V, $\beta_{FB} = 1$, $C_O = 10$ μF, $R_{ESR} = 200$ mΩ, $C_B = 1$ μF,

$f_{BW} = 500$ kHz, $R_{CL} = 300$ mΩ, $I_{SR} = 5$ μA, $G_{M.SO} = 300$ mA/V,

and $C_{PAR} = 100$ pF.

Solution: $\Delta V_{LD} \approx \Delta I_{LOAD} R_{CL} = 100$ mA $\cdot 300$ mΩ $= 30$ mV

$$\Delta v_{DUMP} = \Delta v_{O(MAX)} - \Delta V_{LD} = \Delta v_{ESR} + \Delta v_{C(MAX)} - \Delta V_{LD}$$

$$\Delta v_{ESR} = \left(\frac{\Delta i_{LOAD} C_O}{C_O + C_B}\right) R_{ESR} = \left(\frac{100 \text{ mA} \cdot 10 \text{ μF}}{10 \text{ μF} + 1 \text{ μF}}\right) 0.2 \ \Omega = 18 \text{ mV}$$

$$\Delta v_{C(MAX)} = \left(\frac{\Delta i_{LOAD} C_O}{C_O + C_B}\right)\frac{t_{R(MAX)}}{C_O} = \left(\frac{100 \text{ mA}}{10 \text{ μF} + 1 \text{ μF}}\right) t_{R(MAX)}$$

$$\Delta t_{R(MAX)} \approx t_{BW} + t_{SO.SR(MAX)} \approx \frac{2.3}{2\pi f_{-3dB}} + \frac{C_O}{i_{O.EA(SINK)}}\left(\frac{\Delta i_{LOAD}}{G_{M.SO}}\right)$$

$$= \frac{2.3}{2\pi(500 \text{ kHz})} + \frac{100 \text{ pF}}{5 \text{ μA}}\left(\frac{100 \text{ mA}}{300 \text{ mA}/_V}\right) \approx 730 \text{ ns} + 7 \text{ μs} \approx 8 \text{ μs}$$

5.2. Total Accuracy

Steady-State Error:

→ Linear sum of systemic errors and root-square sum of random errors.

→ Tolerance, gain error, temperature drift, and line and load regulation.

$$\text{Error}_0 \equiv \Delta E_0 = \frac{\Delta V_{GE} + \Delta V_{TD} + \Delta V_{LN} + \Delta V_{LD} \pm V_{OS}^{\ *}}{V_{OUT}}$$

Total Error:

→ Error_0 plus power-supply rejection and load-dump response.

$$\text{Error} \equiv \Delta E = \Delta E_0 + \frac{\Delta v_{PSR} + \Delta v_{DUMP}}{V_{OUT}}$$

Example: Determine the accuracy of a 2.4-V regulator when $v_{REF} = 1.2$ V, $A_{OL} = 60$ dB, $\Delta v_{IN} = \pm 25$ mV at 100 kHz, PSR − 10 dB at 100 kHz, $\Delta v_{LD} = 140$ mV ± 5 mV, $\Delta V_{TC} = 3$ mV ± 24 mV, $\Delta V_{LD} = 20$ mV ± 5 mV, and $\Delta V_{LN} = 8$ mV ± 2.5 mV.

Solution:

$$\Delta V_{GE} = \frac{v_{REF}}{\beta_{FB}}\left(\frac{-1}{1 + A_{OL}\beta_{FB}}\right) = \frac{1.2 \ V}{2}\left(\frac{-1}{1 + 1000 \cdot 2}\right) \approx 0.3 \text{ mV}$$

5.2. Total Accuracy

Solution (continued):

$$\Delta v_{PSR} = \frac{\Delta v_{IN}}{PSR} = \frac{25 \text{ mV at } 100 \text{ kHz}}{\log^{-1}\left(\dfrac{10 \text{ at } 100 \text{ kHz}}{20}\right)} = \frac{25 \text{ mV}}{3.16} = 7.9 \text{ mV}$$

$$\Delta v_{DUMP} = \Delta v_O - \Delta V_{LD} = 140 \text{ mV} - 20 \text{ mV} = 120 \text{ mV}$$

$$V_{OS}^{\ *} \approx \sqrt{\left(\Delta v_{DUMP}^{\ *}\right)^2 + \left(\Delta V_{TD}^{\ *}\right)^2 + \left(\Delta V_{LD}^{\ *}\right)^2 + \left(\Delta V_{LN}^{\ *}\right)^2}$$

$$= \sqrt{\left(5 \text{ mV}\right)^2 + \left(24 \text{ mV}\right)^2 + \left(5 \text{ mV}\right)^2 + \left(2.5 \text{ mV}\right)^2} = 25.1 \text{ mV}$$

$$\text{Error} = \frac{\Delta V_{GE} + \Delta V_{TD} + \Delta V_{LN} + \Delta V_{LD} + \Delta v_{PSR} + \Delta v_{DUMP} \pm V_{OS}^{\ *}}{V_{OUT}}$$

$$\approx \frac{0.3 \text{ mV} + 3 \text{ mV} + 8 \text{ mV} + 20 \text{ mV} + 7.9 \text{ mV} + 120 \text{ mV} \pm 25.1 \text{ mV}}{2.4 \ V}$$

$$= 6.6\% \pm 1.0\%$$

5.2. Power-Conversion Efficiency

Conversion efficiency is the fraction of P_{IN} that reaches the load.

→ Regulator dissipates power as P_{LOSS}.

$$\eta_C \equiv \frac{P_O}{P_{IN}} = \frac{P_{IN} - P_{LOSS}}{P_{IN}} = \frac{P_O}{P_O + P_{LOSS}} < 100\%$$

Conduction Power: Power switch S_O dissipates power.

$$P_{SO} = i_O \left(v_{IN} - v_{OUT} \right) = i_{LOAD} \left(v_{IN} - v_{OUT} \right)$$

Quiescent Power: Controller dissipates power.

→ Quiescent current is lost as ground current.

$$P_{CTRL} = i_{GND} \left(v_{IN} - 0 \right) = i_{GND} v_{IN}$$

Current efficiency is the fraction of i_{IN} that reaches the load.

$$\eta_I \equiv \frac{i_{LOAD}}{i_{IN}} = \frac{i_{LOAD}}{i_{LOAD} + i_{GND}} < 1$$

5.2. Power-Conversion Efficiency

$$\therefore \quad \eta_C = \frac{P_O}{P_O + P_{SO} + P_{CTRL}} = \frac{i_{LOAD} v_{OUT}}{i_{LOAD} v_{OUT} + i_{LOAD} \left(v_{IN} - v_{OUT} \right) + i_{GND} v_{IN}}$$

$$= \frac{i_{LOAD} v_{OUT}}{\left(i_{LOAD} + i_{GND} \right) v_{IN}} = \eta_I \left(\frac{v_{OUT}}{v_{IN}} \right) < \frac{v_{OUT}}{v_{IN}}$$

→ Highest η_C when ground current is close to nil.

→ Even if η_I is 100%, v_{IN}-to-v_{OUT} spread limits η_C.

$\therefore$ Highest η_C when spread is low, when $v_{IN} - v_{OUT} \approx V_{DO}$.

$$\eta_C = \eta_I \left(\frac{v_{OUT}}{v_{IN}} \right) < \eta_I \left(\frac{v_{IN} - V_{DO}}{v_{IN}} \right) < 1 - \frac{V_{DO}}{v_{IN}}$$

Where $\quad V_{DO} = i_{LOAD} R_{ON}$

$$R_{ON} = R_{METAL} + R_{CONTACT} + R_{BOND-WIRE} + R_{SWITCH}$$

→ Since normally $i_{GND} \ll i_{LOAD(MAX)}$, $\eta_I \approx 100\%$ and $\eta_C \approx \eta_{C(MAX)}$ at full load.

→ When i_{LOAD} is zero, however, η_I and η_C are zero.

5.2. Power-Conversion Efficiency

Example: Determine the worst- and best-case full- and no-load η_C's when

$$v_{IN} = 0.9\text{–}1.6 \text{ V}, \ i_{LOAD} = 0\text{–}100 \text{ mA}, \ v_{REF} = 1.2 \text{ V}, \ \beta_{FB} = 1,$$

$$R_{ON} = 500 \text{ m}\Omega, \text{ and } i_{GND} = 10 \text{ }\mu\text{A}.$$

Solution:

Full: $\quad \eta_C = \dfrac{i_{LOAD(MAX)} v_{OUT}}{\left(i_{LOAD(MAX)} + i_{GND}\right) v_{IN(MAX)}} = \dfrac{100 \text{ mA} \cdot 1.2 \text{ V}}{\left(100 \text{ mA} + 10 \text{ }\mu\text{A}\right) 1.6 \text{ V}} \approx \dfrac{1.2 \text{ V}}{1.6 \text{ V}} = 75\%$

$$V_{DO} = i_{LOAD(MAX)} R_{ON} = 100 \text{ mA} \cdot 500 \text{ m}\Omega = 50 \text{ mV}$$

$$\eta_C = \frac{i_{LOAD(MAX)} v_{OUT}}{\left(i_{LOAD(MAX)} + i_{GND}\right) v_{IN(MIN)}} = \frac{i_{LOAD(MAX)} v_{OUT}}{\left(i_{LOAD(MAX)} + i_{GND}\right)\left(v_{OUT} + V_{DO}\right)}$$

$$= \frac{100 \text{ mA} \cdot 1.2 \text{ V}}{\left(100 \text{ mA} + 10 \text{ }\mu\text{A}\right)\left(1.2 \text{ V} + 50 \text{ mV}\right)} \approx \frac{1.20 \text{ V}}{1.25 \text{ V}} = 96\%$$

No Load: $\quad \eta_C = \dfrac{i_{LOAD(MIN)} v_{OUT}}{\left(i_{LOAD(MIN)} + i_{GND}\right) v_{IN(MAX)}} = \dfrac{\left(0 \text{ A}\right) v_{OUT}}{\left(0 \text{ A} + i_{GND}\right) v_{IN(MAX)}} = 0\%$

5.2. Notes

Normally, other blocks use v_{REF}.

$\qquad \therefore v_{REF}$ alone is trimmed to lowest-drift point.

$\qquad\qquad \rightarrow V_{EA.OS}$'s drift with temperature is not compensated.

$\qquad\qquad \therefore$ Low offset $V_{EA.OS}$ is desirable.

Negative feedback counters v_{IN} and i_{LOAD} variations.

$\qquad \therefore$ High loop gain A_{LG} or $A_{OL}\beta_{FB}$ is desirable.

v_{REF} is normally less sensitive to v_{IN} than regulators are.

$\qquad \therefore$ The regulator's A_{IN} and PSR limit performance.

Response time Δt_R produces load-dump variations.

$\qquad \therefore$ High bandwidth $f_{CL.BW}$ or f_{0dB} is desirable.

Output capacitors C_O and C_B supply full load dump at first.

$\qquad \therefore$ High capacitances C_O and C_B are desirable.

5.2. Notes

Load dump drops a voltage across C_O's R_{ESR}.

$\therefore$ Low resistance R_{ESR} is desirable.

Linear sum of random errors is unrealistically pessimistic and

root-square sum of systemic errors is similarly optimistic.

Steady-state error E_0 is normally near 0.5%–3%.

Silicon area and board space are often scarce,

C_O is low and load-dump error Δv_{DUMP} can be 2%–7%.

Controller power is proportional to ground current i_{GND}.

$\therefore$ Low ground current i_{GND} is desirable.

Conduction power is proportional to $v_{IN} - v_{OUT}$.

$\therefore$ Low dropout voltage V_{DO} is desirable.

5.2. Notes

Dropout voltage V_{DO} changes with input-supply v_{IN} variations.

$\rightarrow$ Specification should define conditions.

E.g.: V_{DO} or R_{ON} at full load when v_{IN} is at v_{OUT}'s target $V_O{}'$.

E.g.: $i_{O(MAX)}$ when v_{IN} is at v_{OUT}'s target $V_O{}'$ and

linear regulator drops 200 mV.

Since high $i_{O(MAX)}$ and PSR_{MIN} and low ΔE_0, i_{GND}, V_{DO}, C_O, and

Δt_R are desirable, a figure of merit FoM can be:

$$\text{FoM} \equiv \frac{i_{O(MAX)}PSR_{MIN}}{\Delta E_0 i_{GND} V_{DO} C_O \Delta t_R}\underbrace{\left(\frac{0.01 \cdot 5 \ \mu A \cdot 200 \ mV \cdot 1 \ \mu F \cdot 1 \ \mu s}{100 \ mA \cdot 10}\right)}_{\text{A plausible point of reference.}} = \frac{i_{O(MAX)}PSR_{MIN}}{\Delta E_0 i_{GND} V_{DO} C_O \Delta t_R \left(10^{20}\right)}$$

But since applications *do not* normally weigh factors evenly,

FoM's are hardly used in practice.

5.3. Feedback Control

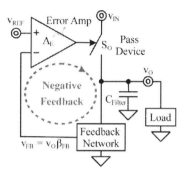

5.3. Equivalent Small-Signal Circuit

The purpose of a filter at the output is to supply sudden load-dump power.

→ High output capacitance C_O is desirable.

Low-cost, high-capacitance capacitors exhibit considerable

equivalent series resistance (ESR) R_{ESR}.

→ Users normally add low-ESR

bypass capacitors C_B near the load.

The feedback network is usually a

voltage-dividing resistor divider

that conducts little current.

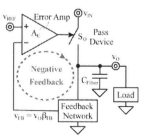

→ High feedback resistances R_{FB1} and R_{FB2}.

5.3. Equivalent Small-Signal Circuit

Transform the error amplifier A_E, the power switch S_O,

and the load into Norton equivalents.

v_{IN} is a low-impedance source, so v_{in} is nearly zero → Small-signal ground.

Simplify circuit by combining parallel components:

→ $C_O' \equiv C_B + C_P + C_L$.

→ $R_O \equiv R_L \| R_P$.

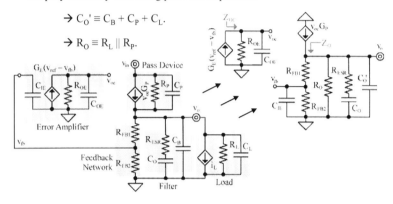

5.3. Relative Resistances and Capacitances

R_{ESR} is parasitic metallic resistance at 50–500 mΩ.

R_P is the output resistance of a large power transistor with

considerable channel-length or base-width modulation

that carries substantial current → Can be 0.1–50 kΩ.

R_{FB1}–R_{FB2} normally carry less than 5 µA → Can be 100–500 kΩ.

E.g.: 1.8 V into 500 kΩ produces 3.6 µA.

R_{OE} sets the loop gain → Usually higher than 500 kΩ.

C_O supplies most of the load dump → Usually high in nF's or µF's.

C_B supplements C_O → Usually about 1/10 of C_O.

C_{IE}, C_{OE}, C_P, and C_L are parasitic → Much lower than C_O and C_B.

S_O and the load are large → S_O's C_{OE} and C_P and the load's $C_L \gg C_{IE}$.

$\therefore R_{ESR} \ll R_P \ll R_{FB1}$–$R_{FB2} < R_{OE}$ and $C_{IE} \ll C_{OE}$, C_P, $C_L \ll C_B \ll C_O$.

5.3. Frequency Response

Loop Gain A_{LG} or $A_{OL}\beta_{FB}$:

$$A_{LG} = A_{OL}\beta_{FB} = \left(\frac{v_o}{v_{ref} - v_{fb}}\right)\left(\frac{v_{fb}}{v_o}\right) = \left(G_E Z_{OE} G_P Z_O\right)\left(\frac{Z_{FB2}}{R_{FB1} + Z_{FB2}}\right)$$

Low-Frequency Loop Gain A_{LG0}:

$$A_{LG0} = G_E R_{OE} G_P\left[\left(R_{FB1} + R_{FB2}\right) \| R_O\right]\left(\frac{R_{FB2}}{R_{FB1} + R_{FB2}}\right) \approx G_E R_{OE} G_P R_P\left(\frac{R_{FB2}}{R_{FB1} + R_{FB2}}\right)$$

Gain drops (pole) when A_E's

$\quad C_{OE}$ shunts R_{OE}

$\qquad$ when $1/sC_{OE} \leq R_{OE}$

$\qquad \therefore p_E = 1/2\pi R_{OE}C_{OE}.$ $\quad \left.\dfrac{1}{sC_{OE}}\right|_{p_E = \frac{1}{2\pi R_{OE}C_{OE}}} \equiv R_{OE}$

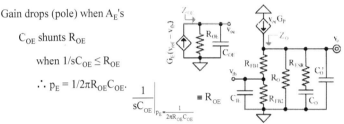

5.3. Frequency Response: Across Z_O

Notes: $C_O \gg C_B \rightarrow C_O$ shorts first.

$\qquad R_{ESR} \ll R_O, R_{FB1}-R_{FB2} \rightarrow R_{ESR}$ is negligible at low frequency.

Gain drops (pole) when C_O and C_O' shunt $R_{FB1}-R_{FB2}\|R_O$:

$$\left.\frac{1}{s\left(C_O + C_O'\right)}\right|_{p_O = \frac{1}{2\pi\left[\left(R_{FB1}+R_{FB2}\right)\|R_L\|R_P\right]\left(C_O+C_B+C_L+C_P\right)}} \equiv \left(R_{FB1} + R_{FB2}\right) \| R_O$$

Gain flattens (zero) when C_O shorts with respect to R_{ESR}:

$\quad \left.\dfrac{1}{sC_O}\right|_{z_{ESR} = \frac{1}{2\pi R_{ESR}C_O}} \equiv R_{ESR}$

C_O' is so much higher than others that

$\quad$ gain drops (pole) when C_O' shunts R_{ESR}:

$\quad \left.\dfrac{1}{sC_O'}\right|_{p_B = \frac{1}{2\pi R_{ESR}(C_B+C_L+C_P)}} \equiv R_{ESR}$

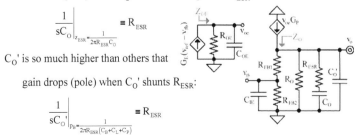

5.3. Frequency Response

Since C_O and C_O' already shorted v_o,

gain drops when C_{IE}' shunts R_{FB1}–R_{FB2}:

$$\left.\frac{1}{sC_{IE}}\right|_{p_{FB}=\frac{1}{2\pi(R_{FB2}\|R_{FB1})C_{IE}}} \equiv R_{FB2}\,\|\,R_{FB1}$$

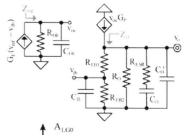

So uncompensated loop-gain response is:

$$A_{LG} \approx \frac{A_{LG0}\left(1+\dfrac{s}{2\pi z_{ESR}}\right)}{\left(1+\dfrac{s}{2\pi p_E}\right)\left(1+\dfrac{s}{2\pi p_O}\right)\left(1+\dfrac{s}{2\pi p_B}\right)\left(1+\dfrac{s}{2\pi p_{FB}}\right)}$$

Note R_{ESR} sets both z_{ESR} and p_B and $C_O \gg C_O'$,

→ z_{ESR} tracks and precedes p_B:

$$\frac{p_B}{z_{ESR}} = \frac{2\pi R_{ESR} C_O}{2\pi R_{ESR} C_O'} = \frac{C_O}{C_O'} = \frac{C_O}{C_B + C_L + C_P}$$

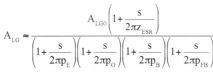

5.3. Frequency Response

Validation

Combine R_{FB1}–R_{FB2} and R_O into R_O' ∴

$$Z_O = \frac{R_O'\left(1+sR_{ESR}C_O\right)}{s^2 R_O' R_{ESR} C_O C_O' + s\left(R_O' + R_{ESR}\right)C_O + sR_O'C_O' + 1}$$

At low frequency, s^2 term $\ll s^1$ term.

∴ s^2 term disappears and

$$p_O \approx 1/2\pi R_O'(C_O + C_O')$$

→ Same as previous.

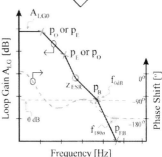

At high frequency, $s^0 \ll s^2$ and s^1 terms.

∴ 1 disappears and

$$p_B \approx 1/2\pi R_{ESR}(C_O \odot C_O')$$

$$\approx 1/2\pi R_{ESR}C_O' \rightarrow \text{Same as previous.}$$

5.3. Frequency Response: Design Notes

A_{LG} incorporates 4 poles and 1 zero.

Since C_{IE} is low, p_{FB} is high.

Still, 3 poles and 1 zero can

produce unstable conditions.

R_L is typically unpredictable.

i_L spans up to 4–5 decades.

E.g.: 1 µA $< i_L <$ 100 mA.

R_{ESR} range spans 1–2 decades

with process and temperature.

z_{ESR} can help, but only if R_{ESR} is high,

which is bad for load-dump response.

Since $R_P \ll R_{FB1}$–R_{FB2},

$p_O \propto 1/R_O' \approx 1/R_P \propto i_L$.

$\therefore p_O$ shifts with i_L

up to 5–6 decades.

z_{ESR} tracks and precedes p_B

by C_O/C_O'.

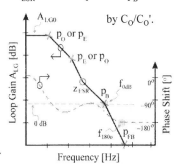

5.3. Frequency Response

Example: Determine the poles and zeros of a linear regulator when

C_O = 4.7 µF, C_B = 0.3 µF, C_L = 0.2 µF, C_P = 10 pF, R_P = 100 Ω,

R_L = 10 kΩ, R_{FB1} + R_{FB2} = 500 kΩ, and R_{ESR} = 100 mΩ.

Solution:

$$p_O = \frac{1}{2\pi\left[\left(R_{FB1}+R_{FB2}\right)\|R_L\|R_P\right]\left(C_O+C_B+C_L+C_P\right)}$$

$$= \frac{1}{2\pi\left[\left(500\ k\Omega\right)\|\left(10\ k\Omega\right)\|\left(100\ \Omega\right)\right]\left(4.7+0.3+0.2\ \mu F+10\ pF\right)} \approx 300\ Hz$$

$$z_{ESR} = \frac{1}{2\pi R_{ESR}C_O} = \frac{1}{2\pi\left(0.1\ \Omega\right)\left(4.7\ \mu F\right)} \approx 340\ kHz$$

$$p_B = \frac{1}{2\pi R_{ESR}\left(C_B+C_L+C_P\right)} = \frac{1}{2\pi\left(0.1\ \Omega\right)\left(0.3+0.2\ \mu F+10\ pF\right)} \approx 2.9\ MHz$$

5.3. Frequency Response

Note: With only one pole p_1, gain falls $10\times$ as frequency rises $10\times$.

$\therefore$ Gain–bandwidth product (GBW) is constant past p_1.

$\therefore$ Unity-gain frequency $f_{0dB} = A_{LG0}p_1 \equiv f_{GBW}$.

Output Compensation: Ensure p_O is the dominant low-frequency pole, so

$$f_{GBW} = A_{LG0}p_O = \frac{G_E R_{OE} G_P \left[\left(R_{FB1} + R_{FB2}\right) \| R_O\right]\beta_{FB}}{2\pi\left[\left(R_{FB1} + R_{FB2}\right)\| R_O\right]\left(C_O + C_B + C_L + C_P\right)} = \frac{A_E G_P \beta_{FB}}{2\pi\left(C_O + C_B + C_L + C_P\right)} \propto G_P$$

Common-Source PMOS Power Device:

$f_{GBW} \propto G_P = g_{mP} \propto \sqrt{i_L}$.

z_{ESR}–p_B pair extends f_{GBW} to f_{0dB}.

$\therefore f_{0dB.PMOS} \approx f_{GBW}(p_B/z_{ESR}) \propto \sqrt{i_L}$.

p_E compromises stability.

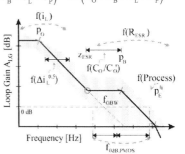

5.3. Frequency Response

Common-Emitter PNP Power Device.

$f_{GBW} \propto G_P = g_{mP} \propto i_L$.

z_{ESR}–p_B pair extends f_{GBW} to f_{0dB}.

$\therefore f_{0dB.PNP} \approx f_{GBW}(p_B/z_{ESR}) \propto i_L$.

p_E compromises stability.

Since i_L can span 4–5 decades

and z_{ESR}–p_B can extend f_{0dB} a decade, f_{0dB} can span

Output Compensation

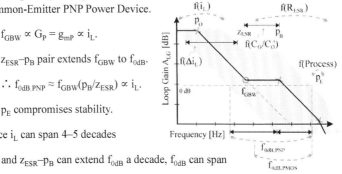

3–4 decades with PMOSFETs and 5–6 decades with PNP BJTs.

$$\frac{f_{0dB(MAX).PMOS}}{f_{0dB(MIN).PMOS}} = \left(\frac{f_{GBW(MAX)}}{f_{GBW(MIN)}}\right)\left(\frac{p_B}{z_{ESR}}\right) = \left(\frac{A_E G_{P(MAX)}\beta_{FB}}{A_E G_{P(MIN)}\beta_{FB}}\right)\left(\frac{p_B}{z_{ESR}}\right) \approx \left(\sqrt{\frac{i_{L(MAX)}}{i_{L(MIN)}}}\right)\left(\frac{C_O}{C_B + C_L + C_P}\right)$$

$$\frac{f_{0dB(MAX).PNP}}{f_{0dB(MIN).PNP}} = \left(\frac{f_{GBW(MAX)}}{f_{GBW(MIN)}}\right)\left(\frac{p_B}{z_{ESR}}\right) = \left(\frac{A_E G_{P(MAX)}\beta_{FB}}{A_E G_{P(MIN)}\beta_{FB}}\right)\left(\frac{p_B}{z_{ESR}}\right) \approx \left(\frac{i_{L(MAX)}}{i_{L(MIN)}}\right)\left(\frac{C_O}{C_B + C_L + C_P}\right)$$

5.3. Frequency Response

Internal Compensation: Ensure p_E is the dominant low-frequency pole, so

$$f_{GBW} = A_{LG0}p_E = \frac{G_E R_{OE} G_P\left[\left(R_{FB1}+R_{FB2}\right)\| R_O\right]\beta_{FB}}{2\pi R_{OE}C_{OE}} \approx \frac{G_E G_P R_O \beta_{FB}}{2\pi C_{OE}} \approx \frac{G_E A_P \beta_{FB}}{2\pi C_{OE}} \propto \frac{A_P}{C_{OE}}$$

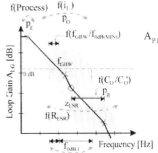

N-Type Follower Power Device

$$A_{P.Follower} = G_{M(DEG)}R_{LOAD} = \left(\frac{g_m}{1+g_m R_{LOAD}}\right)R_{LOAD} \approx 1$$

$\therefore f_{GBW} \neq f(i_L)$.

$z_{ESR}-p_B$ pair extends f_{GBW} to f_{0dB}.

$\therefore f_{0dB} \approx f_{GBW}(p_B/z_{ESR}) \neq f(i_L)$.

p_O compromises stability.

Note that $p_O \approx g_m/2\pi C_O$, so $p_{O(MOS)} \propto g_m \propto \sqrt{i_L}$ and $p_{O(BJT)} \propto g_m \propto i_L$,

so i_L can shift p_O 2–3 decades with PMOSFETs and 4–5 decades with NPN BJTs.

5.3. Frequency Response

Internal Compensation: Ensure p_E is the dominant low-frequency pole, so

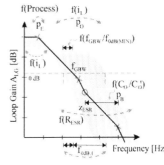

P-Type Miller Power Device

$$\frac{A_{P.Miller}}{C_{OE}} = \frac{g_m R_{LOAD}}{\left(1+g_m R_{LOAD}\right)C_M} \approx \frac{1}{C_M}$$

$\therefore f_{GBW} \neq f(i_L) \rightarrow$ Same as follower.

$z_{ESR}-p_B$ pair extends f_{GBW} to f_{0dB}.

$\therefore f_{0dB} \approx f_{GBW}(p_B/z_{ESR}) \neq f(i_L)$.

p_O compromises stability.

Note that p_O can be within half a decade of f_{0dB}, so p_O can extend f_{0dB} by $\sqrt{10}$.

So even if i_L spans 4–5 decades, f_{0dB} can span up to 1.5 decades.

$$\frac{f_{0dB(MAX)}}{f_{0dB(MIN)}} = \left(\frac{f_{GBW}}{f_{0dB(MIN)}}\right)\left(\frac{p_B}{z_{ESR}}\right) = \left(\frac{f_{GBW}}{f_{0dB(MIN)}}\right)\left(\frac{C_O}{C_B+C_L+C_P}\right) < \left(\sqrt{10}\right)\left(\frac{C_O}{C_B+C_L+C_P}\right)$$

5.3. Frequency Response: Summary and Conclusions

R_{ESR} extends f_{0dB}.

Output Compensation:

   p_O is dominant.

   i_L shifts f_{0dB}.

   p_E is low to moderate at 0.5–1 MHz.

Internal Compensation:

   p_E is dominant.

   i_L shifts p_O, but not f_{0dB}.

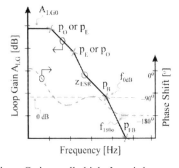

Since C_O suppresses load-dump variations, C_O is usually high $\therefore$ p_O is low.

With low quiescent current, $1/g_m$'s are high $\therefore$ Parasitic poles are low at 1–10 MHz.

→ $f_{0dB(MAX)}$ is usually below 1 MHz $\therefore$ Limited load-dump response.

→ To reach 0 dB at 1 MHz with one pole,

   A_{LG0} must be low at maybe 45–65 dB.

   $\therefore$ Poor line and load regulation and supply rejection.

5.4. Power-Supply Rejection

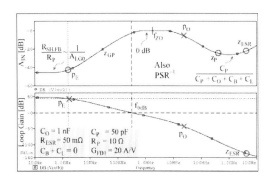

5.4. Definitions

Power-Supply Rejection (PSR):

Ability to reject power-supply noise.

Also known as power-supply ripple rejection.

Inability to amplify supply noise:

$$PSR \equiv \frac{1}{A_{IN}} \equiv \frac{\partial v_{IN}}{\partial v_O} \equiv \frac{v_{in}}{v_o}$$

Line Regulation (LNR):

Variations in v_O in response to steady-state changes in v_{IN}.

Since circuit is in linear mode through v_{IN} range:

$$LNR \equiv \frac{\Delta V_O}{\Delta V_{IN}} \approx \frac{\partial v_O}{\partial v_{IN}}\bigg|_{Low.Freq.} = A_{IN0} = \frac{1}{PSR_0}$$

Power-Supply Rejection Ratio (PSRR):

How much circuit favors processed signals s_I over supply noise in v_O.

$$PSRR \equiv \frac{A_{FWD}}{A_{SUPPLY}} = \left(\frac{\partial s_O}{\partial s_I}\right)\left(\frac{\partial v_{SUPPLY}}{\partial s_O}\right) = A_{FWD}PSR$$

$\therefore$ Power-supply rejection ratio is *not* PSR.

To avoid confusion, use only PSR for supply rejection.

5.4. Voltage-Divider Model

Output stage voltage-divides supply noise v_{in} to v_o.

Top Impedance Z_T: S_O's resistance R_P and capacitance C_P couple v_{in}.

Bottom Impedance Z_B: Feedback resistors R_{FB1}–R_{FB2} and filter C_O–C_B' shunt v_O.

Feedback through S_O's G_P suppresses ripple $\rightarrow$ Shunts v_O with $Z_{SH.FB}$.

$$Z_{SH.FB} \equiv \frac{v_o}{i_{GP}} = \frac{v_o}{v_o \beta_{FB} A_E G_P} \equiv \frac{1}{G_{FB}} = \frac{Z_T \| Z_B}{\beta_{FB} A_E G_P (Z_T \| Z_B)} = \frac{Z_{O.OL}}{\beta_{FB} A_{OL}} = \frac{Z_{O.OL}}{A_{LG}}$$

Note S_O's G_P *can* inject noise into v_O in the form of feed-through noise.

5.4. Feed-Through Noise in Power Transistors

Transistors:

$$i_D \propto (|v_G - v_S| - |v_T|)^2 \quad \text{and} \quad i_C \propto \exp(|v_B - v_E|/V_t)$$

$\therefore$ Noise that is common to gate/base and source/emitter terminals cancels.

Possible Output Transistors:

Voltage Followers	CS/CE Transistors
Sources reproduce gate noise.	Unmatched gate–source noise generates noise current.
$\therefore$ Remove gate noise.	$\therefore$ Reproduce supply noise in gate.

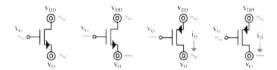

Eliminating feed-through noise from output transistors is possible with balanced mirrored gain stages and common-mode capacitors.

5.4. Feed-Through Noise in Mirrors

Current mirrors receive and reproduce noise currents.

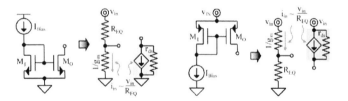

Supply noise and impedance across supply produce noise current.

$$i_{in} = \frac{v_{in}}{R_{EQ} + \dfrac{1}{g_m}} \approx \frac{v_{in}}{R_{EQ}}$$

$\therefore$ High supply impedance limits noise current.

N-type mirrors sink supply-noise current.

P-type mirrors source supply-noise current.

5.4. Feed-Through Noise with N-Type Mirrors

Small-Signal Model: Shunt impedance $Z_{SH.FB}$ already accounts for feedback.

Feedback reproduces v_{REF} in v_{FB} ∴ $v_{id} = 0$.

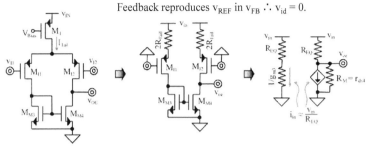

Supply resistance injects supply-noise current to v_{OE}.

N-type mirrors sink supply-noise current from v_{OE} → Reduces v_{in} noise.

$$A_{IN(N.MIR)} = \frac{v_{oe}}{v_{in}} = \frac{\left(\frac{v_{in}R_M}{R_{EQ}+R_M}\right)-\left[i_{in}\left(R_{EQ}\parallel R_M\right)\right]}{v_{in}} \approx \frac{\left(\frac{v_{in}R_M}{R_{EQ}+R_M}\right)-\left[\left(\frac{v_{in}}{R_{EQ}}\right)\left(R_{EQ}\parallel R_M\right)\right]}{v_{in}} = 0$$

With a balanced load, N-type mirrors cancel supply noise v_{in}.

5.4. Feed-Through Noise with N-Type Mirrors

More accurate without i_{in} approximation: When $i_{in} = v_{in}/(R_{EQ} + R_{GM3})$:

$$A_{IN(N.MIR)} \equiv \frac{v_{oe}}{v_{in}} = \frac{\left(\frac{v_{in}R_M}{R_{EQ}+R_M}\right)-\left[i_{in}\left(R_{EQ}\parallel R_M\right)\right]}{v_{in}} \approx \left(\frac{R_M}{R_{EQ}+R_M}\right)-\left(\frac{R_{EQ}\parallel R_M}{R_{EQ}+\frac{1}{g_{mM3}}}\right)$$

Circuit Variations: Applies to mirrors with symmetrical loads.

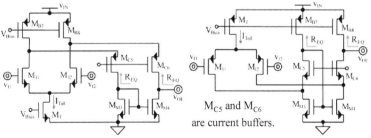

M_{C5} and M_{C6} are current buffers.

Since $i_{c5} \approx i_{c6}$, mirror M_{M3}–M_{M4} sinks and cancels M_{C6}'s i_{in}.

∴ A_E can be designed to cancel v_{IN} ripple.

5.4. Feed-Through Noise with N-Type Mirrors

Example: Determine the supply gain of an error amplifier that incorporates

an N-type current mirror when g_m is 50 μS and resistances are 500 kΩ.

Solution:

$$A_{IN} \equiv \frac{v_{oe}}{v_{in}} \approx \left(\frac{R_M}{R_{EQ} + R_M} \right) - \left(\frac{R_{EQ} \| R_M}{R_{EQ} + \dfrac{1}{g_{mM3}}} \right) \approx \left(\frac{0.5 \ M\Omega}{0.5 \ M\Omega + 0.5 \ M\Omega} \right) - \left(\frac{0.5 \ M\Omega \| 0.5 \ M\Omega}{0.5 \ M\Omega + \dfrac{1}{50 \ \mu S}} \right)$$

$$= 0.5 - \left(\frac{0.25 \ M\Omega}{0.5 \ M\Omega + \dfrac{1}{50 \ \mu S}} \right) \approx 19 \ mV/V = -34 \ dB$$

5.4. Feed-Through Noise with P-Type Mirrors

Small-Signal Model: Shunt impedance $Z_{SH.FB}$ already accounts for feedback.

Feedback reproduces v_{REF} in v_{FB} ∴ $v_{id} = 0$.

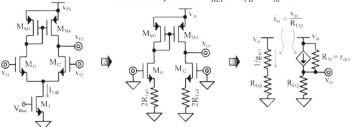

Output resistance in P-type mirrors injects supply-noise current to v_{OE}.

P-type mirrors supply supply-noise current to v_{OE} → Reinforces v_{in} noise.

$$A_{IN(P.MIR)} = \frac{v_{oe}}{v_{in}} = \frac{\left(\dfrac{v_{in} R_{EQ}}{R_{EQ} + R_M} \right) + \left[i_{in} \left(R_{EQ} \| R_M \right) \right]}{v_{in}} \approx \frac{\left(\dfrac{v_{in} R_{EQ}}{R_{EQ} + R_M} \right) + \left[\left(\dfrac{v_{in}}{R_{EQ}} \right) \left(R_{EQ} \| R_M \right) \right]}{v_{in}} = 1$$

With a balanced load, P-type mirrors reproduce supply noise v_{in}.

5.4. Feed-Through Noise with P-Type Mirrors

More accurate without i_{in} approximation: When $i_{in} = v_{in}/(R_{EQ} + R_{GM3})$:

$$A_{IN(P.MIR)} \equiv \frac{v_{oe}}{v_{in}} = \frac{\left(\frac{v_{in}R_{EQ}}{R_{EQ}+R_M}\right) + \left[i_{in}\left(R_{EQ} \| R_M\right)\right]}{v_{in}} \approx \left(\frac{R_{EQ}}{R_{EQ}+R_M}\right) + \left(\frac{R_{EQ} \| R_M}{R_{EQ} + \frac{1}{g_{mM3}}}\right)$$

Circuit Variations: Applies to mirrors with symmetrical loads.

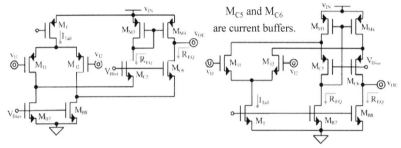

M_{C5} and M_{C6} are current buffers.

Since $i_{c5} \approx i_{c6}$, g_{m4} sources and reinforces r_{ds4}'s i_{in}.

5.4. Feed-Through Noise with P-Type Mirrors

Example: Determine the supply gain of an error amplifier that incorporates

an P-type current mirror when g_m is 50 μS and resistances are 500 kΩ.

Solution:

$$A_{IN} \equiv \frac{v_{oe}}{v_{in}} \approx \left(\frac{R_{EQ}}{R_{EQ}+R_M}\right) + \left(\frac{R_{EQ} \| R_M}{R_{EQ} + \frac{1}{g_{mM3}}}\right) \approx \left(\frac{0.5 \ M\Omega}{0.5 \ M\Omega + 0.5 \ M\Omega}\right) + \left(\frac{0.5 \ M\Omega \| 0.5 \ M\Omega}{0.5 \ M\Omega + \frac{1}{50 \ \mu S}}\right)$$

$$= 0.5 + \left(\frac{0.25 \ M\Omega}{0.5 \ M\Omega + \frac{1}{50 \ \mu S}}\right) \approx 0.98 \ V/V = -0.17 \ dB$$

5.4. Feed-Through Noise with Miller Capacitors

Miller capacitors diode-connect P-type S_O's at high frequencies.

$\therefore C_M$ reduces Z_T and therefore couples supply noise v_{in} to v_O.

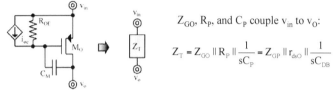

Z_{GO}, R_P, and C_P couple v_{in} to v_O:

$$Z_T = Z_{GO} \| R_P \| \frac{1}{sC_P} = Z_{GP} \| r_{dsO} \| \frac{1}{sC_{DB}}$$

C_M diode-connects M_O and shunts R_P when $Z_{GP} \leq R_P$, past Miller pole p_M:

$$Z_{GP} = \frac{1}{\left(\dfrac{G_P R_{OE}}{R_{OE} + Z_{CM}} \right)} \approx \left. \frac{R_{OE} + \dfrac{1}{sC_M}}{G_P R_{OE}} \right|_{\frac{1}{sC_M} \gg R_{OE}} \approx \left. \frac{1}{sC_M G_P R_{OE}} \right|_{p_M = \frac{1}{2\pi R_{OE}(G_P R_P C_M)}} \equiv R_P$$

Z_{GO} flattens at $1/G_P$ when $1/sC_M < R_{OE}$, past zero z_{GP}:

$$\left. \frac{1}{sC_M} \right|_{z_{GP} = \frac{1}{2\pi R_{OE} C_M}} \equiv R_{OE}$$

C_P couples v_{in} when $1/sC_P < 1/G_P$, past pole p_{CP}:

$$\left. \frac{1}{sC_P} \right|_{p_{CP} = \frac{G_P}{2\pi C_P}} \equiv \frac{1}{G_P}$$

$\therefore Z_T$ is equivalent to R_P with two poles and one zero.

5.4. Feed-Through Noise: Design Conclusions

Followers propagate gate/base noise.

→ Since N-type mirrors with symmetrical loads cancel supply noise, they should drive N-type S_O's.

Common-source transistors cancel in-phase (common-mode) gate/base noise.

→ Since P-type mirrors with symmetrical loads reproduce supply noise, they should drive P-type S_O's.

Miller capacitors that diode-connect P-type S_O's couple supply noise.

→ Avoid *conventional* Miller compensation when possible.

Output capacitor C_O shunts noise in v_O, but C_O's R_{ESR} limits suppression.

→ Favor high-C_O and low-R_{ESR} designs → Better if dominant pole at v_O.

5.4. Analysis

Voltage-Divider Model: Derive supply gain A_{IN} from voltage divider.

Assume G_P does not feed-through noise $\rightarrow$ Reasonable design assumption.

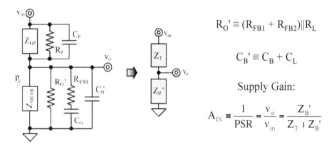

$$R_O' \equiv (R_{FB1} + R_{FB2})\|R_L$$

$$C_B' \equiv C_B + C_L$$

Supply Gain:

$$A_{IN} \equiv \frac{1}{PSR} = \frac{v_o}{v_{in}} = \frac{Z_B'}{Z_T + Z_B'}$$

Low-Frequency Supply Gain A_{IN}: C_O and C_B' are open.

$$A_{IN0} = \frac{1}{PSR_0} = \frac{R_O'\|R_{SH.FB}}{R_P + (R_O'\|R_{SH.FB})} \approx \frac{R_{SH.FB}}{R_P} = \frac{1}{(\beta_{FB}A_{E0}G_P)R_P} \approx \frac{1}{A_{LG0}} \approx LNR$$

5.4. Analysis: Output Compensation

At low frequency: $A_{IN} = R_{SH.FB}/R_P$.

Past p_O: C_O and C_B' shunt R_O', but not $R_{SH.FB}$

$$A_{IN} = \frac{Z_B'}{Z_T + Z_B'}$$

because $R_{SH.FB} \ll R_O'$ $\therefore$ No effect in Z_B' or A_{IN}.

Past p_E: p_E lowers A_E $\therefore$ Raises $Z_{SH.FB}$ and $A_{IN} = Z_{SH.FB}/R_P$.

Past f_{0dB}: C_O and C_B' shunt $Z_{SH.FB} \rightarrow Z_B'$ and $A_{IN} = Z_{CO}/R_P \ll 1$ fall.

Past z_{ESR}: R_{ESR} limits Z_{CO} and A_{IN} to R_{ESR}/R_P.

Past p_B: C_B' shunts R_{ESR} and $A_{IN} = Z_{CB}/R_P$ falls.

Past z_P: C_P shunts R_P and $A_{IN} = Z_{CB}/Z_{CP}$ flattens.

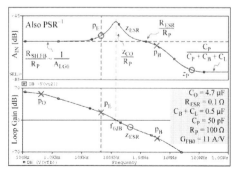

5.4. Analysis: Output Compensation

Example: Determine line regulation and power-supply rejection

at low frequency, at the system's bandwidth, and past z_{ESR} when

$\beta_{FB} = 0.5$ V/V, $A_{E0} = 440$ V/V, $G_P = 50$ μS, $R_P = 100$ Ω,

$R_L = 10$ kΩ, $R_{FB1} + R_{FB2} = 500$ kΩ, $R_{ESR} = 0.1$ Ω,

$f_{0dB} = 100$ kHz, $C_O = 4.7$ μF, $C_B = 0.3$ μF, $C_L = 0.2$ μF, and $C_P = 10$ pF.

Solution:

$$LNR = A_{IN0} = \frac{1}{PSR_0} \approx \frac{R_{SH.FB}}{R_P} = \frac{1}{\left(\beta_{FB}A_{E0}G_P\right)R_P}$$

$$\approx \frac{1}{\left(0.5 \text{ V/V}\right)\left(440 \text{ V/V}\right)\left(50 \text{ mA/V}\right)\left(100 \text{ Ω}\right)} \approx 0.9 \text{ mV/V} = -61 \text{ dB}$$

$$PSR_{0dB} = \frac{1}{A_{IN(0dB)}} \approx \frac{R_P}{Z_{CO}} = s\left(C_O + C_B + C_L\right)R_P$$

$$\approx 2\pi\left(100 \text{ kHz}\right)\left[\left(4.7 + 0.3 + 0.2 \text{ μF}\right)\right]\left(100 \text{ Ω}\right) \approx 330 \text{ V/V} \approx 50 \text{ dB}$$

$$PSR = \frac{1}{A_{IN}}\bigg|_{f > z_{ESR}} \approx \frac{R_P}{R_{ESR}} = \frac{100 \text{ Ω}}{0.1 \text{ Ω}} = 1 \text{ kV/V} = 60 \text{ dB}$$

5.4. Analysis: Internal Compensation

At low frequency: $A_{IN} = R_{SH.FB}/R_P$.

$$A_{IN} = \frac{Z_B'}{Z_T + Z_B'}$$

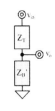

Past p_E: p_E lowers A_E ∴ Raises $Z_{SH.FB}$ and $A_{IN} = Z_{SH.FB}/R_P$.

Past f_{0dB}: $Z_{SH.FB} > R_P \rightarrow A_{IN} \approx Z_{SH.FB}/Z_{SH.FB} = 1$ flattens.

Past p_{ZO}: C_O and C_B' shunt $Z_{SH.FB} \rightarrow$ Still, $A_{IN} \approx Z_{CO}/Z_{CO} = 1$.

Past p_O: $Z_{CO} < R_P \rightarrow A_{IN} \approx Z_{CO}/R_P$ falls.

Past z_P: C_P shunts R_P and

$A_{IN} = Z_{CO}/Z_{CP}$ flattens.

Past z_{ESR}: R_{ESR} limits Z_{CO}

and $A_{IN} \approx R_{ESR}/Z_{CP}$ rises.

Past p_B: C_B' shunts R_{ESR} and

$A_{IN} = Z_{CB}/Z_{CP}$ flattens.

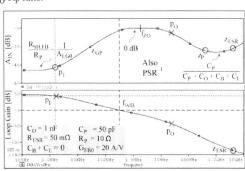

5.4. Summary and Conclusions

Derive PSR from the supply gain A_{IN} of the equivalent voltage divider.

And track how A_{IN} changes with shunting capacitors.

For high PSR:

Raise supply impedance Z_T → High R_P and low C_P.

Lower ground impedance Z_B' → Low $Z_{SH.FB}$, high C_O and C_B, and low R_{ESR}.

High PSR hinges on shunt feedback:

High loop gain A_{LG}.

High feedback bandwidth → High p_E → Output Compensation.

Benefits disappear past f_{0dB} → Worst near f_{0dB}, which can be 50 kHz–1 MHz.

∴ Feedback does not suppress

switched-inductor ripples well at 20 kHz–10 MHz.

Past f_{0dB}, PSR hinges on C_O and C_B → Low-ESR capacitors are important.

5.4. Comparison of Compensation Strategies

	Output Compensation	Internal Compensation
Dominant Pole	Output Pole p_O	Error-Amplifier Pole p_E
C_O	Higher	Lower
Integration	Off-chip or in-package C_O	On-chip or in-package C_O
Load-Dump Variation	Lower	Higher
Stability Requirement	Low p_O and high p_E	Low p_E and high p_O
Worst-Case Stability	High p_O, low p_E, and no R_{ESR}	High p_E, low p_O, and no R_{ESR}
PSR	Wider bandwidth	Lower bandwidth
Typical Application	Higher power	Lower power

Load-dump and PSR performance degrade with integration.

5.5. Integrated Circuits

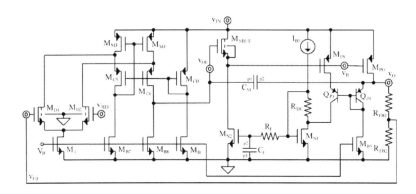

5.5. Design Process

Usually begins with specifications at the output and ends with the input.

For high bandwidth, drive large power transistor S_O with a buffer A_B

to unload S_O's large C_{SW} from A_E's large, gain-setting R_{OE}.

→ Split one low-frequency pole into two higher-frequency poles p_E and p_{BUF}.

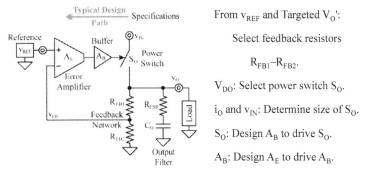

From v_{REF} and Targeted V_O':

Select feedback resistors

R_{FB1}–R_{FB2}.

V_{DO}: Select power switch S_O.

i_O and v_{IN}: Determine size of S_O.

S_O: Design A_B to drive S_O.

A_B: Design A_E to drive A_B.

5.5. Power Transistors: Options

The ideal power transistor drops 0 V, outputs ∞ A, leaks 0 A, and outputs 0 Ω,

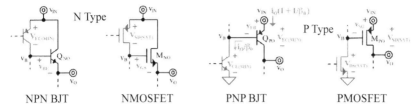

| NPN BJT | NMOSFET | PNP BJT | PMOSFET |

Parameter	N Type		P Type	
	NPN	NMOS	PNP	PMOS
V_{DO}	$V_{EC(MIN)} + V_{BE}$	$V_{SD(SAT)} + V_{GS}$	$V_{EC(MIN)}$	$V_{SD(SAT)}$
Drive	$i_{O(MAX)}/\beta_N$	$v_B - v_O$	$-i_{O(MAX)}/\beta_P$	$v_{IN} - v_B$
$i_{O(MAX)}$	Highest	Low	High	Moderate
i_{GND}	0 A	0 A	$i_{O(MAX)}/\beta_P$	0 A
R_O	$1/g_{m(BJT)}$	$1/g_{m(MOS)}$	r_o	r_{ds}

5.5. Power Transistors: Performance Considerations

Fast load-dump response → High bandwidth.

Low output resistance R_O ∴ N-type Followers.

High output power:

High output current i_O and high breakdown V_{BD} ∴ BJTs.

Extended battery life → High power-conversion efficiency η_C.

$$\eta_C \equiv \frac{P_O}{P_{IN}} = \frac{P_O}{P_{SO} + P_O} = \frac{P_O}{\left(v_{IN} - v_O\right)i_O + v_{IN}i_{GND} + P_O} \leq \frac{P_O}{V_{DO}i_O + v_{IN}i_{GND} + P_O}$$

Low dropout V_{DO} ∴ P-type Transistors ⎤

Low ground current i_{GND} ∴ MOSFETs ⎦ ⊢ PMOSFETs

5.5. Power Transistors: Design Example

Design Example: Design a power transistor that outputs 50 mA into 1 V with less than 200 mV of dropout and no ground current when $v_{IN} = 0.9$–1.6 V, $|V_{TP0}| = 0.6 \pm 0.15$ V, $K_p' = 40$ $\mu A/V^2 \pm 20\%$, and $L \geq 0.35$ μm.

Solution:

For low V_{DO} and zero i_{GND}, PMOSFET.

$$V_{DO} \leq R_{DS(MAX)} i_{O(MAX)} \approx \frac{i_{O(MAX)}}{K_{P(MIN)}' \left(\dfrac{W}{L} \right) \left(v_{IN(MIN)} - \left| v_{TP(MAX)} \right| \right)} \leq 100 \text{ mV}$$

$$\therefore \quad \frac{W}{L} \geq \frac{50m}{(32\mu)(200m)(0.9 - 0.75)} = 52083$$

For minimum capacitance, $L = L_{MIN} = 0.35$ μm $\therefore$ W = 18.3 mm.

$$V_{DS(SAT)} \leq \sqrt{\frac{2 i_{O(MAX)}}{K_{P(MIN)}' \left(\dfrac{W}{L} \right)}} = \sqrt{\frac{2(50m)}{(32\mu)\left(\dfrac{18300}{0.35} \right)}} \approx 244 \text{ mV} \left.\begin{array}{l} \\ \\ \\ \end{array}\right\} \begin{array}{l} \text{PFET enters dropout} \\ \text{when } v_O \text{ is within} \\ 250 \text{ mV of } v_{IN}. \end{array}$$

5.5. Power Transistors: Physical Structure

Vertical NPN BJT

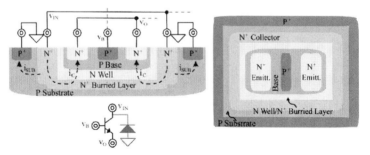

For High $i_{O(MAX)}$ $\therefore$ Large emitter area.

Fast large-signal response $\therefore$ Low base resistance R_B.

Uniform response $\therefore$ Embedded base strips.

Low substrate noise and power (as i_{SUB}) $\therefore$ Peripheral collecting P^+ ring.

5.5. Power Transistors: Physical Structure

Lateral PNP BJT

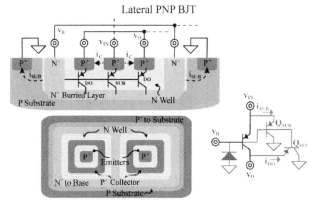

For High $i_{O(MAX)}$ $\therefore$ Long periphery → Multiple "emitter dots".

Fast large-signal response $\therefore$ Low R_B → N^+ plugs and buried layer.

Low i_{SUB} $\therefore$ Low vertical PNP β_{PAR} → N^+ buried layer and collecting P^+ ring.

5.5. Power Transistors: Physical Structure

Substrate N-Channel MOSFET

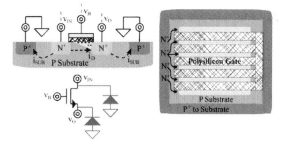

For High $i_{O(MAX)}$ $\therefore$ Low channel resistance R_{DS}

→ Wide and short channel → High W and low L.

Fast large-signal response $\therefore$ Low gate resistance R_G

→ Parallel tree-like length-limited gate fingers.

Low i_{SUB} $\therefore$ Collecting P^+ ring.

5.5. Power Transistors: Physical Structure
Welled P-Channel MOSFET

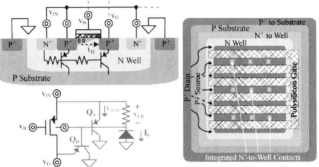

For High $i_{O(MAX)}$ ∴ Low R_{DS} → Wide and short channel → High W and low L.

Fast large-signal response ∴ Low R_G → Parallel length-limited gate fingers.

Low i_{SUB} ∴ N⁺ ring in N well, collecting P⁺ ring, and butted or

      source-integrated bulk contacts, which normally violate layout rules.

5.5. Power Transistors: Physical Structure

Metallization: Metal and bond-wire resistances raise dropout voltage.

$V_{DO} = i_O R_{ON} = i_O \left(R_{SW} + R_M + R_{BW} \right)$ → E.g.: 100 mΩ + 25 mΩ + 50 mΩ.

For reliability and low R_M and R_{BW}, reduce and balance current densities.

Steering i_O within the power transistor:

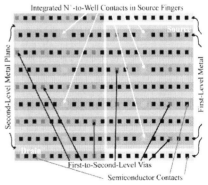

    Longitudinal Metal-1 fingers

        for input and output terminals.

    Stacked Semiconductor–Metal 1

        and Metal 1–2 vias, if possible.

    Orthogonal Metal-2 planes.

    Stack other metal planes

        to lower series resistance.

5.5. Power Transistors: Physical Structure

Metallization

Steering i_O to and from the power transistor:

Use top-level low-resistance metals.

Use large-area vias.

Keep current densities consistent:

To avoid current crowding.

→ Avoid hot spots.

To maximize metal efficiency.

→ Lower resistance.

From v_{IN}: Decrease width

as device sinks more i_O.

To v_O: Raise width as device sources more i_O.

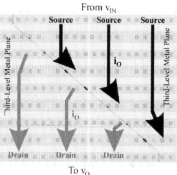

5.5. Power Transistors: Physical Structure

Layout Design

Place S_O next to output v_O and input v_{IN} pads.

Parallel multiple bond pads and/or bond wires when possible.

Place current-sense device in the middle of the power transistor

to improve matching performance.

Place S_O away from match-sensitive devices

to keep thermal gradients from introducing offsets.

Place thermal-shutdown sensor next to heat source → Next to S_O

to sense S_O and keep S_O in safe-operating area (SOA).

5.5. Buffers: Requirements

Accurate → High loop gain → Establish a light load.

∴ High input resistance R_{IB}.

Fast load-dump response → High bandwidth.

∴ Low input capacitance C_{IB}.

∴ Low output resistance R_{OB}.

Large power transistor is a highly capacitive load.

∴ Low output resistance R_{OB}.

∴ High output current i_B.

Long operational life → Low power consumption.

∴ Low ground current i_{GND}.

∴ Low headroom limit $v_{IN(MIN)}$.

Wide load-current range → Wide output swing Δv_B.

5.5. Buffers: N-Type Power Transistors

Class-A Follower Buffers

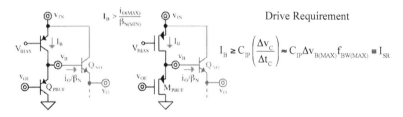

Output resistance R_{OB} is moderately low at $1/g_m$.

P-Type Buffer: $V_{DO} \approx v_{BE} + V_{EC(MIN)}$ → Moderate dropout voltage V_{DO}.

Limited $i_{B(SOURCE)}$ → Low base/gate drive.

→ Slow response to rising load dumps.

N-Type Buffer: $V_{DO} \approx 2v_{BE} + V_{EC(MIN)}$ → High dropout voltage V_{DO}.

5.5. Buffers: N-Type Power Transistors

Class-AB Follower Buffers: With On-Demand Drive

Use shunt feedback to:

Raise $i_{B(SOURCE)}$ *only when needed* to: Extend NPN's $i_{O(MAX)}$.

Accelerate load-dump response.

Incurrent current efficiency.

Reduce R_{OB} to extend bandwidth.

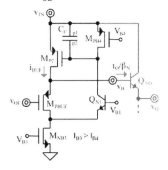

M_{PBUF} series-mixes v_{OE} and v_B.

→ Virtual ac short: $v_{oe} \approx v_b$.

M_{PBUF} shunt-samples v_B.

→ Low R_{OB}.

$$R_{OB} \approx \frac{1}{g_{m.BUF}A_{LG}} \approx \frac{1}{g_{m.BUF}\left(r_{ds4}g_{m2}\right)}$$

5.5. Buffers: P-Type Power Transistors

Class-A Follower Buffers

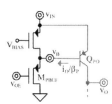

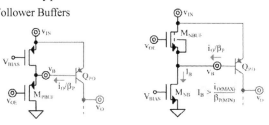

Output resistance R_{OB} is moderately low at $1/g_m$.

P-Type Buffer: High $v_{B(MIN)}$ → Low gate drive.

Limited $i_{B(SOURCE)}$ → Slewed response to falling load dumps.

N-Type Buffer: Low $v_{B(MAX)}$ → Difficult to shut S_{PO}.

Limited $i_{B(SINK)}$ → Low base drive.

→ Slow response to rising load dumps.

5.5. Buffers: P-Type Power Transistors
Class-A Follower Buffers

A lower-v_T NMOS raises $v_{B(MAX)}$, so it can more easily shut S_O.

v_T for native NMOSFETs is nearly zero.

→ Skipping threshold-adjust implant step requires extra mask.

v_{BS} for isolated MOSFETs can be zero → No bulk/body effects.

→ Deep N⁺ plug ring and buried layer can isolate NMOSFETs.

Isolated Native NMOSFET M_{NBUF}

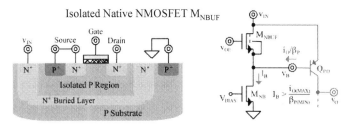

5.5. Buffers: P-Type Power Transistors
Class-AB Follower Buffers: With On-Demand Drive

Use shunt feedback to:

Raise $i_{B(SOURCE)}$ *only when needed* to: Extend NPN's $i_{O(MAX)}$.

Accelerate load-dump response.

Incurrent current efficiency.

Reduce R_{OB} to extend bandwidth.

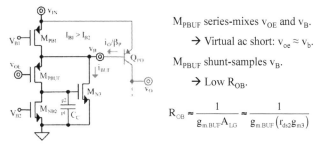

M_{PBUF} series-mixes v_{OE} and v_B.

→ Virtual ac short: $v_{oe} \approx v_b$.

M_{PBUF} shunt-samples v_B.

→ Low R_{OB}.

$$R_{OB} \approx \frac{1}{g_{m.BUF} A_{LG}} \approx \frac{1}{g_{m.BUF}\left(r_{ds2}g_{m3}\right)}$$

5.5. Buffers: P-Type Power Transistors

Class-AB Follower Buffers: With On-Demand Drive

Shunt feedback raises $i_{B(SINK)}$ *only when needed* and lowers R_{OB}.

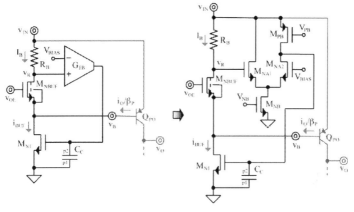

M_{NBUF} series-mixes v_{OE} and v_B and M_{NBUF} shunt-samples $v_B \to v_b \approx v_{oe}$ and R_{OB} is low.

5.5. Buffers: P-Type Power Transistors

Regenerative Drive:

Accelerates response.

Is positive feedback.

$\to$ Compromises feedback stability.

Negative feedback to v_{OE} reduces R_{OB}, but only up to system's bandwidth f_{0dB}.

$\therefore$ Positive loop gain should be less than 1 without negative feedback:

$$A_{LG+} = G_{FB+}Z_{OB} = G_{FB+}\left(\frac{R_{OB}}{A_{REG}} \middle\| \frac{1}{sC_{SW}}\right) < G_{FB+}\left(R_{OB} \middle\| \frac{1}{sC_{SW}}\right) < 1$$

Side Note: Since p_O and f_{0dB} rise with i_O, buffer-pole requirement rises with i_O.

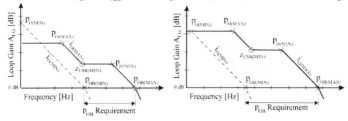

5.5. Buffers: P-Type Power Transistors

Regenerative Load-Tracking Class-A Follower Buffer

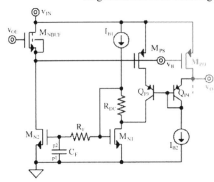

M_{NBUF} is the buffer.

M_{PS}'s i_S mirrors M_{PO}'s i_O.

Q_{P3} current-buffers M_{PS}'s i_S.

M_{N1}–M_{N2} mirrors i_S.

Q_{P4} biases Q_{P3} so $v_{SD.PS} \approx v_{SD.PO}$.

$\therefore M_{PS}$ mirrors M_{PO} better.

R_{DC} level-shifts M_{N1}'s v_{G1} to keep Q_{P3} out of deep saturation.

M_{PS} and M_{N1}–M_{N2} ensure $i_2 \propto i_O$ $\quad \therefore i_{B(SINK)}$ rises with $i_O \rightarrow$ On-demand drive.

$\quad \therefore p_{OB} \propto g_{mBUF} \propto \sqrt{i_O} \rightarrow$ Tracks load.

R_F–C_F attenuates positive-feedback gain A_{LG+}.

I_{B1} keeps Q_{P3} and M_{N1}–M_{N2} from shutting when i_O nears zero.

5.5. Buffers: Design Example

Design Example: Design the regenerative load-tracking buffer discussed for the PMOS power transistor designed in the previous example, where

$W_O = 18.3$ mm, $L_O = 0.35$ µm, $v_{IN} = 1.1$–1.6 V, $v_O = 1$ V, and $i_O \leq 50$ mA, so p_{OB} at 0 A ≥ 100 kHz, p_{OB} at 50 mA ≥ 1 MHz, I_Q at 0 A ≤ 4 µA,

$v_{B(MAX)} = v_{IN} - |V_{TP0(MIN)}|$, and $v_{B(MIN)} = 0.2$ V.

Process: $V_{TN0} = |V_{TP0}| = 0.6 \pm 0.15$ V, $V_{TN0.NAT} = 0.6 \pm 0.15$ V,

$K_p' = 40$ µA/V^2 ± 20%, $K_N' = 100$ µA/V^2 ± 20%, $L \geq 0.35$ µm,

$1/\lambda_{L(MIN)} = 2$ V, $1/\lambda_{3L(MIN)} = 500$ V, $L_{OV} = 35$ nm, $C_{OX}'' = 5$ fF/µm^2,

$\beta_{P0} = 50$–150 A/A, and $V_A = 15$ V.

Solution:

Parasitic zero-load capacitance $C_{IP(0)}$ at v_B:

$$C_{IP(0)} \approx C_{SG.PO} \approx \frac{2}{3} C_{OX}'' W_{PO} L_{PO} + C_{OX}'' W_{PO} L_{OV}$$

$$\approx \frac{2}{3}(5f)(18.3k)(0.35) + (5f)(18.3k)(0.035) \approx 25 \text{ pF}$$

5.5. Buffers: Design Example

Equivalent full-load capacitance $C_{IP(50mA)}$ at v_B:

$$C_{IP(50mA)} \approx C_{GS.PO} + C_{GD.PO(Miller)} \approx \frac{2}{3}C_{OX}"W_{PO}L_{PO} + C_{OX}"W_{PO}L_{OV}\left(g_{m.PO}r_{ds.PO}\right)$$

$$\approx \frac{2}{3}C_{OX}"W_{PO}L_{PO} + C_{OX}"W_{PO}L_{OV}\left(\frac{\sqrt{2i_{O(MAX)}K_P'\left(\frac{W}{L}\right)_{PO}}}{i_{O(MAX)}\lambda_{L(MIN)}}\right)$$

$$\approx \frac{2}{3}\left(5f\right)\left(18.3k\right)\left(0.35\right) + \left(5f\right)\left(18.3k\right)\left(0.035\right)\left(\frac{\sqrt{2\left(50m\right)\left(40\mu\right)\left(\frac{18.3k}{0.35}\right)}}{\left(50m\right)\left(500m\right)}\right) \approx 80 \ pF$$

5.5. Buffers: Design Example

Full-load bandwidth $p_{OB(50mA)}$:

$$p_{OB(50mA)} \approx \frac{1}{2\pi C_{IP(50mA)}R_{OB}} \approx \frac{g_{m.NBUF}}{2\pi C_{IP(50mA)}} = \frac{\sqrt{2i_{NBUF(50mA)}K_N'\left(\frac{W}{L}\right)_{NBUF}}}{2\pi C_{IP(50mA)}} \geq 1 \ MHz$$

$$\therefore$$

$$i_{NBUF(50mA)}\left(\frac{W}{L}\right)_{NBUF} \geq \frac{\left(2\pi C_{IP(50mA)}p_{OB(50mA)}\right)^2}{2K_{N(MIN)}'} = \frac{\left[\left(2\pi\right)\left(80p\right)\left(1M\right)\right]^2}{2\left(80\mu\right)} \approx 1.6 \ mA\left(\frac{m}{m}\right)$$

If $W_{NBUF} \equiv 12 \ \mu m$ and $L_{NBUF} \equiv 0.35 \ \mu m$, $i_{NBUF(50mA)} = 46 \ \mu A$.

If $(W/L)_{N1} \equiv (W/L)_{N2}$,

$$\frac{i_O}{i_{PS}} = \frac{\left(\frac{W}{L}\right)_{PO}}{\left(\frac{W}{L}\right)_{PS}} = \frac{\left(\frac{18.3k}{0.35}\right)}{\left(\frac{W}{L}\right)_{PS}} \equiv \frac{50 \ mA}{46 \ \mu A}$$

$\therefore (W/L)_{PS} \geq 48 \rightarrow W_{PS} \equiv 17 \ \mu m$ when $L_{PS} \equiv L_{MIN} \equiv 0.35 \ \mu m$ (smallest).

5.5. Buffers: Design Example

Zero-load bandwidth $p_{OB(0)}$:

$$p_{OB(0)} \approx \frac{1}{2\pi C_{IP}R_{OB}} \approx \frac{g_{m.NBUF}}{2\pi C_{IP(0)}} = \frac{\sqrt{2i_{NBUF(0)}K_N'\left(\frac{W}{L}\right)_{NBUF}}}{2\pi C_{IP(0)}} \geq 100 \text{ kHz}$$

$$i_{NBUF(0)} \geq \frac{\left(2\pi C_{IP(0)}p_{OB(0)}\right)^2}{2K_{N(MIN)}'\left(\frac{W}{L}\right)_{NBUF}} = \frac{\left[2\pi(25p)(100k)\right]^2}{2(80\mu)\left(\frac{12}{0.35}\right)} \approx 0.05 \ \mu A$$

$\therefore$ Adding margin to overwhelm coupled noise, $i_{NBUF(0)} \equiv 0.5 \ \mu A$.

$v_{B(MIN)}$:

$$v_{B(MIN)} \approx V_{DS.N2(SAT)} \leq \sqrt{\frac{2i_{NBUF(MAX)}}{K_{K(MIN)}'\left(\frac{W}{L}\right)_{N2}}} \leq 0.2 \text{ V}$$

$$\left(\frac{W}{L}\right)_{N2} \geq \frac{2i_{NBUF(MAX)}}{V_{DS.N2(SAT)}{}^2 K_{N(MIN)}'} = \frac{2i_{NBUF(50mA)}}{V_{DS.N2(SAT)}{}^2 K_{N(MIN)}'} = \frac{2(46\mu)}{(0.2)^2(80\mu)} = 28.7$$

$\therefore W_{N1} \equiv W_{N2} \equiv 30 \ \mu m$ when $L_{N1} \equiv L_{N2} \equiv 3L_{MIN} = 3(0.35) \ \mu m$ (higher $1/\lambda_L$).

5.5. Buffers: Design Example

$R_{FB}\text{–}C_{FB}$: Set pole to $f_{pFB} \equiv 100$ kHz.

$$p_{FB+} \approx \frac{1}{2\pi C_F R_F} \leq 100 \text{ kHz}$$

$\therefore$ With $C_F \equiv 5$ pF,

$$R_F \geq \frac{1}{2\pi C_F p_{FB+}} = \frac{1}{2\pi(5p)(100k)} \approx 320 \text{ k}\Omega$$

Keep Q_{P3} out of deep saturation:

$$V_{EC.P3(MIN)} \approx v_O - \left(v_{GS.N1(MAX)} - I_{B1}R_{DC}\right) \approx v_O - v_{TN(MAX)} - \sqrt{\frac{2i_{NBUF(MAX)}}{K_{N(MIN)}'\left(\frac{W}{L}\right)_{N1}}} + I_{B1}R_{DC} \geq 0.3 \text{ V}$$

Since $M_{N1} \equiv M_{N2}$ and $i_{NBUF(0)} \equiv 0.5 \ \mu A$, $I_{B1} \equiv 0.5 \ \mu A$.

$$R_{DC} \geq \frac{V_{EC.P3(MIN)} - v_O + v_{TN(MAX)} + \sqrt{\frac{2i_{NBUF(MAX)}}{K_{N(MIN)}'\left(\frac{W}{L}\right)_{N1}}}}{I_{B1}} \approx \frac{0.3 - 1 + 0.75 + \sqrt{\frac{2(46\mu)}{(80\mu)\left(\frac{30}{1.05}\right)}}}{0.5\mu} = 501 \text{ k}\Omega$$

$\therefore R_{DC} \equiv 500$ kΩ.

5.5. Buffers: Design Example

I_{B2}: Choosing $i_{P4} \equiv 0.5$ μA. $\quad I_{B2(MIN)} \geq \dfrac{i_{P3(MAX)}}{\beta_{P0(MIN)}} + I_{P4} \approx \dfrac{46\mu}{50} + 0.5\mu = 1.4$ μA

∴ Adding margin to accommodate ±30% variation, $i_{B2} \equiv 2$ μA.

Design Checks

No-Load Feedback Stability:

M_{PS}'s $i_S \approx 0$ when $i_O \approx 0$ ∴ $A_{LG+(0)} \approx 0$ → No positive feedback ∴ Stable.

Loaded Feedback Stability:

$$A_{LG+} \equiv \frac{v_b}{v_b} = \left(\frac{v_{g.N1}}{v_b}\right)\left(\frac{v_b}{v_{g.N1}}\right) \approx \left[g_{m.PS}\left(\frac{1}{g_{m.N1}}\right)\left(\frac{1}{1+R_F C_F s}\right)\right]\left[g_{m.N2}\left(\frac{R_{OB}}{A_{REG}} \| \frac{1}{sC_{IP}}\right)\right] < g_{m.PS}R_{OB}$$

R_F–C_F and C_{IP} attenuate A_{LG+}.

$R_{OB} \approx 1/g_{m.NBUF}$.

$$= \frac{g_{m.PS}}{g_{m.NBUF}} \approx \frac{\sqrt{2i_{PS}K_P'\left(\frac{W}{L}\right)_{PS}}}{\sqrt{2i_{PS}K_N'\left(\frac{W}{L}\right)_{NBUF}}} = \sqrt{\frac{K_P'\left(\frac{W}{L}\right)_{PS}}{K_N'\left(\frac{W}{L}\right)_{NBUF}}} = \sqrt{\frac{(40\mu)\left(\frac{17}{0.35}\right)}{(100\mu)\left(\frac{12}{0.35}\right)}} \approx 0.75 < 1 \quad ∴ \text{ Stable.}$$

5.5. Buffers: Design Example

Small-Signal Gain across Buffer A_B:

Decomposing M_{NBUF}'s $g_{m.NBUF}$ reveals that:

A T connection at v_B shunt-mixes $g_{m.NBUF}$'s i_i and M_{N2}'s i_{fb}.

M_{NBUF}'s source ($g_{m.NBUF}$) shunt-samples v_b.

∴

$$A_{ROL0} \equiv \frac{v_b}{i_i - i_{fb}} = r_{ds2} \| \frac{1}{g_{m.NBUF}} \approx \frac{1}{g_{m.NBUF}}$$

$$A_{B0} = \frac{v_b}{v_{oe}} = \left(\frac{i_i}{v_{oe}}\right)\left(\frac{v_b}{i_i}\right) = \left(\frac{i_i}{v_{oe}}\right)A_{RCL0} = g_{m.NBUF}\left(\frac{A_{ROL0}}{1-A_{LG0}}\right) \approx g_{m.NBUF}\left[\frac{1}{g_{m.NBUF}\left(1-0.75\right)}\right] \approx 4$$

Where $\quad A_{LG0} \approx g_{m.PS}\left(\frac{1}{g_{m.N1}}\right)g_{m.N2}R_{OB} = g_{m.PS}\left(\frac{1}{g_{m.N1}}\right)g_{m.N2}\left(\frac{1}{g_{m.NBUF}}\right) = \frac{g_{m.PS}}{g_{m.NBUF}} \approx 0.75$

Feedback: Shifts p_{FB+} to $(1-A_{LG0})p_{FB+}$ or $0.25p_{FB+}$ or 25 kHz.

Creates the effects of a zero when A_{LG} and its p_{FB+} disappear

near p_{FB+} or 100 kHz.

5.5. Buffers: Design Example

$$A_{RCL} = \frac{A_{ROL}}{1 - \left(\dfrac{A_{LG0}}{1+\dfrac{s}{2\pi p_{FB+}}}\right)} = \frac{\left(\dfrac{A_{ROL}}{1-A_{LG0}}\right)\left(1+\dfrac{s}{2\pi p_{FB+}}\right)}{1+\dfrac{s}{2\pi\left(1-A_{LG0}\right)p_{FB+}}} = \frac{A_{ROL0}\left(1+\dfrac{s}{2\pi p_{FB+}}\right)}{1+\dfrac{s}{2\pi\left(1-A_{LG0}\right)p_{FB+}}}$$

C_{IP} then shunts R_{OB} at $p_{OB} \approx 1$ MHz.

A_B near p_{FB+} excludes +FB $\therefore A_{B(MF)} \approx g_{m.NBUF}/g_{m.NBUF} = 1 = 0$ dB.

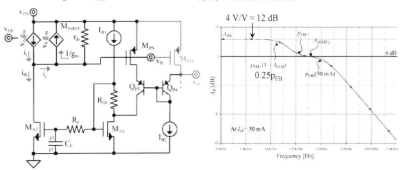

5.5. Buffers: Design Example

More Design Checks

$v_{B(MAX)}$ when assuming $v_{OE(MAX)}$ is $v_{IN} - 0.3$ V:

$$v_{B(MAX)} > v_{OE(MAX)} - v_{GS.NBUF(0)} = v_{OE(MAX)} - \left(v_{TN.NAT(MAX)} + \sqrt{\frac{2i_{NBUF(0)}}{K_{N(MIN)}'\left(\dfrac{W}{L}\right)_{NBUF}}}\right)$$

$$\approx \left(v_{IN} - 0.3\right) - \left(0.15 + \sqrt{\frac{2\left(0.5\mu\right)}{\left(80\mu\right)\left(\dfrac{12}{0.35}\right)}}\right) \approx v_{IN} - 0.47 \text{ V} < v_{IN} - \left|v_{TP(MIN)}\right|$$

Zero-load quiescent current $i_{Q(0)}$:

$$i_{Q(0)} = i_{N2(0)} + i_{N1(0)} + i_{p4} \approx I_{B1} + I_{B1} + I_{B2} = 0.5\mu + 0.5\mu + 2\mu = 3 \text{ }\mu A$$

$\therefore$ A 30% variation in currents raises $i_{Q(0)}$ to 3.9 μA < 4 μA.

5.5. Buffers: Design Example

Full-load quiescent current $i_{Q(50mA)}$:

$$i_{Q(50mA)} = i_{N2(50mA)} + i_{N1(50mA)} + i_{P4} \approx 46\mu + 46\mu + 2\mu = 94 \ \mu A$$

∴ A 30% variation in currents raises $i_{Q(50mA)}$ to 120 μA << 50 mA.

$v_{IN(MIN)}$ assuming the minimum voltage across I_{B1} is 150 mV:

$$v_{IN(MIN)} = v_{GS.N1(MAX)} + V_{B1(MIN)} = \left[v_{TN(MAX)} + \sqrt{\frac{2i_{NBUF(MAX)}}{K_{N(MIN)}'\left(\dfrac{W}{L}\right)_{N1}}} \right] + V_{B1(MIN)}$$

$$\approx 0.75 + \sqrt{\frac{2(46\mu)}{(80\mu)\left(\dfrac{30}{1.05}\right)}} + 0.15 \approx 1.1 \ V$$

End of Example.

5.5. Error Amplifiers: Requirements

Accurate

→ High gain A_E.

→ High power-supply rejection.

→ Low input-referred offset V_{OS}.

Fast load-dump response

→ High bandwidth → High pole p_E.

Long operational life

→ Low quiescent current I_Q.

→ Low headroom $v_{IN(MIN)}$.

Wide load-current range

→ Wide output swing Δv_{OE}.

5.5. Error Amplifiers: Headroom

$$v_{IN(MIN)} = Max\left\{V_{ROOM+} + V_{ROOM-}\right\}$$

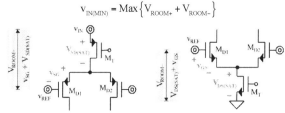

P-Type Differential Pairs

$$v_{IN(MIN)} = V_{ROOM+} + v_{REF} = V_{SD(SAT)} + v_{SG} + v_{REF} = 2V_{SD(SAT)} + |v_{TP}| + v_{REF}$$

v_{REF} is usually the bandgap voltage at about 1.2 V.

$\therefore v_{REF}$ and v_{SG} limit $v_{IN(MIN)}$ to roughly 2.2 V.

N-Type Differential Pairs

$$v_{REF} > V_{ROOM-} = v_{GS} + V_{DS(SAT)} = v_{TN} + 2V_{DS(SAT)}$$

This requirement is usually met because v_{REF} is roughly 1.2 V.

Note that a lower v_{REF} reduces signal-to-noise ratio (SNR) → Lowers dynamic range.

5.5. Error Amplifiers: Headroom

Load Mirror: v_{SG} of conventional mirror limits V_{ROOM+}.

$$v_{IN(MIN)} = V_{ROOM+} + v_{REF} = v_{SG} + V_{CE(MIN)} - v_{BE} + v_{REF}$$

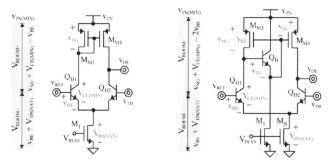

Level-shifting the diode connection reduces v_{SG} to $v_{SG} - v_{BE}$.

Except, the v_{BE} of an NPN follower does not track v_{SG}.

The v_{GS} of an NMOSFET tracks better, but not perfectly.

5.5. Error Amplifiers: Headroom

Folding differential currents via cascodes reduces v_{SG} to V_{BP}'s $v_{SG(BIAS)} - v_{SG5,6}$.

And now, the v_{SG} of the cascodes track across temperature and fabrication corners.

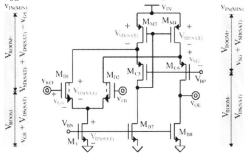

If $v_{SD3,4}$ is close to $V_{SD(SAT)}$, $v_{IN(MIN)}$ is nearly at its lowest possible setting.

$$v_{IN(MIN)} = V_{ROOM+} + v_{REF} = V_{SD(SAT)} + V_{DS(SAT)} - v_{GS} + v_{REF} = V_{SD(SAT)} - v_{TN} + v_{REF}$$

Low v_{REF} reduces $v_{IN(MIN)}$ further, and also SNR.

With such a low $v_{IN(MIN)}$, other paths may also limit $v_{IN(MIN)}$:

$$v_{IN(MIN)} = V_{ROOM+} + V_{ROOM-} = \left(v_{SG} + V_{SD(SAT)}\right) + V_{SD(SAT)} = \left|v_{TP}\right| + 3V_{SD(SAT)}$$

5.5. Error Amplifiers: Power-Supply Rejection

N-type mirrors cancel supply ripple v_{in} → Good for N-type power transistors.

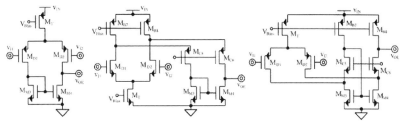

P-type mirrors reproduce supply ripple v_{in} → Good for P-type power transistors.

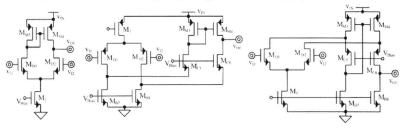

5.5. Error Amplifiers: Input-Referred Offset

Feedback resistors amplify A_E's input-referred offset V_{OS}.

$$v_O = v_{FB}\left(\frac{R_{FB1} + R_{FB2}}{R_{FB1}}\right) \approx \left(v_{REF} + V_{OS}\right)\left(\frac{R_{FB1} + R_{FB2}}{R_{FB1}}\right)$$

Mismatched gate–source Δv_{GS} and mismatched drain voltages Δv_M

produce an offset current that an input-referred offset V_{OS} cancels.

Δv_{GS} are small and random to produce a random component $V_{OS}{}^*$.

Δv_M produce a linear and systemic component $V_{OS(S)}$.

$V_{OS}{}^*$ and $V_{OS(S)}$ are very low (e.g., in millivolts).

$\therefore$ Linear models predict them well $\rightarrow$ Use small-signal models.

And $\quad V_{OS} = V_{OS(S)} \pm V_{OS}{}^*$

5.5. Error Amplifiers: Random Component

Random mismatches are uncorrelated $\rightarrow$ $V_{OS}{}^*$ is the root of summed squares.

All pair currents mismatch $\rightarrow$ All pairs contribute to $V_{OS}{}^*$:

$$V_{OS}{}^* = \sqrt{\left(\frac{\Delta i_{12}}{g_{m12}}\right)^2 + \left(\frac{\Delta i_{34}}{g_{m12}}\right)^2 + \left(\frac{\Delta v_{56} G_{M56(DEG)}}{g_{m12}}\right)^2 + \left(\frac{\Delta i_{78}}{g_{m12}}\right)^2}$$

$$\approx \sqrt{\left(\frac{\Delta i_{12}}{g_{m12}}\right)^2 + \left(\frac{\Delta i_{34}}{g_{m12}}\right)^2 + \left(\frac{\Delta i_{78}}{g_{m12}}\right)^2}$$

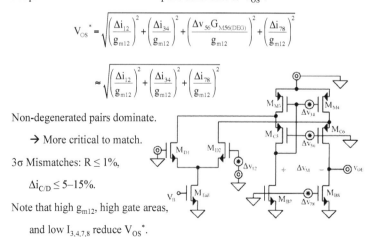

Non-degenerated pairs dominate.

$\rightarrow$ More critical to match.

3σ Mismatches: $R \leq 1\%$,

$\Delta i_{C/D} \leq 5\text{–}15\%$.

Note that high g_{m12}, high gate areas,

and low $I_{3,4,7,8}$ reduce $V_{OS}{}^*$.

5.5. Error Amplifiers: Systemic Component

$V_{OS(S)}$: Δv_M produces $V_{O(S)}$: $\quad V_{OS(S)} = \dfrac{\Delta v_M}{A_E} = \dfrac{\Delta v_M}{g_{m12} R_{OE}}$

$\therefore$ High gain A_E lowers $V_{OS(S)}$.

Load Regulation: Feedback adjusts v_{OE} and v_B to accommodate the load.

$\rightarrow v_{OE}$ changes with output current i_O.

$\therefore V_{OS(S)}$ changes with i_O $\rightarrow$ Load regulation effect.

$$\Delta V_{OS(S)} = \frac{\Delta v_M(i_O)}{A_E} \approx \frac{\Delta v_B}{A_E} = \left| \frac{i_{O(MAX)}}{G_{P(MAX)}} - \frac{i_{O(MIN)}}{G_{P(MIN)}} \right| \left(\frac{1}{A_E} \right)$$

This is how load regulation manifests in v_{FB},

which R_{FB1} and R_{FB2} then amplify in v_O to:

$$\Delta V_{LD} = \Delta v_{FB} \left(\frac{R_{FB1} + R_{FB2}}{R_{FB1}} \right) \equiv \Delta V_{OS(S)} \left(\frac{R_{FB1} + R_{FB2}}{R_{FB1}} \right)$$

5.5. Error Amplifiers: Input-Referred Offset

In the regenerative load-tracking buffer and PMOS power transistor:

$v_{OE} = v_B + v_{GS.NBUF}$

$v_{SG.PO} \propto i_O$ $\rightarrow$ v_B falls with rising i_O.

$i_{NBUF} \propto i_O$ $\rightarrow$ $v_{GS.NBUF}$ rises with rising i_O.

$\therefore v_{GS}$ variations offset v_B variations

to produce lower v_{OE} variations:

$$\Delta v_{OE} = \Delta v_{GS.NBUF} - \Delta v_B \approx \left(\frac{i_{NBUF(MAX)}}{g_{m(MAX)}} - \frac{i_{NBUF(MIN)}}{g_{m(MIN)}} \right) - \left(\frac{i_{O(MAX)}}{G_{P(MAX)}} - \frac{i_{O(MIN)}}{G_{P(MIN)}} \right)$$

$$\approx \frac{i_{NBUF(MAX)}}{g_{m(MAX)}} - \frac{i_{O(MAX)}}{G_{P(MAX)}} = \frac{i_{O(MAX)} A_I}{g_{m(MAX)}} - \frac{i_{O(MAX)}}{G_{P(MAX)}} \approx \Delta i_{O(MAX)} \left(\frac{A_I}{g_{m(MAX)}} - \frac{1}{G_{P(MAX)}} \right)$$

$\therefore$ The load-tracking feature lowers load regulation effect ΔV_{LD}.

Caution: Higher A_I lowers ΔV_{LD} and raises A_{LG+}.

$\therefore$ For stable feedback conditions, limit A_I and lower A_{LG+}'s pole p_{FB+}.

5.5. Error Amplifiers: Layout Design

Matching Hierarchy

Critical for low $V_{OS}{}^*$: Non-degenerated input, mirror, and bias pairs.

Apply all matching techniques (e.g., close, modular -square-,

same orientation, common centroid, cross-coupled, dummy transistors,

uniform sheet(s) of metal and no metal routes immediately above, etc.)

Good for predictable performance: Biasing current mirrors.

Apply few basic matching techniques (e.g., close, modular -square-,

same orientation, etc.).

Nominal for low 2nd-order effects: Cascode transistors.

Apply one or two basic matching techniques (e.g., close, etc.).

Thick–thin oxide height difference between poly strips causes etching errors.

∴ Use dummy devices or dummy thin-oxide polysilicon strips.

5.5. Error Amplifiers: Design Example

Design Example: Design a 6-μA error amplifier for the regenerative load-

tracking buffer and PMOS power transistor from the previous examples,

where $W_O = 18.3$ mm, $L_O = 0.35$ μm, $v_{IN} = 1.1$–1.6 V, $v_O = 1$ V,

$v_{REF} = 0.9$ V, 10 μA $\leq i_O \leq 50$ mA, $f_{0dB} \geq 1$ MHz, $0.2 \leq v_{OE} \leq v_{IN} - 0.3$ V,

$V_{OS} \leq \pm 25$ mV, $\Delta V_{LD} \leq 10$ mV, and p_{OE} is dominant.

Process: $V_{TN0} = |V_{TP0}| = 0.6 \pm 0.15$ V, $V_{TN0.NAT} = 0.6 \pm 0.15$ V,

$K_p' = 40$ μA/V^2 ± 20%, $K_N' = 100$ μA/V^2 ± 20%, $L \geq 0.35$ μm,

$1/\lambda_{L(MIN)} = 2$ V, $1/\lambda_{3L(MIN)} = 500$ V, $L_{OV} = 35$ nm, $C_{OX}'' = 5$ fF/μm^2,

$\beta_{P0} = 50$–150 A/A, and $V_A = 15$ V.

Solution:

Architectural Design

Differential Input Pair:

Since $v_{REF} = 0.9$ V, use native NFETs.

Since $v_{TN.NAT(MIN)} = -0.15$ V, connect bulk to ground to raise $v_{TN.NAT}$.

5.5. Error Amplifiers: Design Example

Load Mirror:

Since S_O is a PFET, use P-type mirror to reproduce v_{in} in v_{OE} for PSR.

Since $v_{IN(MIN)}$ = 1.1 V, use cascode transistors to fold currents for ICMR.

Use a diode-connected PFET to bias the cascode transistors.

Internal Compensation:

Use Miller C_M across A_B and M_{PO} to ensure v_{OE} is dominant.

Negative Feedback:

Since M_{PO} inverts and A_B does not, A_E should not invert.

∴ v_{FB} should connect to A_E's non-inverting input.

Low Random Offset:

Differential and Load-Mirror Transistors ≡ Large and critically matched.

∴ $L_{D1,2} \equiv L_{M3,4} \equiv 10L_{MIN}$ = 3.5 μm.

Since A_E should not be too high, L_{MIN} for non-degenerated bias transistors.

∴ $L_{B7,8} \equiv L_{MIN}$ = 0.35 μm, but still critically matched.

5.5. Error Amplifiers: Design Example

Internally Compensated Low-Dropout PMOS Regulator

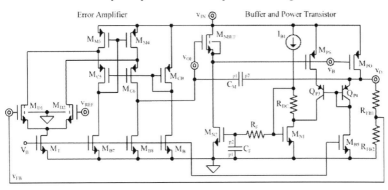

Component Design

Feedback Resistors R_{FB1} and R_{FB2}:

$$\frac{v_O}{v_{REF}} = \frac{R_{FB1} + R_{FB2}}{R_{FB2}} \equiv \frac{1}{0.9} = 1.11 \text{ V/V}$$

5.5. Error Amplifiers: Design Example

To ensure R_{FB1} and R_{FB2} can sink M_{PO}'s subthreshold current:

$$i_R = \frac{v_O}{R_{FB1} + R_{FB2}} \approx 3 \ \mu A$$

$\therefore R_{FB2} \equiv 300 \ k\Omega$ and $R_{FB1} \equiv 33.3 \ k\Omega$.

Error-Amplifier Gain A_E: Set to roughly 40 dB.

$$A_{E0} \approx g_{m.D1} r_{ds.B8} \approx \frac{\sqrt{2 I_{D1} K_N' \left(\dfrac{W}{L}\right)_{D1}}}{I_{B8} \lambda_{L(MIN)}} = \frac{\sqrt{2 \left(\dfrac{I_{Tail}}{2}\right) K_N' \left(\dfrac{W}{L}\right)_{D1}}}{I_{B8} \lambda_{L(MIN)}} \equiv 100$$

$$\therefore \quad \frac{\sqrt{I_{Tail} \left(\dfrac{W}{L}\right)_{D1}}}{I_{B8}} \equiv \frac{A_{E0} \lambda_{L(MIN)}}{\sqrt{K_N'}} = \frac{(100)(0.1)}{\sqrt{100\mu}} \approx 1000$$

And choosing $I_{Tail} \equiv 2 \ \mu A$ and $I_{B8} \equiv 1 \ \mu A$,

$$\left(\frac{W}{L}\right)_{D1} \approx \frac{(1000)^2 (1\mu)^2}{2\mu} = 0.5 \quad \therefore W_{D1,2} \equiv 0.5 L_{D1,2} = 1.75 \ \mu m.$$

5.5. Error Amplifiers: Design Example

Highest Output Voltage $v_{OE(MAX)}$: To shut M_{PO},

$$v_{OE(MAX)} = v_{IN} - v_{SD.M4} - V_{SD.C6(SAT)} \geq v_{IN} - 0.3 \ V$$

$$\therefore \quad V_{SD.M4(SAT)} = \sqrt{\frac{2 I_{M4}}{K_K' \left(\dfrac{W}{L}\right)_{M4}}} \leq \sqrt{\frac{2 \left(I_{D2} + I_{B8}\right)}{K_{K(MIN)}' \left(\dfrac{W}{L}\right)_{M4}}} \leq 0.15 \ V$$

Or $\quad \left(\dfrac{W}{L}\right)_{M4} \geq \dfrac{2\left(I_{D2} + I_{B8}\right)}{V_{SD.M4(SAT)}^2 K_{P(MIN)}'} = \dfrac{2(1\mu + 1\mu)}{(0.15)^2 (32\mu)} = 5.55$

$\therefore W_{M3,4} \equiv 6 L_{M3,4} = 21 \ \mu m.$

And $\quad V_{SD.C6(SAT)} = \sqrt{\dfrac{2 I_{C6}}{K_P' \left(\dfrac{W}{L}\right)_{C6}}} \leq \sqrt{\dfrac{2 I_{B8}}{K_{P(MIN)}' \left(\dfrac{W}{L}\right)_{C6}}} \leq 0.15 \ V$

Or $\quad \left(\dfrac{W}{L}\right)_{C6} \geq \dfrac{2 I_{B8}}{V_{SD.C6(SAT)}^2 K_{P(MIN)}'} = \dfrac{2(1\mu)}{(0.15)^2 (32\mu)} = 2.8$

$\therefore W_{C5,6} \equiv 1.05 \ \mu m$ and $L_{C5,6} \equiv L_{MIN} \equiv 0.35 \ \mu m.$

5.5. Error Amplifiers: Design Example

Choosing $v_{SD.M4} \equiv 0.15$ V and noting that

$$v_{G.CB} = v_{IN} - v_{SG.CB} \equiv v_{IN} - v_{SD.M4} - v_{SG.C6}$$

$$\therefore \quad v_{SG.CB} = |v_{TP}| + \sqrt{\frac{2I_{BP}}{K_P'\left(\frac{W}{L}\right)_{CB}}} \equiv v_{SD.M4} + v_{SG.C6} = v_{SD.M4} + |v_{TP}| + \sqrt{\frac{2I_{C6}}{K_P'\left(\frac{W}{L}\right)_{C6}}}$$

And choosing $I_{BP} \equiv 0.5$ μA,

$$\left(\frac{W}{L}\right)_{CB} = \frac{2I_{BP}}{\left[K_P'\left|v_{SD.M4} + \sqrt{\frac{2I_{C2}}{K_P'\left(\frac{W}{L}\right)_{C6}}}\right|\right]^2} = \frac{2(0.5\mu)}{\left[(40\mu)\left|0.15 + \sqrt{\frac{2(1\mu)}{(40\mu)\left(\frac{1.05}{0.35}\right)}}\right|\right]^2} = 0.32$$

$\therefore W_{CB} \equiv 1$ μm and $L_{CB} \equiv 3$ μm.

5.5. Error Amplifiers: Design Example

Lowest Output Voltage $v_{OE(MIN)}$: To fully engage M_{PO},

$$v_{OE(MIN)} = V_{DS.B8(SAT)} \leq \sqrt{\frac{2I_{B8}}{K_{N(MIN)}'\left(\frac{W}{L}\right)_{B8}}} \leq 0.2 \text{ V}$$

$$\therefore \quad \left(\frac{W}{L}\right)_{B8} \geq \frac{2I_{B8}}{K_{N(MIN)}'v_{OE(MIN)}^2} = \frac{2(1\mu)}{(80\mu)(0.2)^2} = 0.62$$

And $W_{B8} \equiv 2$ μm and $L_{B8} \equiv L_{MIN} \equiv 0.35$ μm.

Miller Capacitor C_M: Since $f_{0dB} = f_{GBW}$,

$$f_{0dB} \approx A_E A_B A_P p_{OE} \approx \frac{A_E A_B A_P}{2\pi C_M \left(A_B A_P\right) R_{OE}} \approx \frac{\left(g_{m.D1} R_{OE}\right) A_B A_P}{2\pi C_M \left(A_B A_P\right) R_{OE}} = \frac{g_{m.D1}}{2\pi C_M} \equiv 1 \text{ MHz}$$

$$\therefore C_M = \frac{g_{m.D1}}{2\pi f_{0dB}} = \frac{\sqrt{2I_{D1} K_N'\left(\frac{W}{L}\right)_{D1}}}{2\pi f_{0dB}} = \frac{\sqrt{2(1\mu)(100\mu)\left(\frac{1.75}{3.5}\right)}}{2\pi(1M)} = 1.59 \text{ pF} \rightarrow C_M \equiv 1.6 \text{ pF}.$$

5.5. Error Amplifiers: Design Example

Design Checks

Quiescent Current i_Q:

$$i_Q = i_{M3} + i_{M4} + I_{BP} = 2\mu + 2\mu + 0.5\mu = 4.5 \ \mu A$$

And with a 30% variation is 5.85 $\mu A \leq 6 \ \mu A$.

Headroom $v_{IN(MIN)}$ when $V_{IBP(MIN)} = 0.2$ V:

$$v_{IN(MIN)} = Max \begin{cases} V_{SG.M3} + V_{DS.B7(SAT)} = \left|V_{TP(MAX)}\right| + V_{SD.M3(SAT)} + V_{DS.B7(SAT)} \\ \\ V_{SG.CB} + V_{I_{BP}} = \left|V_{TP(MAX)}\right| + V_{SD.CB(SAT)} + V_{IBP(MIN)} \end{cases}$$

$$\approx Max \begin{cases} \left|V_{TP(MAX)}\right| + \sqrt{\dfrac{2I_{M3}}{K_{P(MIN)}'\left(\dfrac{W}{L}\right)_{M3}}} + \sqrt{\dfrac{2I_{B7}}{K_{P(MIN)}'\left(\dfrac{W}{L}\right)_{B7}}} \\ \\ \left|V_{TP(MAX)}\right| + \sqrt{\dfrac{2I_{BP}}{K_{P(MIN)}'\left(\dfrac{W}{L}\right)_{CB}}} + V_{IBP(MIN)} \end{cases}$$

5.5. Error Amplifiers: Design Example

$$v_{IN(MIN)} \approx Max \begin{cases} 0.75 + \sqrt{\dfrac{2(2\mu)}{(32\mu)\left(\dfrac{21}{3.5}\right)}} + \sqrt{\dfrac{2(1\mu)}{(80\mu)\left(\dfrac{2}{0.35}\right)}} \approx 0.96 \\ \\ 0.75 + \sqrt{\dfrac{2(0.5\mu)}{(32\mu)\left(\dfrac{1}{3}\right)}} + 0.2 \approx 1.26 \end{cases} \approx 1.26 \ V > 1.1 \ V$$

$\therefore$ To reduce $v_{IN(MIN)}$ to 1.05 V,

→ Lower M_{CB}'s $v_{SG.CB}$ by 150 mV.

→ Lower $M_{C5,6}$'s $V_{SD5,6(SAT)}$ by 75 mV.

→ Lower $M_{M3,4}$'s $V_{SD3,4(SAT)}$ by 50 mV.

$\therefore$ $M_{M3,4}$ in triode by 25 mV, but okay because $A_E \neq f(r_{ds3,4})$.

5.5. Error Amplifiers: Design Example

$$\rightarrow \quad \left(\frac{W}{L}\right)_{C5} \equiv \left(\frac{W}{L}\right)_{C6} \geq \frac{2I_{B8}}{V_{SD.C6(SAT)}{}^{2}K_{P(MIN)}{}'} = \frac{2(1\mu)}{(0.075)^2(32\mu)} = 11$$

$\therefore W_{C5,6} \equiv 3.85\ \mu m$ and $L_{C5,6} \equiv L_{MIN} \equiv 0.35\ \mu m$.

$$\rightarrow \quad \left(\frac{W}{L}\right)_{M3} \equiv \left(\frac{W}{L}\right)_{M4} \geq \frac{2(I_{D2}+I_{B8})}{V_{SD.M4(SAT)}{}^{2}K_{P(MIN)}{}'} = \frac{2(1\mu+1\mu)}{(0.1)^2(32\mu)} = 12.5$$

$\therefore$ Reduce $L_{M3,4}$ to keep dimensions from growing excessively.

$\therefore W_{M3,4} \equiv 12.5L_{M3,4}\ \mu m = 22\ \mu m$ and $L_{M3,4} \equiv 5L_{MIN} \equiv 1.75\ \mu m$.

$$\rightarrow \quad \left(\frac{W}{L}\right)_{CB} = \frac{2I_{D'}}{K_{P}{}'\left[v_{SD.M4}+\sqrt{\dfrac{2I_{C6}}{K_{P}{}'\left(\dfrac{W}{L}\right)_{C6}}}\right]^2} = \frac{2(0.5\mu)}{(40\mu)\left[0.075+\sqrt{\dfrac{2(1\mu)}{(40\mu)\left(\dfrac{3.85}{0.35}\right)}}\right]^2} = 1.2$$

$\therefore W_{CB} \equiv 1.2\ \mu m$ and $L_{CB} \equiv 1\ \mu m$.

5.5. Error Amplifiers: Design Example

Systemic Offset $V_{OS(S)}$:

$$V_{OS(S)} = \frac{V_{DS.B8}-V_{DS.B7}}{A_E} = \frac{V_{OE}-\left(v_{IN}-v_{SG.M3}\right)}{A_E}$$

$$V_{OS(S)(MAX)} \leq \frac{V_{OE(MAX)}-\left\{v_{IN}-\left[|v_{TP(MAX)}|+\sqrt{\dfrac{2I_{M3}}{K_{P(MIN)}{}'\left(\dfrac{W}{L}\right)_{M3}}}\right]\right\}}{A_E}$$

$$V_{OS(S)(MIN)} \leq \frac{v_{OE(MIN)}-\left\{v_{IN(MAX)}-\left[|v_{TP(MIN)}|+\sqrt{\dfrac{2I_{M3}}{K_{P(MAX)}{}'\left(\dfrac{W}{L}\right)_{M3}}}\right]\right\}}{A_E}$$

$\therefore -5.7\ mV \leq V_{OS(S)} \leq 4.6\ mV$

5.5. Error Amplifiers: Design Example

Load regulation Δv_{LD}:

$$\Delta v_{OE} = \Delta v_{GS.NBUF} - \Delta v_B \approx \Delta i_{O(MAX)} \left(\frac{A_I}{g_{m(MAX)}} - \frac{1}{G_{P(MAX)}} \right)$$

$$\approx 50m \left[\left(\frac{17}{18.3k} \right)(1) \left(\frac{1}{\sqrt{2(46\mu)(100\mu)(12/0.35)}} \right) - \frac{1}{\sqrt{2(50m)(40\mu)(18.3k/0.35)}} \right] \approx -27 \text{ mV}$$

$$\therefore \ \Delta V_{OS(S)} = \frac{\Delta v_{OE}}{A_E} \approx \frac{27m}{100} = 270 \ \mu V \quad \text{And} \quad \Delta v_{O(LD)} = \Delta V_{OS(S)} \left(\frac{v_O}{v_{REF}} \right) \approx (270\mu) \left(\frac{1}{0.9} \right) < 1 \text{ mV}$$

Random offset $V_{OS}{}^*$: Assume $3\sigma \ \Delta i_D$ of critical transistors is $\pm 5\%$.

$$V_{OS}{}^* \approx \sqrt{ \left(\frac{\Delta i_{12}}{g_{m12}} \right)^2 + \left(\frac{\Delta i_{34}}{g_{m12}} \right)^2 + \left(\frac{\Delta i_{78}}{g_{m12}} \right)^2 }$$

$$\approx \sqrt{ \frac{(5\% I_{12})^2 + (5\% I_{34})^2 + (5\% I_{78})^2}{2 I_{12} K_N{}'(W/L)_{D12}} } = \sqrt{ \frac{(5\% \cdot 1\mu)^2 + (5\% \cdot 2\mu)^2 + (5\% \cdot 1\mu)^2}{2(1\mu)(100\mu)(0.5)} } \approx 12 \text{ mV}$$

Chapter 6. Linear-Regulator Systems

6.1. Low Dropout

6.2. High Bandwidth

6.3. Self-Referenced

6.4. Noise Suppressors

6.5. Other Enhancements

6.6. Circuit Protection

6.7. Characterization

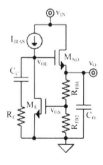

6.1. Output-Compensated PMOS LDO

Low Dropout (LDO): P-type power transistor S_O.

Low Power: MOS power transistor M_{PO}.

Low Load-Dump Variation: High output capacitance C_O.

High Power-Supply Rejection: Output compensation.

P-type mirror reproduces supply ripple v_{in}.

Low-ESR C_O.

Extend Bandwidth:

N-type follower.

Low Headroom:

Level-shift P-type

mirror's $v_{SG.M3}$.

Low Offset: NPN

differential pair.

Phase-Saving Zero:

C_{FF} bypasses R_{FB1}.

6.1. Output-Compensated PMOS LDO

Compensation Strategy

C_O and C_B establish dominant pole p_O.

R_{ESR} extends f_{0dB} with a zero z_{ESR}.

A_E's output pole p_{OE} near $f_{0dB(MIN)}$.

A_B's output pole p_{OB} near $f_{0dB(MAX)}$.

C_{FF}'s feed-forward zero z_{FF} near $f_{0DB(MAX)}$.

Near $10f_{0dB}$:

C_B shunts R_{ESR} past bypass pole p_B.

Mirror pole p_M.

Mirror zero z_M.

C_{GSBUF}'s feed-forward zero z_{BUF}.

C_{GDO}'s Miller zero z_{PO}.

v_{FB}'s feedback pole p_{FB}.

C_{GD2}'s Miller zero z_{D2}.

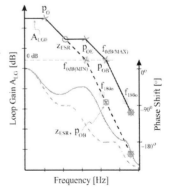

6.1. Output-Compensated PMOS LDO

Single-pole drop to $f_{0dB(MIN)}$ without z_{ESR}:

$$\frac{A_{LG0}}{1+\frac{s}{2\pi p_O}} \approx \left.\frac{A_{LG0}}{\left(\frac{s}{2\pi p_O}\right)}\right|_{f_{0dB(MIN)}\approx A_{LG0}p_O} \equiv 1$$

A_E's output pole:

$$p_{OE} \approx \frac{1}{2\pi\left(r_{ds4}\|r_{o2}\right)C_{D4}} \approx f_{0dB(MIN)}$$

A_B's output pole:

$$p_{OB} \approx \frac{g_{mBUF}}{2\pi C_{SGO}} \approx f_{0dB(MAX)}$$

R_{ESR} current-limits C_O:

$$\frac{1}{2\pi R_{ESR(MAX)}C_O} \le z_{ESR} \le \frac{1}{2\pi R_{ESR(MIN)}C_O}$$

R_{ESR} extends f_{0dB} to $f_{0dB(MAX)}$:

$$f_{0dB(MAX)} \approx f_{0dB(MIN)}\left(\frac{p_{OE}}{z_{ESR(MIN)}}\right)$$

C_{FF} bypasses R_{FB1} after C_O and C_B shunt:

$$\left.\frac{1}{sC_{FF}}\right|_{z_{FF}=\frac{1}{2\pi R_{FB1}C_{FF}}\approx 5f_{0dB(MAX)}} \equiv R_{FB1}$$

Highest C_B shunts R_{ESR} near $10f_{0dB(MAX)}$:

$$p_B \approx \frac{1}{2\pi R_{ESR}C_{B(MAX)}} \approx 10f_{0dB(MAX)}$$

6.1. Output-Compensated PMOS LDO

$$p_M = A_{V0}p_{D3} \approx \frac{g_{m3}\left(r_{ds3}\|r_{o1}\right)}{2\pi\left(r_{ds3}\|r_{o1}\right)C_{D3}} \approx \frac{g_{m3}}{2\pi C_{D3}} \approx 5f_{0dB(MAX)} \quad \leftarrow \text{Mirror Pole}$$

Pole in Mirror. $\rightarrow \quad p_{G3} \approx \frac{g_{mMD}}{2\pi\left(C_{GS3}+C_{GS4}+C_{GSMD}\right)} \approx p_M \approx 5f_{0dB(MAX)}$

$$i_C = \left.\frac{v_{gs}}{sC_{GSBUF}}\right|_{z_{BUF}=\frac{g_{mBUF}}{2\pi C_{GSBUF}}\approx 5f_{0dB(MAX)}} \equiv i_{gm} = v_{gs}g_{mBUF} \quad \leftarrow C_{GSBUF}\text{'s }i_C \text{ exceeds }i_{gm}.$$

C_{GDO}'s i_C exceeds i_{gm}. $\rightarrow \quad i_C = \frac{v_{sgO}-v_{sdO}}{sC_{GDO}} = \left.\frac{v_{sgO}}{sC_{GDO}}\right|_{z_{PO}=\frac{g_{mO}}{2\pi C_{GDO}}\ge 10f_{0dB(MAX)}} \equiv i_{gm} = v_{sg}g_{mO}$

$$\left.\frac{1}{s\left(C_{\mu2}+C_{\pi2}+C_{FF}\right)}\right|_{p_{FB}=\frac{1}{2\pi\left(R_{FB1}\|R_{FB2}\right)\left(C_{\pi2}+C_{FF}\right)}\approx 10f_{0dB(MAX)}} \equiv R_{FB1}\|R_{FB2} \quad \leftarrow v_{fb} \text{ drops after } C_O \text{ and } C_B \text{ shunt.}$$

$C_{\mu2}$'s i_C exceeds i_{gm}. $\rightarrow \quad i_C = \frac{v_{be2}-v_{ce2}}{sC_{\mu2}} = \left.\frac{v_{be2}}{sC_{\mu2}}\right|_{z_{D2}=\frac{g_{m2}}{2\pi C_{\mu2}}\ge 10f_{0dB(MAX)}} \equiv i_{gm} = v_{be2}g_{m2}$

6.1. Miller-Compensated PMOS LDO

Low Dropout: P-type power transistor S_O.

Low Power: MOS power transistor M_{PO}.

System-on-Chip Integration: Internal compensation.

Reject Power-Supply Ripple: P-type mirror reproduces supply ripple v_{in}.

Load-Dump Response: C_O supplies supplementary power.

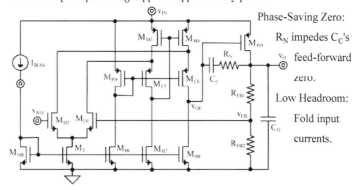

Phase-Saving Zero:
R_N impedes C_C's feed-forward zero.

Low Headroom:
Fold input currents.

6.1. Miller-Compensated PMOS LDO

Compensation Strategy

Miller C_C establishes dominant pole p_{OE}.

C_O sets secondary pole p_O.

R_N's zero z_N cancels p_O.

Near $10f_{0dB}$:

Mirror pole p_M.

Mirror zero z_M.

v_{FB}'s feedback pole p_{FB}.

Cascode pole $p_{S5,6}$.

C_{GD1}'s Miller zero z_{D1}.

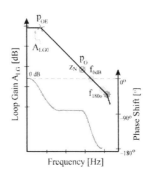

6.1. Miller-Compensated PMOS LDO

Single-pole
drop to $f_{0dB(MIN)}$. →
$$\frac{A_{LG0}}{1+\dfrac{s}{2\pi p_{OE}}} \approx \frac{A_{LG0}}{\left(\dfrac{s}{2\pi p_{OE}}\right)} \approx \frac{g_{m2}r_{ds8}A_{PO}}{r_{ds8}\left[A_{PO}\left(C_C+C_{GDO}\right)\right]s}\Bigg|_{f_{0dB}=\frac{g_{m2}}{2\pi\left(C_C+C_{GDO}\right)}} \equiv 1$$

$$\frac{1}{s\left(C_O+C_{DBO}\right)}\Bigg|_{p_O=\frac{g_{mO}}{2\pi\left(C_O+C_{DBO}\right)}\le\frac{f_{0dB}}{10}} \equiv \frac{1}{g_{mO}} \quad \leftarrow C_O \text{ shunts } v_O \text{ after } C_M \text{ shorts.}$$

R_N impedes C_C's
feed-forward i_C. →
$$i_R = \frac{v_{sgO}-v_{sdO}}{R_N+\dfrac{1}{sC_C}} = \frac{v_{sgO}}{R_N+\dfrac{1}{sC_C}}\Bigg|_{z_N=\frac{1}{2\pi\left(R_N-\frac{1}{g_{mO}}\right)C_C}=p_O} \equiv i_{gm} = v_{sgO}g_{mO}$$

$$\frac{1}{s\left(C_{GS3}+C_{GS4}+C_{GD3}+C_{GD4}+C_{GD5}+C_{GD7}\right)}\Bigg|_{p_M=\frac{g_{m3}}{2\pi\left(C_{GS3}+C_{GS4}\right)}=5f_{0dB}} \equiv \frac{1}{g_{m3}} \quad \leftarrow \text{Mirror Pole}$$

v_{fb} drops after C_O
and C_B shunt. →
$$\frac{1}{s\left(C_{GD1}+C_{GS1}\right)}\Bigg|_{p_{FB}=\frac{1}{2\pi\left(R_{FB1}\|R_{FB2}\right)C_{GS1}}=10f_{0dB(MAX)}} \equiv R_{FB1}\|R_{FB2}$$

6.1. Miller-Compensated PMOS LDO

M_{C5}'s and M_{C6}'s $1/g_{m5}$ and $1/g_{m6}$ drop half of the differential gain.

∴ Combined, they constitute one pole:

$$\frac{1}{s\left(C_{GSC}+C_{GDM}+C_{GDD}\right)}\Bigg|_{p_{S5,6}=\frac{g_{mC}}{2\pi\left(C_{GSC}+C_{GDM}+C_{GDD}\right)}=10f_{0dB}} \equiv \frac{1}{g_{mC}}$$

C_{GD1}'s i_C exceeds i_{gm}. →
$$i_C = \frac{v_{gs1}-v_{ds1}}{sC_{GD1}} = \frac{v_{gs1}}{sC_{GD1}}\Bigg|_{z_{D1}=\frac{g_{m1}}{2\pi C_{GD1}}\ge10f_{0dB(MAX)}} \equiv i_{gm} = v_{gs1}g_{m1}$$

Note: If C_O is high enough, C_O establishes dominant pole p_O.

$$\frac{1}{s\left(C_O+C_{DBO}\right)}\Bigg|_{p_O=\frac{1}{2\pi\left[r_{dsO}\|\left(R_{FB1}+R_{FB2}\right)\right]\left(C_O+C_{DBO}\right)}} \equiv r_{dsO}\|\left(R_{FB1}+R_{FB2}\right)$$

C_C shunts A_E's R_{OE}.

$$\frac{1}{s\left(C_C+C_{GDO}\right)}\Bigg|_{p_{OE}=\frac{1}{2\pi r_{ds8}\left(C_C+C_{GDO}\right)}\ge\frac{f_{0dB}}{10}} \equiv r_{ds8}$$

R_N current-limits C_C.

$$\frac{1}{sC_C}\Bigg|_{z_N=\frac{1}{2\pi R_N C_C}=p_{OE}} \equiv R_N$$

∴ z_N cancels p_{OE} → System is stable for a wide range of C_O's.

6.1. Miller-Amplified PMOS LDO

For higher on-chip integration:

→ Reduce C_M.

→ Or raise C_M's efficacy → Amplify Miller effects.

Premise:

Loop gain A_{LG} around Miller stage sets Miller multiplication factor:

→ $C_M = (1 + A_{LG})C_M$

Magnify Miller Effect:

Amplify C_M's feedback current i_{CM} by A_I.

→ $C_M = (1 + A_{LG}A_I)C_M$

How:

Amplifying current mirror.

6.1. Miller-Amplified PMOS LDO

M_{B7A}–M_{B7} amplify C_M's i_{CM} and M_{M3}–M_{M4} steers it to v_{OE}.

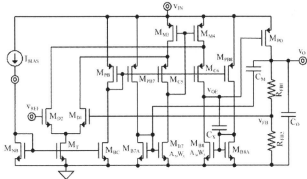

Caution: M_{B7A}'s $1/g_m$ current-limits C_M → Zero peaks A_B's gain near f_{0dB}.

Possible Band-Aid: Damp peaking effect with capacitance.

→ M_{B8A}–M_{B8} amplify and steer C_X's i_{CX} to v_{OE} for $(1 + A_M)C_X$.

$$i_{EQ} = i_{CX} + i_{B8} = i_{CX}(1 + A_M) \approx v_{oe}sC_X(1 + A_M) \equiv v_{oe}sC_{EQX}$$

6.2. High Bandwidth

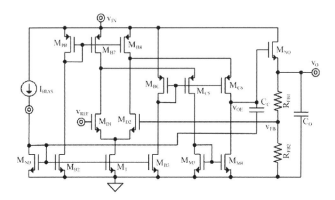

6.2. Internally Compensated NMOS

High Bandwidth: N-type power transistor S_O.

→ Follower's shunt feedback is fast, but with a high dropout voltage.

System-on-Chip Integration: Internal compensation.

Reject Power-Supply Ripple: N-type mirror cancels supply ripple v_{in}.

Suppress Power-Supply Ripple: Low-ESR output capacitor C_O.

Phase-Saving Zero: M_{NB}'s $1/g_m$ current-limits C_C.

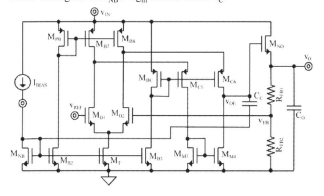

6.2. Internally Compensated NMOS

Compensation Strategy

C_C establishes dominant pole p_{OE}.

C_O sets secondary pole p_O.

M_{NB}'s $1/g_m$ zero z_C cancels p_O.

Near 5–$10f_{0dB}$:

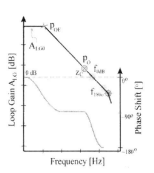

C_{GSNO}'s feed-forward zero z_{NO}.

Mirror pole p_M.

Mirror zero z_M.

Cascode pole $p_{S5,6}$.

v_{FB}'s feedback pole p_{FB}.

C_{GD2}'s Miller zero $z_{D2.RHP}$.

6.2. Internally Compensated NMOS

Single-pole drop to $f_{0dB(MIN)}$. $\rightarrow$
$$\frac{A_{LG0}}{1+\dfrac{s}{2\pi p_{OE}}} \approx \frac{A_{LG0}}{\left(\dfrac{s}{2\pi p_{OE}}\right)} \approx \left.\frac{g_{m1}r_{ds4}}{r_{ds4}\left(C_C+C_{GDNO}\right)s}\right|_{f_{0dB}\approx\frac{g_{m1}}{2\pi\left(C_C+C_{GDNO}\right)}} \equiv 1$$

C_O shunts M_{NO}'s $1/g_m$:
$$\left.\frac{1}{s\left(C_O+C_{GSNO}\right)}\right|_{p_{O(MIN)}\approx\frac{g_{mNO}}{2\pi\left(C_{O(MAX)}+C_{GSNO}\right)}\geq\frac{f_{0dB}}{10}} \equiv \frac{1}{g_{mNO}}$$

M_{NB}'s $1/g_m$ current-limits C_C:
$$\left.\frac{1}{sC_C}\right|_{z_C=\frac{g_{mNB}}{2\pi C_C}\approx p_O} \equiv \frac{1}{g_{mNB}}$$

C_{GSNO}'s i_C exceeds i_{gm}:
$$\left.i_C=\frac{v_{gsNO}}{sC_{GSNO}}\right|_{z_{NO}=\frac{g_{mNO}}{2\pi C_{GSNO}}\geq 5f_{0dB}} \equiv i_{gm} = v_{gsNO}g_{mNO}$$

6.2. Internally Compensated NMOS

$$\text{Mirror Pole} \rightarrow \left.\frac{1}{s\left(C_{GS3}+C_{GS4}+C_{GD4}+C_{GD5}\right)}\right|_{P_M=\frac{g_{m3}}{2\pi\left(C_{GS3}+C_{GS4}\right)}\approx 5f_{0dB}} \equiv \frac{1}{g_{m3}}$$

M_{C5}'s and M_{C6}'s $1/g_{m5}$ and $1/g_{m6}$ drop half of the differential gain.

$\therefore$ Combined, they constitute one pole:

$$\left.\frac{1}{s\left(C_{GSC}+C_{GDB}+C_{GDD}\right)}\right|_{P_{S5,6}=\frac{g_{mC}}{2\pi\left(C_{GSC}+C_{GDB}+C_{GDD}\right)}\approx 10f_{0dB}} \equiv \frac{1}{g_{mC}}$$

v_{fb} drops after C_O and C_B shunt:

$$\left.\frac{1}{s\left(C_{GS2}+C_{GD2}\right)}\right|_{P_{FB}=\frac{1}{2\pi\left(R_{FB1}\|R_{FB2}\right)C_{GS2}}\approx 10f_{0dB(MAX)}} \equiv R_{FB1}\|R_{FB2}$$

$$C_{GD2}\text{'s } i_C \text{ exceeds } i_{gm} \rightarrow \left.i_C=\frac{v_{gs2}-v_{ds2}}{sC_{GD2}}=\frac{v_{gs2}}{sC_{GD2}}\right|_{z_{D2}=\frac{g_{m2}}{2\pi C_{GD2}}\geq 10f_{0dB(MAX)}} \equiv i_{gm}=v_{gs2}g_{m2}$$

6.3. Self-Referenced

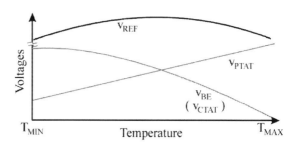

6.3. Temperature Dependence

Diode or Base–Emitter Voltage Primitive

$$v_D \approx v_{BE} \approx 0.6\text{--}0.7 \text{ V} \pm 2\% \text{ at } T_{ROOM} \text{ and falls } -2.2 \text{ mV/°C.}$$

Gate–Source Voltage Primitive

$$\Delta v_T \approx \pm 100\text{--}150 \text{ mV}, \Delta K' \approx \pm 20\%, \text{ and both fall with temperature.}$$

$$\therefore \Delta v_{GS} \approx \pm 5\% \text{ to } 10\% \text{ at } T_{ROOM} \rightarrow \text{ Less accurate than diode.}$$

Proportional-to-absolute temperature (PTAT) Voltage

Rises with temperature → $v_{PTAT} \propto T$.

$$V_t = \frac{KT}{q}$$

Usually, derived from Thermal voltage V_t.

The difference of two matched, but ratioed diode voltages or

gate–source voltages in subthreshold produces v_{PTAT}.

$$\Delta v_D = v_{D1} - v_{D2} \approx V_t \ln\left(\frac{i_{D1}I_{S2}}{I_{S1}i_{D2}}\right) = V_t \ln\left(\frac{i_{D1}A_{D2}}{A_{D1}i_{D2}}\right) = v_{PTAT}$$

Complementary-to-absolute temperature (CTAT) Voltage

Falls with temperature → v_D, v_{BE}, v_T, and K'.

6.3. Zero-Order Independence

Temperature dependence can be decomposed and described by a polynomial:

$$p_X = \sum_{A=0}^{N} K_A T^A = K_0 + K_1 T^1 + K_2 T^2 + \ldots + K_N T^N$$

Zero-Order Temperature Independence

No independence → Regulate a voltage primitive.

Define v_{BE} or v_{GS} with Q_E or M_E.

Voltage-divide *up* to target v_O.

Close feedback loop with

a source follower.

→ Fast response.

→ High dropout.

Internal Compensation:

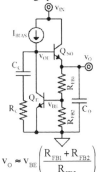 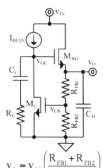

$$v_O \approx v_{BE}\left(\frac{R_{FB1} + R_{FB2}}{R_{FB2}}\right) \qquad v_O \approx v_{GS}\left(\frac{R_{FB1} + R_{FB2}}{R_{FB2}}\right)$$

C_C lowers p_{OE} and R_C's z_C offsets C_O's p_O.

6.3. Temperature Compensation

First-Order Temperature Independence

Balanced v_{GS}: Cancel falling v_T with rising $V_{DS(SAT)}$.

$$v_{GS} = v_T + V_{DS(SAT)} = v_T + \sqrt{\frac{2i_D}{K'\left(\dfrac{W}{L}\right)}}$$

→ Tolerance (of v_T and K') is high.

Bandgap Approach:

Cancel falling v_{BE} with rising V_t.

PTAT core generates i_{PTAT}.

PTAT Core

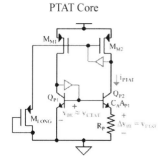

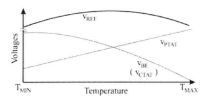

Mirror M_{M1}–M_{M2}: $i_{C1} \approx i_{C2}$.

Δv_{BE} Cell: $v_R \approx v_{BE1} - v_{BE2}$.

Starter M_{LONG}: Ensures $i_{PTAT} \neq 0$.

6.3. Temperature Compensation

First-Order Temperature Independence

Bandgap Conversion: Add v_{PTAT} to regulated v_{BE}.

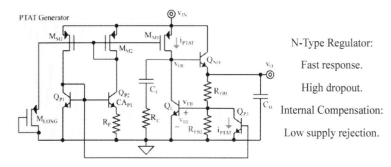

N-Type Regulator:

Fast response.

High dropout.

Internal Compensation:

Low supply rejection.

$$v_O = v_{BE} + \left(\frac{v_{BE}}{R_{FB2}} + i_{PTAT}\right)R_{FB1} = v_{BE} + \left(\frac{v_{BE}}{R_{FB2}} + \frac{\Delta v_{BE}}{R_P}\right)R_{FB1} = v_{BE}\left(1 + \frac{R_{FB1}}{R_{FB2}}\right) + \Delta v_{BE}\left(\frac{R_{FB1}}{R_P}\right)$$

6.3. Temperature Compensation

First-Order Temperature Independence

Bandgap Integration: Embed PTAT core into regulated v_{BE}.

→ PTAT core (Q_{P1}) introduces positive-feedback path.

∴ Core's R_p to degenerate positive-feedback gain A_{LG+}.

∴ Use C_{FF} to filter positive-feedback gain A_{LG+}.

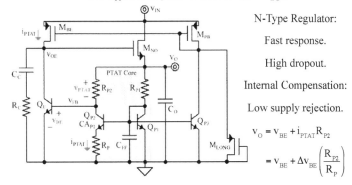

N-Type Regulator:

Fast response.

High dropout.

Internal Compensation:

Low supply rejection.

$$v_O = v_{BE} + i_{PTAT} R_{P2}$$

$$= v_{BE} + \Delta v_{BE} \left(\frac{R_{P2}}{R_P} \right)$$

6.3. Temperature Compensation

First-Order Temperature Independence

Bandgap Integration: Replace N-type follower with P-type transconductor.

Miller C_C splits p_{OE} (to low frequency) and p_O (to high frequency).

R_C impedes C_C's feed-forward path and its zero cancels p_O.

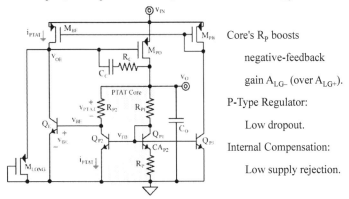

Core's R_p boosts

negative-feedback

gain A_{LG-} (over A_{LG+}).

P-Type Regulator:

Low dropout.

Internal Compensation:

Low supply rejection.

6.3. Temperature Compensation

First-Order Temperature Independence

Bandgap Integration:

Embed PTAT core into

differential pair.

Miller C_C splits p_{OE} and p_O.

R_C's zero cancels p_O.

R_P boosts A_{LG-} over A_{LG+}.

R_{B2}– C_{FF} filters A_{LG+}.

R_{B1} balances R_{B2}'s

base-voltage drop.

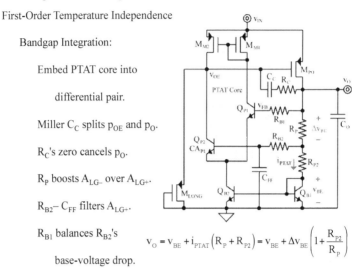

$$v_O = v_{BE} + i_{PTAT}\left(R_P + R_{P2}\right) = v_{BE} + \Delta v_{BE}\left(1 + \frac{R_{P2}}{R_P}\right)$$

6.4. Noise Suppressors

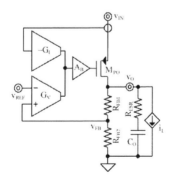

6.4. Shunt Supply Noise

Supply Filter:	Low-Dropout (LDO) Filter:
C_F shunts high-frequency noise.	Only shunts low-frequency noise.
R_F raises dropout voltage.	Raises dropout voltage.
$\rightarrow P_{LOSS} = i_{IN}{}^2 R_F.$	$\rightarrow P_{LOSS} = i_{IN}(v_{IN} - v_{IN}') \geq i_{IN} V_{DO}$

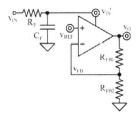
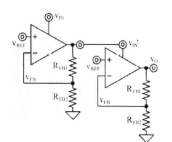

6.4. Impede Supply Noise

Charge-Pumped Cascode:

Cascode M_C raises the impedance to the supply v_{IN}.

$\rightarrow$ Keep M_C in saturation to ensure r_{dsC} is high.

Switched-capacitor charge pump biases M_C's gate above v_{IN}.

$\rightarrow$ Reduces dropout between v_{IN} an v_{IN}'.

$\rightarrow$ Injects high-frequency (10 MHz) noise.

$\rightarrow$ C_F shunts switching noise (past 3 kHz).

$\therefore$ r_{dsC} suppresses all-frequency supply noise

(by maybe 25–30 dB).

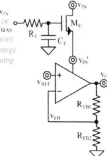

M_C leaks some switching noise into v_{IN}'.

M_C raises dropout voltage: $P_{LOSS} = i_{IN}(v_{IN} - v_{IN}') \geq i_{IN} V_{DSC(SAT)}.$

6.4. Impede Supply Noise

Series Feedback:

Shunt feedback to v_O shunts supply noise up to f_{0dB}.

Series feedback raises M_{PO}'s resistance, and with high bandwidth,

can impede high-frequency supply noise.

How: Sample i_O and feed sampled i_O across loop.

$A_{LG(SHUNT)} \gg A_{LG(SERIES)}$ below f_{0dB}.

∴ $v_O \approx v_{REF}$ → Degenerate G_I.

$A_{LG(SERIES)} \gg A_{LG(SHUNT)}$ above f_{0dB}:

∴ Impede v_{in} → Bypass G_I's degeneration with C_{FF}.

∴ Rejects high-frequency noise near f_{0dB} (by another 20 dB).

G_I's bandwidth limits high-frequency rejection.

G_I consumes quiescent power.

Dropout voltage is unaffected.

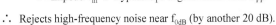

6.5. Other Enhancements

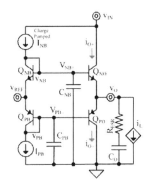

6.5. Power-Transistor Enhancements

Challenge: $v_{IN(MIN)}$ and $|v_{TP}|$ limit M_{PO}'s gate drive $\rightarrow$ Limit $i_{O(MAX)}$ and V_{DO}.

Bulk Boost: Forward-biasing the bulk–source junction lowers $|v_{TP}|$.

Caution:

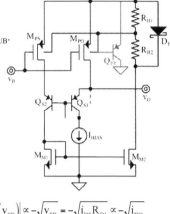

    Forward-biasing the bulk activates

        parasitic PNP BJT $\rightarrow$ Injects i_{SUB}.

    $\therefore$ Forward-bias only

        when needed $\rightarrow$ With i_O.

    $\therefore$ Limit forward-biasing

        voltage to a fraction of v_D.

M_{PS}, $Q_{S2,1}$, and $M_{M1,2}$ sense i_O fraction.

$R_{B1,2}$ and D_B raise v_{SB}

    (lower $|v_{TP}|$) with i_O.

$\therefore$ M_{PO}'s gate drive $\rightarrow$ $v_{SGT} = v_{SG} - \left|v_{TP}\left(v_{SB}\right)\right| \propto -\sqrt{v_{SB}} = -\sqrt{i_{DS}R_{B1}} \propto -\sqrt{i_{DO}}$

6.5. Power-Transistor Enhancements

Challenge: M_{PO}'s large gate slows loop response $\rightarrow$ Limits load-dump response.

Linear Slave: Drive a smaller M_{PO} that induces a slave transistor to conduct.

    $\therefore$ Gate capacitance of slave PMOS M_{PX} is outside of v_O loop.

Caution:

    Slave loop must be stable.

    Slave loop should be as fast as v_O loop.

    Sense resistor R_S raises dropout voltage.

        $\therefore$ R_S should be low.

$Q_{P1,2}$ is a base-coupled differential pair that

    amplifies the difference of emitter voltages $v_{SO} - v_{SW}$.

    $\therefore$ $v_{SO} \approx v_{SX}$ $\rightarrow$ $i_{DX} = \dfrac{v_{RX}}{R_X} = \dfrac{v_{RS}}{R_X} = \dfrac{i_{DO}R_S}{R_X} = A_1 i_{DO}$

6.5. Power-Transistor Enhancements

Nonlinear Slave: Drive a smaller M_{PO} and

Steer unregulated current i_{DX} when v_O drops below threshold V_{THR}.

v_O loop adjusts i_{DO} about imposed dc offset i_{DX} to supply i_L.

Caution:

CP$_{AUX}$'s threshold V_{THR}

should be well below

v_{REF} to avoid interfering

with v_O loop.

Slave loop should be fast

to keep it from extending

load-dump response.

6.5. Buffer Enhancements

Challenge: Buffer slews → Limits load-dump response.

Bulk Feedback: Use parasitic BJT to assist buffer.

Caution: BJT conducts substrate current i_{SUB} → Generates Noise.

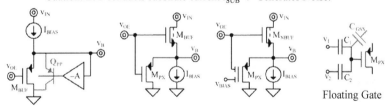

Floating Gate

Speed-Up Transistor: Assist buffer when heavily slewed.

Limit: Helps only when slew voltage $v_{GS.BUF} = v_{OE} - v_B < -|v_{TP.PX}|$.

Reduce $|v_{TP}|$ by coupling a voltage that partially inverts the channel:

$$v_{GX} = \frac{v_1 Z_{C2}}{Z_{C1} + Z_{C2}} + \frac{v_2 Z_{C1}}{Z_{C1} + Z_{C2}} = v_1 \left(\frac{C_1}{C_1 + C_2} \right) + v_2 \left(\frac{C_2}{C_1 + C_2} \right) \rightarrow \text{Limited improvement.}$$

6.5. Loop-Gain Enhancement

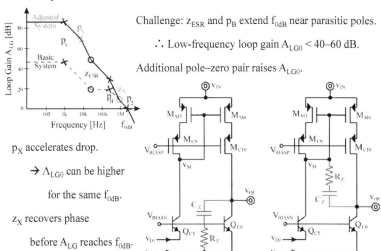

Challenge: z_{ESR} and p_B extend f_{0dB} near parasitic poles.

$\therefore$ Low-frequency loop gain $A_{LG0} < 40\text{--}60$ dB.

Additional pole–zero pair raises A_{LG0}.

p_X accelerates drop.

$\rightarrow A_{LG0}$ can be higher

for the same f_{0dB}.

z_X recovers phase

before A_{LG} reaches f_{0dB}.

How: C_Z shunts $R_{OE} + R_Z + 1/g_m$ for p_X and $R_Z + 1/g_m$ current-limit C_Z for z_X.

6.5. Load-Regulation Enhancement

Challenge: Loop gain is normally low $\rightarrow$ Load-regulation drop can be significant.

Shift v_{REF}: Raise v_{REF} when i_O rises.

How: M_{PS} and $Q_{P1,2}$ sense i_O.

i_S, i_Q, and R_{OS} raise v_{REF}.

$$v_O = v_{REF} - i_O R_{O.CL} + v_{OS}$$

$$= v_{REF} - i_O R_{O.CL} + \left(i_Q + i_s\right) R_{OS}$$

Notes: i_Q is undesired offset.

$\therefore$ Keep i_Q low.

Cancel variation when $i_s R_{OS} = i_O R_{O.CL}$.

$\therefore$ Trim R_{OS} to cancel error or center to reduce error.

v_{REF} is dedicated (no longer accurate for other circuits).

$\rightarrow$ Trim v_O (instead of v_{REF}) for lowest offset and temperature drift.

v_{OS} is in mV's, so its effects on small-signal response are negligible.

6.5. Load-Dump Enhancement

Challenge: Low quiescent current → Slow response.

Base/Gate-Coupled Pairs: Follower's local feedback is fast.

How:

    With dc bases/gates, Q_{NO} and Q_{PO}

        respond almost immediately.

    Fix V_{NB+} and V_{PB-} with C_{NB} and C_{PB}.

    Charge-pump Q_{NB} to raise V_{NB+} above v_{IN}.

    → For low dropout voltage V_{DO}.

Notes:

    v_{REF} should be able to sink and supply some current.

    v_{REF} should suppress coupled (kickback) noise → Be low impedance.

    Loop gain is low → Can add slow feedback loop to improve accuracy.

6.6. Circuit Protection

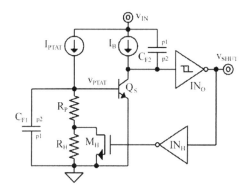

6.6. Generalities

Objective: Protect power transistor against extreme operating conditions.

∴ Keep in safe operating area (SOA).

Below power limit across temperature.

→ $P_{SW} = v_{SW}i_{SW} = (v_{IN} - v_O)i_O \leq P_{SOA(MAX)}$

Below breakdown voltages $V_{DSS(BD)}$ and $V_{GSS(BD)}$.

Away from secondary breakdown, which hot spots or large

thermal gradients cause from uneven distribution of current.

Types: Over Current (overload or short Circuit)   Thermal Shutdown

Electrostatic Discharge (ESD)   Reverse Battery

Note: Protection should be *transparent* (i.e., $i_Q \approx 0$ and $v_{SERIES} \approx 0$),

alert (i.e., always ready to engage), and *deglitched* (desensitized to noise).

6.6. Overcurrent Protection: Fixed Limit

With low i_Q, trip point I_{OCP} is inaccurate.

∴ Include margin → $I_{OCP(MIN)} > i_{O(MAX)}$.

$P_{O(MAX)} = v_O i_{O(MAX)} \approx V_{O(TAR)}I_{OCP(MIN)}$

A short-circuit load pulls v_O to 0 V.

∴ $v_{SW(MAX)} = v_{IN}$ and $i_{O(MAX)} = i_{SC(MAX)}$.

$P_{SW(MAX)} = (v_{IN} - 0)i_{SW(MAX)} \approx v_{IN}I_{OCP(MAX)}$

$\dfrac{P_{O(MAX)}}{P_{SW(MAX)}} = \left(\dfrac{V_{O(TAR)}}{v_{IN}}\right)\left(\dfrac{I_{OCP(MIN)}}{I_{OCP(MAX)}}\right) < \dfrac{V_{O(TAR)}}{v_{IN}}$

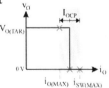

How: M_{PS} senses i_O and compares i_S with I_{OCP}/A_I.

Feedback loop regulates (limits) i_O to I_{OCP}.

C_C establishes dominant low-frequency pole.

6.6. Overcurrent Protection: Fold-Back Limit

Limitation with Fixed Limit: $i_{O(MAX)} = i_{SC(MAX)} \rightarrow P_{O(MAX)} \ll P_{SC(MAX)}$.

Fold-Back Limit: Lower i_{OCP} with v_O to $I_{OCP(MAX)}'$ so $i_{O(MAX)} > i_{SC(MAX)}$.

Objective: $P_{O(MAX)} \equiv P_{SW(MAX)}$ $\because$

$$P_{SW(MAX)} = v_{IN} i_{SC(MAX)} = v_{IN} I_{OCP(MAX)}' \equiv \left(v_{IN} - V_{O(TAR)}\right) I_{OCP(MAX)}$$

$$\frac{I_{OCP(MAX)}}{i_{SC(MAX)}} = \frac{I_{OCP(MAX)}}{I_{OCP(MAX)}'} = \frac{v_{IN}}{v_{IN} - V_{O(TAR)}} > 1$$

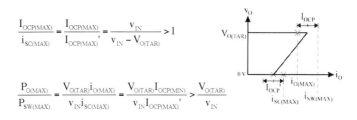

$$\frac{P_{O(MAX)}}{P_{SW(MAX)}} = \frac{V_{O(TAR)} i_{O(MAX)}}{v_{IN} i_{SC(MAX)}} = \frac{V_{O(TAR)} I_{OCP(MIN)}}{v_{IN} I_{OCP(MAX)}'} > \frac{V_{O(TAR)}}{v_{IN}}$$

6.6. Overcurrent Protection: Fold-Back Limit

How:

M_{PS} senses i_O.

R_S translates i_{PS} to v_R.

$\rightarrow v_R$ and v_N rise with i_O.

$R_{T1,2}$ *drops more* than $R_{B3,4}$.

$\therefore$ The amplifier A_{OCP} activates and

regulates v_R when v_N reaches v_P.

$\rightarrow$ Regulates i_O.

$\therefore v_R$ rises as v_O falls.

$\rightarrow$ Lower values of i_O balance A_{OCP}.

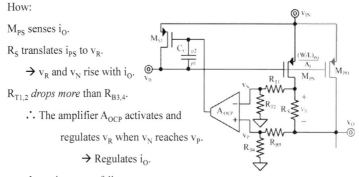

$$v_N = \left(v_O + i_{PS} R_S\right) A_T = \left[v_O + \left(\frac{i_O}{A_I}\right) R_S\right] A_T \approx v_P = v_O A_B \quad \therefore \quad i_O \approx v_O A_I \left(\frac{A_B - A_T}{R_S A_T}\right)$$

C_C establishes dominant low-frequency pole.

6.6. Thermal Shutdown

Since chip dissipates power, junction temperature T_J > ambient temperature T_A.

$$T_{J(MAX)} = T_A + P_{REG(MAX)}\theta_P \approx T_A + P_{SW(MAX)}\theta_P = T_A + v_{IN}I_{OCP(MAX)}\theta_P$$

Protection: Keep T_J below the melting point T_P of the package.

E.g.: Plastic packages melt at roughly 170° C.

Culprit: Power transistor S_O ∴ Sense near S_O.

Temperature changes slowly.

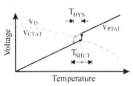

∴ Use hysteresis to avoid noise-triggered oscillations.

How: Sense T_J with $(Q_S's)$ v_{BE} near S_O.

Trip when v_{BE} exceeds $I_{PTAT}R_P$ (at T_{SHUT}).

Overdrive with $V_{HYS} = I_{PTAT}R_H$.

Use $C_{F1,2}$ to deglitch response.

Use v_{SHUT} to shut system.

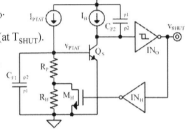

6.6. Reverse-Battery Protection

Protection: Block or shunt *sustained* reverse-battery current.

Transparency: No quiescent current i_Q because i_Q loads battery.

No series voltage v_{SERIES} because v_{SERIES} consumes power.

No reverse battery i_R because i_R drains battery.

Types: Shunt steers i_R away from IC back to V_{BAT} ∴ i_R drains V_{BAT}.

Series blocks i_R and conducts i_{IN} ∴ i_{IN} drops $v_{SERIES} \neq 0$ V.

Physical tracks/guides orient V_{BAT} properly ∴ i_Q, v_{SERIES}, $i_R = 0$.

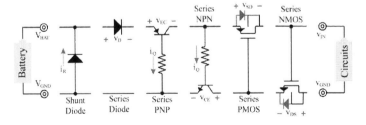

6.6. Electrostatic-Discharge Protection

Protection: Shunt electrostatic discharges (ESD).

Event: Discharge 100–300-pF pre-charged to 200–5000-V.

$\therefore$ *Temporary* high-voltage and high-current conditions.

Types:

Human Touch (e.g., after walking across a carpet).

→ Human-Body Model (HBM): E.g. 2-kV 100 pF through 1.5 kΩ.

Machine Touch (e.g., during bundling and shipping process).

→ Machine Model (MM): E.g. 200-V 200 pF.

Charged IC Discharges (e.g., after chip slides through plastic tube holder).

→ Charged-Device Model (CDM): E.g. 500-V C_{CHIP}.

6.6. Electrostatic-Discharge Protection

Ideal Objective: Shunt positive- and negative-strike currents to ground.

Stacked Diode Clamp

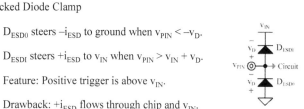

D_{ESD0} steers $-i_{ESD}$ to ground when $v_{PIN} < -v_D$.

D_{ESDI} steers $+i_{ESD}$ to v_{IN} when $v_{PIN} > v_{IN} + v_D$.

Feature: Positive trigger is above v_{IN}.

Drawback: $+i_{ESD}$ flows through chip and v_{IN}.

Dual-Mode Diode Clamp

D_{BE} and Q_{ESD} steer $-i_{ESD}$ to ground when $v_{PIN} < -v_D$.

D_{BE} steers $+i_{ESD}$ to ground when $v_{PIN} > V_{BE(BD)}$.

Feature: ESD currents flow to ground.

Drawback: Zener breakdown voltage $V_{BE(BD)}$ is usually 6.8 V.

6.6. Electrostatic-Discharge Protection

Capacitor-Coupled BJT Clamp

C_{TRIG} triggers Q_{ESD} when $dv_{PIN}/dt \gg \tau_{RC}$.

→ Q_{ESD} steers $+i_{ESD}$ to ground.

Feature: $+i_{ESD}$ flows to ground.

Drawback: Depends on dv_{PIN}/dt.

Latching BJT Clamp (silicon-controlled rectifier)

ESD events first trickle currents into bases.

Q_P and Q_N then feed each other until

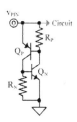

circuit clamps and steers $+i_{ESD}$ to ground.

Feature: $+i_{ESD}$ flows to ground.

Drawback: Depends on v_{IN} range and dv_{PIN}/dt.

6.6. Electrostatic-Discharge Protection

Polysilicon Gates are especially sensitive

to charged-device strikes.

∴ Limit strike current with a series resistor.

∴ Shunt current near exposed gate with a local clamp.

Notes:

Parasitic devices in large power devices also steer ESD currents.

→ Self protecting if guard-ringed to carry ESD currents.

ESD devices carry substantial currents.

∴ Should be large, well-routed, and next to corresponding pad.

Conduction properties of ESD devices depend on layout.

→ Difficult to model and predict.

→ Must characterize each layout.

6.7. Characterization

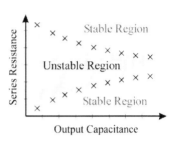

Output Capacitance

6.7. Measurements

Soak Time

Allow sufficient time for measurement value to settle because

→ Parasitic capacitances and resistances slow measurement.

→ Thermal response is slow.

Soak time extends test time in production, so avoid excessive soak time.

Soak time may be short if the rising response to steady-state variations

in temperature, i_{LOAD}, and v_{IN} is different from the falling response.

Reliability

Test devices from different parts of the wafer, different wafers,

and different fabrication lots.

Input Supply

A low-cost, high-ESR capacitor shunts considerable low-frequency noise.

A low-ESR ceramic capacitor shunts high-frequency noise.

6.7. Emulating the Load

Variable Resistor

Value: $R_L \equiv v_O/i_L$ → 10 Ω for 200 mA and 2 V.

→ 40 Ω for 50 mA and 2 V.

→ 2 kΩ for 1 mA and 2 V.

Feature: Simple to implement in simulations and measurements.

Drawback: Does not match all possible loads.

→ E.g.: R_L for 3-V, 100-μA amplifier is not necessarily 30 kΩ.

→ Problem because R_I affects the feedback dynamics of the system.

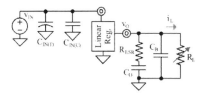

6.7. Emulating the Load

Variable Current Source

Feature: Resistance is high → R_L does not affect feedback dynamics.

∴ Emulates high worst-case extreme of R_L.

Drawbacks: Does not emulate low worst-case extreme of R_L.

Requires off-chip components, board space,

and programming voltage source.

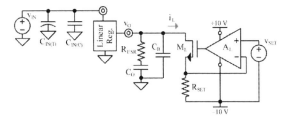

∴ Use variable resistor for low worst-case extreme of R_L.

Use variable resistor and variable current source for high worst-case extreme of R_L.

6.7. Regulation and Drift

Load Regulation

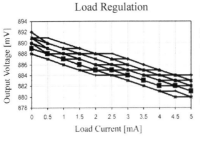

Temperature Drift

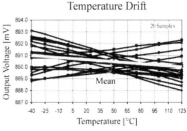

Line Regulation

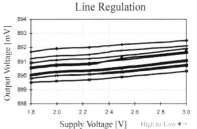

To avoid startup dynamics

from affecting line-regulation

measurements, start at $v_{IN(MAX)}$

and ramp input supply v_{IN} down.

6.7. Load-Dump Response

Delay sets load-dump response.

∴ The rise and fall times t_R and t_F
of the load dump affect the response.

→ Excessively short t_R and t_F
are unrealistically pessimistic.

→ Excessively long t_R and t_F
are unrealistically optimistic.

Load-Dump Response

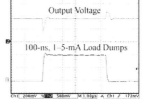

Although not as accurate, pulsing a resistor is often easier than pulsing a current source.

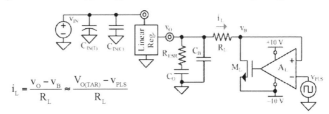

$$i_L = \frac{V_O - V_B}{R_L} \approx \frac{V_{O(TAR)} - V_{PLS}}{R_L}$$

6.7. Power-Supply Rejection

Power-Supply Rejection

Power-Supply Rejection

→ Opposite and reciprocal
  of supply gain.

→ Measure of power-supply
  ripple rejection.

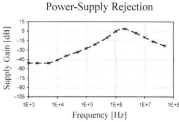

Power-Supply Rejection

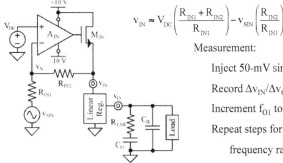

$$v_{IN} \approx V_{DC}\left(\frac{R_{IN1}+R_{IN2}}{R_{IN1}}\right) - v_{SIN}\left(\frac{R_{IN2}}{R_{IN1}}\right)$$

Measurement:

Inject 50-mV sine into v_{IN} at f_{O1}.

Record $\Delta v_{IN}/\Delta v_O$ at f_{O1}.

Increment f_{O1} to f_{O2}.

Repeat steps for desired
frequency range.

6.7. Power Performance and Headroom

Power-Conversion Efficiency

Fraction of input power that reaches v_O → $\eta_C = \dfrac{P_O}{P_{IN}} = \dfrac{i_L v_O}{i_{IN} v_{IN}} = \eta_I\left(\dfrac{v_O}{v_{IN}}\right)$

Application often sets v_{IN} and v_O.

∴ Current efficiency sets η_C → $\eta_I \equiv \dfrac{i_L}{i_{IN}} = \dfrac{i_L}{i_{GND}+i_L} = \dfrac{i_L}{i_Q+i_L}$

→ Highest η_I and η_C when quiescent current is a small fraction of i_L: at $i_{L(MAX)}$.

→ Lowest η_I and η_C when i_{GND} is a small fraction of i_L: at $i_{L(MIN)}$.

Dropout Voltage

Set $v_{IN} \equiv$ Targeted v_O.

$V_{DO} = v_{IN} - v_O$ at $i_{L(MAX)}$.

Headroom

Set v_O above expected $v_{IN(MIN)}$.

$v_{IN(MIN)}$ is roughly v_{IN} when

$v_{IN} - v_O = 1.5 V_{DO}$.

Note: v_O deviates from target near dropout region because loop gain is low.

6.7. Startup

Startup: Ability to reach and settle to targeted v_O without oscillations.

Test: Ramp input supply v_{IN} from 0 V in 1 s, 1 ms, 100 μs, 10 μs,

1 μs, 100 ns, and 10 ns.

Enabled Start

Digital signal enables regulator.

Startup Time

Time required to reach and settle

within 5% of target.

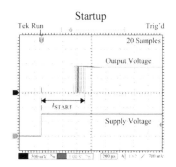

6.7. Stability

Stability: Ability to recover from noise and sudden electrical excursions.

Setup: Noise is wide spectrum, so use 10–100-μs pulses

with 1–10-ns rise and fall times.

Bank of connectible filter resistors and low-ESR ceramic capacitors.

Test: Select R_{ESR} and C_O.

Pulse i_L or v_{IN} across wide range.

If more than 4 rings, record R_{ESR} and C_O.

Increment R_{ESR} or C_O and repeat.

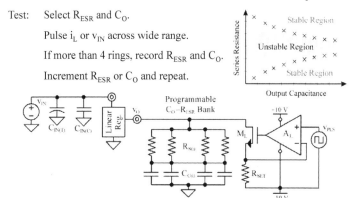

6.7. Sample Specification Report

Parameter	Test Conditions	Measured
Trimmed v_O	At i_{LOAD} = 100 mA	0.997–1.003 V
Δv_O across Load	0–200 mA at v_{IN} = 2 V	14–18 mV
Δv_O across Line	1.5–4.2 V at i_{LOAD} = 10 mA	2–8 mV
Trimmed Drift	–40° to 125° C (Box Method)	14 ± 21 ppm/°C
Load-Dump Response	100-ns 1–100 mA at v_{IN} = 2 V	30–50 mV
Power-Supply Rejection	Δv_{IN} = 50 mV at 2 V and 10 kHz	> 40 dB
	Δv_{IN} = 50 mV at 2 V and 100 kHz	> 25 dB
	Δv_{IN} = 50 mV at 2 V and 1 MHz	> 5 dB
Quiescent Current	At i_{LOAD} = 1 mA	7–13 μA
	At i_{LOAD} = 200 mA	115–145 μA
Dropout Voltage	At i_{LOAD} = 200 mA	< 150 mV
Headroom $v_{IN(MIN)}$	At i_{LOAD} = 200 mA	1.24–1.26 V
t_{START}	When R_{LOAD} = 1 kΩ	350–650 μs
Output Capacitor	R_{ESR}	> 50 mΩ
	C_O	> 0.5 μF

Chapter 7. Switched-Inductor Supplies

7.1. Power Stages

7.2. Output Ripple

7.3. Power Losses

7.4. Frequency Response

7.5. Feedback Control

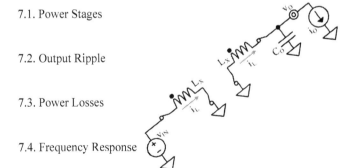

7.1. Switched Inductor: Continuous-Conduction Mode

Objective: Inductor transfers energy from v_{IN} to v_O.

Characterizing Feature: Inductor conducts continuously.

Inductor: $v_L = L_X \left(\dfrac{di_L}{dt} \right)$ → $\dfrac{di_L}{dt} = \dfrac{v_L}{L_X}$ And $E_L = 0.5 L_X i_L^{\ 2}$

$\therefore i_L$ rises with a positive voltage and falls with a negative voltage.

Operation: Energize L_X from v_{IN} → i_L rises.

Drain L_X into v_O → i_L falls in alternating phases.

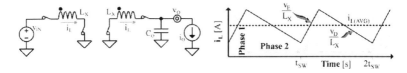

Duty Cycle $d_E \equiv$ Fraction of time energizing switches are on → t_E/t_{SW}.

$1 - d_E =$ Fraction of time energizing switches are off → t_D/t_{SW}.

7.1. Switched Inductor: Discontinuous-Conduction Mode

Characterizing Feature: Inductor conducts discontinuously.

Operation: Energize L_X from v_{IN} → i_L rises to $i_{L(PK)}$.

Deplete L_X into v_O → i_L falls to zero.

Open- or short-circuit L_X until next t_{SW}.

→ v_L and i_L remain zero.

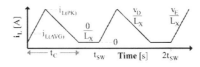

$\therefore L_X$ delivers discrete energy packets to v_O.

Duty Cycle $d_E \equiv$ Fraction of conduction time energizing switches are on → t_E/t_C.

$1 - d_E =$ Fraction of conduction time energizing switches are off → t_D/t_C.

7.1. Buck or Step-Down DC–DC Converter

Insightful (intuitive) Analysis: Inductor L_O is a low-frequency short.

$\therefore v_{SW(AVG)} \equiv v_{O(AVG)} \equiv V_O$ and $i_{L(AVG)} \equiv i_{O(AVG)} \equiv I_O$.

$V_O = v_{SW(AVG)} = V_{IN}\left(\dfrac{t_E}{t_{SW}}\right) = V_{IN}d_E \;\therefore\; V_O$ is a fraction of V_{IN}.

Operation: S_I energizes L_O from v_{IN}, so $v_L = v_{IN} - v_O > 0 \rightarrow i_L$ rises.

Open S_I, so i_L lowers v_{SW} until D_G forward-biases.

D_G drains L_O into v_O, so $v_L \approx -v_O < 0 \rightarrow i_L$ falls.

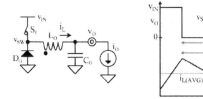

S_I conducts a d_E fraction of $i_{L(AVG)} \;\therefore\; i_{IN} < i_{L(AVG)} = i_O$.

7.1. Buck or Step-Down DC–DC Converter

Example: Determine d_E and Δi_L for a buck dc–dc converter when

$v_{IN} = 4.0$ V, $v_O = 1.8$ V, $L_O = 22\ \mu H$, and $t_{SW} = 1\ \mu s$.

Solution:

$$v_{O(AVG)} = v_{IN(AVG)}d_E \;\rightarrow\; d_E = \frac{v_{O(AVG)}}{v_{IN(AVG)}} = \frac{1.8}{4} = 45\%$$

$$d_E = \frac{t_E}{t_{SW}} \;\rightarrow\; t_E = d_E t_{SW} = 450\ ns$$

$$v_L = L_O\left(\frac{di_L}{dt}\right)$$

$$\therefore \quad \Delta i_L = \left(\frac{v_E}{L_O}\right)t_E = \left(\frac{v_{IN} - v_O}{L_O}\right)t_E = \left(\frac{4 - 1.8}{22\mu}\right)450n = 45\ mA$$

7.1. Boost or Step-Up DC–DC Converter

Insightful Analysis: Inductor L_O is a low-frequency short.

$$\therefore \quad v_{SW(AVG)} = v_{IN} = v_{SW(PEAK)}\left(\frac{t_O}{t_{SW}}\right)$$

D_O–C_O is a positive peak detector. $\quad \therefore \quad v_O \approx v_{SW}$'s positive peak.

$$v_{SW(AVG)} = v_{IN} = v_O d_{DO} = v_O(1 - d_E).$$

$$v_{IN} \text{ is a fraction of } v_O.$$

Operation: S_G energizes L_O from v_{IN}, so $v_L = v_{IN} > 0 \rightarrow i_L$ rises.

Open S_G, so i_L raises v_{SW} until D_O forward-biases.

D_O drains L_O into v_O, so $v_L \approx v_{IN} - v_O < 0 \rightarrow i_L$ falls.

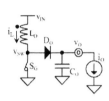 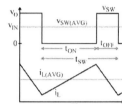

Since D_O duty-cycles i_L:

$$i_O \approx d_O i_{L(AVG)}$$

$$< i_{L(AVG)} = i_{IN}.$$

i_O discharges C_O across t_E.

$\therefore v_O$ ripple can be high.

7.1. Inverting Buck–Boost DC–DC Converter

Insightful Analysis: Inductor L_O is a low-frequency short.

$$\therefore \quad v_{SW(AVG)} = v_{IN}\left(\frac{t_E}{t_{SW}}\right) + v_{SW(PEAK)}\left(\frac{t_O}{t_{SW}}\right) = 0$$

D_O–C_O is a negative peak detector.

$\therefore v_O \approx v_{SW}$'s negative peak.

$$v_{SW(AVG)} = 0 = v_{IN}d_E + v_O(1 - d_E).$$

Or $\quad v_O = -\dfrac{v_{IN}d_E}{\left(1 - d_E\right)}$

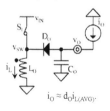

$$i_O \approx d_O i_{L(AVG)}.$$

Operation: S_I energizes L_O from v_{IN}, so $v_L = v_{IN} > 0 \rightarrow i_L$ rises.

Open S_I, so i_L lowers v_{SW} until D_O forward-biases.

D_O drains L_O into v_O, so $v_L \approx -v_O < 0 \rightarrow i_L$ falls.

If $d_E < 0.5 \rightarrow |v_O| < v_{IN}$. ⎤
⎥ Inverting buck or boost.
If $d_E > 0.5 \rightarrow |v_O| > v_{IN}$. ⎦

7.1. Non-Inverting Buck–Boost DC–DC Converter

Insightful Analysis: Inductor L_O is a low-frequency short.

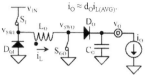

$\therefore v_{SWI(AVG)} = v_{SWO(AVG)}.$

D_O–C_O is a positive peak detector.

$\therefore v_O \approx v_{SWO}$'s positive peak.

$$v_{SWI(AVG)} = v_{IN}\left(\frac{t_E}{t_{SW}}\right) = v_{IN}d_E \equiv v_{SWO(AVG)} = v_O\left(\frac{t_O}{t_{SW}}\right) = v_O d_{DO} = v_O\left(1 - d_E\right) \;\rightarrow\; v_O = \frac{v_{IN}d_E}{\left(1 - d_E\right)}$$

Operation: S_I–S_{GO} energizes L_O from v_{IN}, so $v_L = v_{IN} > 0$ $\rightarrow$ i_L rises.

Open S_I–S_{GO}, so i_L lowers v_{SWI} until D_{GI}–D_O forward-biases.

D_{GI}–D_O drains L_O into v_O, so $v_L \approx -v_O < 0$ $\rightarrow$ i_L falls.

If $d_E < 0.5$ $\rightarrow$ $v_O < v_{IN}$.⎤
⎥ Non-inverting buck or boost.
If $d_E > 0.5$ $\rightarrow$ $v_O > v_{IN}$.⎦

Note: S_I–D_{GI}–L_O buck feeds L_O–S_{GO}–D_O boost to perform buck–boost function.

7.1. Power Switches

Diodes are asynchronous because stored i_L forward-biases them automatically

when other switches are off. $\rightarrow$ They drop 0.6–0.9 V in v_D when engaged.

Transistors are synchronous because a synchronizing signal switches them.

$\rightarrow$ Practicable transistors drop 50–300 mV in v_{DS} when engaged.

$\therefore$ Transistors drop and dissipate less ohmic conduction power.

$\rightarrow$ Transistors often replace diodes.

$\rightarrow$ To keep adjacent transistors from momentarily shorting v_{IN} to 0 V,

dead time t_{DT} separates their conduction periods.

$\therefore$ Parasitic diodes conduct asynchronously across t_{DT}.

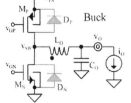

Buck

When $i_L > 0$,

D_N carries i_L

across t_{DT}.

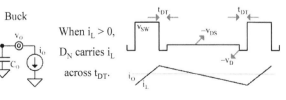

7.1. Asynchronous Switches

Ideally asynchronous switches should drop 0 V, require 0 A, and respond instantly.

→ No ohmic power, no quiescent power, and high bandwidth.

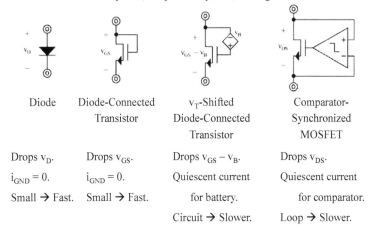

Diode	Diode-Connected Transistor	v_T-Shifted Diode-Connected Transistor	Comparator-Synchronized MOSFET
Drops v_D.	Drops v_{GS}.	Drops $v_{GS} - v_B$.	Drops v_{DS}.
$i_{GND} = 0$.	$i_{GND} = 0$.	Quiescent current	Quiescent current
Small → Fast.	Small → Fast.	for battery.	for comparator.
		Circuit → Slower.	Loop → Slower.

∴ Sacrifice quiescent power P_Q and speed for lower ohmic power P_R.

7.1. Asynchronous Operation

Asynchronous switch blocks negative current ∴.

When $i_{L(AVG)} > 0.5\Delta i_L$: L_O conducts continuously in CCM.

When $i_{L(AVG)} < 0.5\Delta i_L$: L_O conducts discontinuously in DCM.

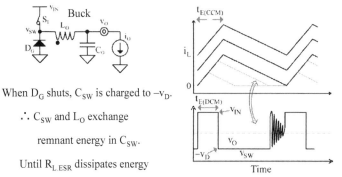

When D_G shuts, C_{SW} is charged to $-v_D$.

∴ C_{SW} and L_O exchange

remnant energy in C_{SW}.

Until $R_{L.ESR}$ dissipates energy

and v_{SW} reaches $v_{SW(AVG)} \approx v_O$ → Generates noise.

7.1. Synchronous Operation

Synchronous switch also conducts negative current $\therefore$

L_O is never in DCM $\rightarrow$ Negative conduction dissipates power.

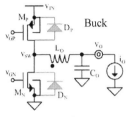

Body diodes conduct across t_{TD}:

M_N's D_N when $i_L > 0$ toward v_O.

M_P's D_P when $i_L < 0$ toward v_{IN}.

Body diodes conduct substrate current i_{SUB}.

$\therefore$ Generate noise.

For lower losses, avoid synchronous operation when loads are light.

7.1. MOS Switches

Non-Blocking MOSFET: Body diode conducts i_L across dead-time period.

$\rightarrow$ Bulk connection directs appropriate body diode.

Examples: Bulk in buck NFET connects to ground.

Bulk in boost PFET connects to v_O.

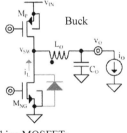

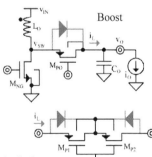

Blocking MOSFET:

Block body diode with an opposing body diode.

$\rightarrow$ With another transistor $\therefore$ Series resistance *or* gate capacitance is higher.

7.2. Output Ripple

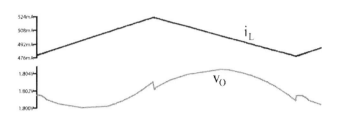

7.2. Continuously Supplied Outputs

When L_O connects to v_O directly, like in a buck: $i_{CO} = i_L - i_{LD} = \Delta i_L$.

L_O's ripple Δi_L flows through C_O and C_O's R_{ESR} and L_{ESL}.

∴ Δi_L into C_O produces a parabola in v_{CO}.

Δi_L into R_{ESR} reproduces i_L's triangular ripple in v_{ESR}.

Constant di_L/dt's into L_{ESL} produce a square in v_{ESL}.

$$\Delta v_O = v_{CO} + v_{ESR} + v_{ESL} = \int \left(\frac{\Delta i_L}{C_O}\right) dt + R_{ESR}\Delta i_L + L_{ESL}\left(\frac{di_L}{dt}\right)$$

$L_O = 22\ \mu H$
$C_O = 1\ \mu F$
$R_{ESR} = 25\ m\Omega$
$L_{ESL} = 5\ nH$

$i_{CO} < 0$

$i_{CO} > 0$

$i_{LD} = 0.5\ A$

v_O

$\Delta v_O \approx 4\ mV$

v_{ESL}

v_{ESR}

v_{CO}

Time

7.2. Continuously Supplied Outputs: Switching Noise

Parabola in v_{CO} mostly produces a quasi-sinusoidal tone at f_{SW}.

Triangle in v_{ESR} and square in v_{ESL} produce harmonic noise.

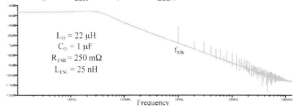

Eliminating R_{ESR} and L_{ESR} eliminates nearly all harmonic noise.

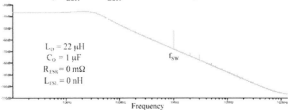

Connecting low-ESR and low-ESL capacitors in parallel also helps.

7.2. Duty-Cycled Outputs

When D_O disconnects v_O from L_O, like in a boosting circuit: $i_{CO} = i_{DO} - i_{LD}$.

Δi_L is usually a tiny fraction of D_O's i_{DO}.

i_{DO} is discontinuous $\rightarrow$ i_{CO} changes abruptly $\therefore$ High output ripple Δv_O.

$i_{DO} - i_{LD}$ and i_{LD} and their di/dt's are nearly constant.

$\therefore$ $i_{DO} - i_{LD}$ charges C_O and i_{LD} discharges C_O $\rightarrow$ Triangular v_{CO}.

$i_{DO} - i_{LD}$ and i_{LD} into R_{ESR} drop constant voltages $\rightarrow$ Pulsing v_{ESR}.

Abrupt i_{CO} into L_{ESL} produces spikes $\rightarrow$ Spiked v_{ESL}.

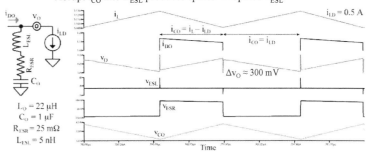

7.2. Duty-Cycled Outputs: Switching Noise

Triangular v_O, spiked v_{ESL}, and pulsing v_{ESR} produce considerable noise.

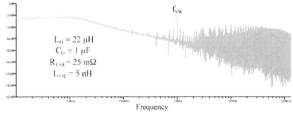

Eliminating R_{ESR} and L_{ESR} reduces, but does not eliminate harmonic noise.

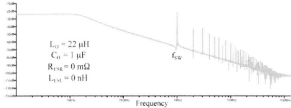

Root cause for high harmonic noise and output ripple Δv_O

is that D_O disconnects the load from its source L_O.

7.2. Load-Dump Response

C_O supplies/absorbs sudden load dumps Δi_{LD} until the system recovers.

$$\Delta v_O = \Delta v_{CO} + \Delta v_{ESL} + \Delta v_{ESR} = \int \left(\frac{\Delta i_{LD}}{C_O}\right) dt + \left(\frac{di_{LD}}{dt}\right) L_{ESL} + \Delta i_{LD} R_{ESR}$$

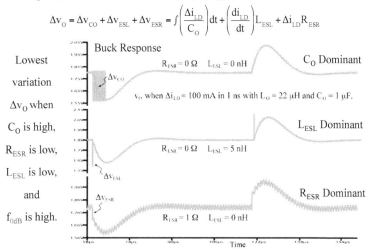

Lowest variation Δv_O when C_O is high, R_{ESR} is low, L_{ESL} is low, and f_{0dB} is high.

Δv_{ESL} and Δv_{ESR} in duty-cycled v_O's is less noticeable because i_{DO} is already abrupt.

7.2. Small-Signal Simulations

Challenge: The steady-state bias of a switched-inductor circuit is a ripple

(not a dc signal), so ac SPICE simulations do not work.

Fix: Break loop at measurable analog feedback point like s_O.

Reproduce rippling bias s_O' with a closed-loop replica of the system.

Feed bias s_O' to the system.

Inject a small sinusoid s_{sin} at f_i, where $s_{sin} \ll S_I$ and $f_i \ll f_{SW}$.

Loop gain A_{LG} at f_i is s_o/s_{sin}.

Repeat at other f_i's to reproduce response across frequency.

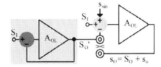

7.2. Small-Signal Simulations: Example – Buck

Break Loop: At v_O.

Bias Loop: Produce rippling steady-state bias V_O' with a replica

of the system and feed bias V_O' to feedback point.

Stimulate: Inject sine v_{sin} at f_i into the reference v_{REF}.

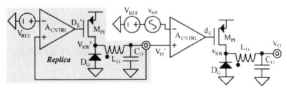

Signal Flow: $v_{sin} \rightarrow d_e \rightarrow i_l \rightarrow v_o$.

Loop Gain: $v_o/v_{sin} \approx \Delta v_{O(PP)}/v_{sin(PP)}$ at f_i with Δv_O-to-v_{sin}'s phase shift.

Note: $v_{sin}A_{LG} \le v_{sin}$ above f_{0dB} ∴ To decipher v_O variations, raise v_{sin}

as f_i rises, but only as long as v_{sin} produces small-signal variations.

7.3. Power Losses

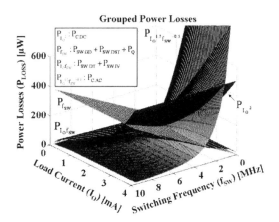

7.3. Power-Conversion Efficiency

Fraction of input power P_{IN} that reaches the output v_O as P_O.

$$\eta_C \equiv \frac{P_O}{P_{IN}} = \frac{P_{IN} - P_{LOSS}}{P_{IN}} = \frac{P_O}{P_O + P_{LOSS}} = \frac{v_O i_O}{v_O i_O + P_{LOSS}}$$

Power losses determine power-conversion efficiency η_C.

→ Switches drop mV's, so loss is very low.

→ Inductors drop mV's on average, so loss is very low.

→ Capacitors conduct nA's on average, so loss is very low.

∴ Losses in P_{LOSS} are very low and η_C is very high at 80% to 95%.

→ Substantially higher than in linear regulators.

Possible because

i_L cannot change instantaneously ∴ v_L does → $v_{SWITCH(AVG)} \approx 0$ V.

v_C cannot change instantaneously ∴ Δv_O is very low → Accurate.

7.3. Loss Mechanisms

In practice, parasitic components dissipate power.

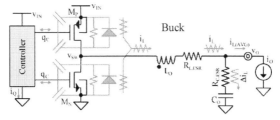

Series Resistances: Ohmic conduction power → $i_{L(RMS)}{}^2 R_{PAR}$.

Switching Gates: Gate drive power required to charge gates → $q_C v_{IN} f_{SW}$.

Quiescent Current: Controller power → $i_Q v_{IN} \propto$ Speed $\propto f_{SW}$.

Other Losses: Transitional i_D–v_{DS} overlap power in switches.

Diode-conduction power during dead time.

Transitional shoot-through power in gate drivers.

7.3. CCM DC Conduction Losses in a Buck

Equivalent Power Circuit

i_L flows through M_P and M_N in alternating cycles.

∴ i_L *always* flows through an equivalent resistance R_{SW}.

$$R_{SW} = R_{MP} D_{MP} + R_{MN} D_{MN} \approx R_{ON}\left(D_{MP} + D_{MN}\right) \approx R_{ON} \approx R_{MP} \approx R_{MN}$$

And although not always equal, R_{MP} and R_{MN} are on the same order.

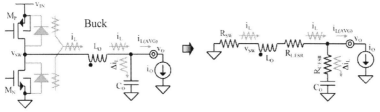

$i_{L(AVG)}$ flows through R_{SW}, L_O, and $R_{L.ESR}$ ∴

$$P_{R(DC)} = i_{L(AVG)}{}^2 \left(R_{SW} + R_{L.ESR}\right) = i_O{}^2 \left(R_{SW} + R_{L.ESR}\right) \equiv i_O{}^2 R_{DC}$$

7.3. CCM AC Conduction Losses

Δi_L flows through R_{SW},

L_O, $R_{L.ESR}$, $R_{C.ESR}$, and C_O $\therefore$

$$P_{R(AC)} \approx \Delta i_{L(RMS)}{}^2 \left(R_{SW} + R_{L.ESR} + R_{C.ESR} \right) \equiv \Delta i_{L(RMS)}{}^2 R_{AC}$$

$R_{C(\Delta)}$ dissipates power when i_L is greater and lower than $i_{L(AVG)}$, so derive $i_{L(RMS)}$:

$$\Delta i_L = \left(\frac{v_E}{L_O} \right) t_E = \frac{v_E d_E}{L_O f_{SW}}$$

$$\Delta i_{L(RMS)} = \sqrt{ \frac{2}{t_{SW}} \left[\int_0^{0.5 t_{ON}} \left(\frac{\Delta i_L{}^2 t^2}{t_{ON}{}^2} \right) dt + \int_0^{0.5 t_{OFF}} \left(\frac{\Delta i_L{}^2 t^2}{t_{OFF}{}^2} \right) dt \right] } = \sqrt{ \frac{2 \Delta i_L{}^2}{3 t_{SW}} \left(\frac{t_{ON}}{8} + \frac{t_{OFF}}{8} \right) } = \frac{0.5 \Delta i_L}{\sqrt{3}}$$

$$\therefore \quad P_{R(AC)} \approx \Delta i_{L(RMS)}{}^2 R_{AC} = \left(\frac{v_E d_E}{2 L_O f_{SW} \sqrt{3}} \right)^2 R_{AC} = K_{RMS} \left(\frac{R_{AC}}{f_{SW}{}^2} \right)$$

Raising f_{SW} reduces ripple Δi_L and ripple-conduction losses $P_{R(AC)}$.

7.3. DCM Conduction Losses

$i_{L(AVG)}$ is no longer a dc offset in DCM $\therefore$ $P_R \equiv P_{R(DC)} + P_{R(AC)} = i_{L(RMS)}{}^2 R_{C(EQ)}$.

$i_{L(RMS)}$ flows through R_{SW} and $R_{L.ESR}$ and $i_L - i_O$ flows through $R_{C.ESR}$.

$$\therefore \quad P_R = i_{L(RMS)}{}^2 \left(R_{SW} + R_{L.ESR} \right) + \left(i_{L(RMS)}{}^2 - i_O{}^2 \right) R_{C.ESR}$$

Energy packets (and conduction losses) drop when i_O falls and frequency rises.

$$i_{L(RMS)}{}^2 = \left(\frac{\Delta i_L}{\sqrt{3}} \right)^2 \left(\frac{t_C}{t_{SW}} \right)$$

$$i_{L(AVG)} = \frac{q_L}{t_{SW}} = \frac{\text{Area}}{t_{SW}} = \frac{0.5 t_C i_{L(PK)}}{t_{SW}} \quad \rightarrow \quad \Delta i_L = i_{L(PK)} = 2 i_{L(AVG)} \left(\frac{t_{SW}}{t_C} \right) = 2 i_O \left(\frac{t_{SW}}{t_C} \right)$$

$$d_E = \frac{t_E}{t_C} \quad \rightarrow \quad t_C = \frac{t_E}{d_E} = \frac{i_{L(PK)} L_O}{d_E \left(v_{IN} - v_O \right)} = \sqrt{ \frac{2 i_O t_{SW} L_O}{d_E \left(v_{IN} - v_O \right)} } \quad \therefore \quad i_{L(RMS)}{}^2 = \frac{4}{3} \left(\frac{i_O{}^{1.5}}{f_{SW}{}^{0.5}} \right) \sqrt{ \frac{d_E \left(v_{IN} - v_O \right)}{2 L_O} }$$

7.3. Gate-Drive Losses

v_{IN} loses energy every cycle to charge gate capacitances.

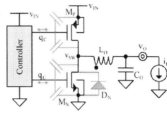

→ $E_G = q_C \Delta v_C = (C_G \Delta v_C) \Delta v_C = C_G \Delta v_C^2$.

→ $P_G = E_G/t_{SW} = E_G f_{SW}$.

v_{IN} supplies C_{GSN}, C_{GDN}, C_{GSP}, and C_{GDP}.

C_{GSN} and C_{GSP} charge across v_{IN}.

C_{GDN} starts at v_D and ends at v_{IN}.

→ $\Delta v_{GDN} = v_{FIN} - v_{INI} = v_{IN} - v_D$.

C_{GDP} starts at $v_{IN} + v_D$ and ends at $-v_{IN}$.

→ $\Delta v_{GDP} = (-v_{IN}) - (v_{IN} + v_D)$.

∴ $E_G = C_{GSN} v_{IN}^2 + C_{GSP} v_{IN}^2 + C_{GDN}(v_{IN} - v_D)^2 + C_{GDP}(2v_{IN} + v_D)^2$ and $P_G = \sum C_G \Delta v_C^2 f_{SW}$

Note v_{IN} delivers $C_G \Delta v_C^2$, C_G stores $0.5 C_G \Delta v_C^2$, and drivers dissipate

$0.5 C_G \Delta v_C^2$ when charging and C_G's $0.5 C_G \Delta v_C^2$ when discharging.

7.3. Other Losses: i_D–v_{DS} Overlap

Loss: Transitional i_D–v_{DS} overlap across power switches.

M_N's Δv_{DS} (before and after dead time) is v_D → Can often neglect.

M_P's Δv_{SD} (before and after dead time) is $v_{IN} + v_D$ → Can be considerable.

M_P's Transitions:

v_{SW} rises (and v_{SDP} falls)

    after i_P surpasses $i_{L(-PK)}$.

v_{SW} falls (and v_{SDP} rises)

    when i_P falls below $i_{L(+PK)}$.

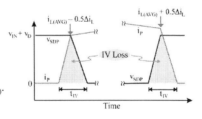

Overlap Loss:

$$P_{IV} = \frac{0.5 t_{IV-} P_{PK-} + 0.5 t_{IV+} P_{PK+}}{t_{SW}} \approx 0.5\left(\frac{t_{IV}}{t_{SW}}\right)(v_{IN} + v_D)(i_{L(PK)-} + i_{L(PK)+}) = \left(\frac{t_{IV}}{t_{SW}}\right)(v_{IN} + v_D) i_{L(AVG)}$$

If $v_{IN} \gg v_D$, $P_{IV} \approx (t_{IV} f_{SW}) v_{IN} i_O$.

t_{IV} depends on how fast C_{GD}'s and C_{DB}'s charge and discharge.

If C_{GD}'s dominate, drivers current-limit t_{IV}. If C_{DB}'s dominate, M_P current-limits t_{IV}.

7.3. Other Losses: Dead-Time Conduction and Shoot-Through

Dead Time: When synchronous switches

open, i_L discharges v_{SW}'s C_{SW}

until D_N forward-biases.

$\therefore D_N$ conducts i_L through t_{DT}.

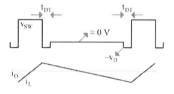

$$P_{DT} \approx v_D \left(i_{L(PK)+} + i_{L(PK)-} \right) \left(\frac{t_{DT}}{t_{SW}} \right) = v_D \left(2i_{L(AVG)} \right) t_{DT} f_{SW} = 2v_D i_O t_{DT} f_{SW}$$

Shoot-Through: Since drivers do not include

dead time, their transistors conduct

transitional shoot-through current.

Two drivers transition twice $\therefore$

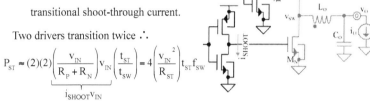

$$P_{ST} \approx (2)(2) \underbrace{\left(\frac{v_{IN}}{R_P + R_N} \right) v_{IN}}_{i_{SHOOT} v_{IN}} \left(\frac{t_{ST}}{t_{SW}} \right) = 4 \left(\frac{v_{IN}}{R_{ST}} \right)^2 t_{ST} f_{SW}$$

7.3. Power Losses: Example

Example: Determine η_C for a synchronous buck dc–dc converter in CCM

when $v_{IN} = 4.0$ V, $v_O = 1.8$ V, $i_O = 250$ mA, $t_{SW} = 1$ μs, $t_{IV} \approx 3$ ns, $t_{DT} \approx 30$ ns,

$t_{ST} \approx 3$ ns, $L_O = 22$ μH, $R_{L.ESR} = 100$ mΩ, $R_{C.ESR} = 25$ mΩ, $R_{DRV} = 5$ Ω,

$R_P = R_N = 0.5$ Ω, $C_{GSN} = C_{GSP} = 350$ pF, $C_{GDN} = C_{GDP} = 70$ pF, and $v_D \approx 0.7$ V.

Solution: From last example, $d_E = 45\%$, $t_E = 450$ ns, and $\Delta i_L = 45$ mA.

$$P_{R(DC)} = i_{L(AVG)}^2 \left(R_{SW} + R_{L.ESR} \right) = (0.25)^2 (0.5 + 0.1) = 37.5 \text{ mW}$$

$$\text{Since } \Delta i_{L(RMS)} = \frac{0.5 \Delta i_L}{\sqrt{3}} = \frac{0.5(45m)}{\sqrt{3}} = 13 \text{ mA}$$

$$P_{R(AC)} \approx \Delta i_{L(RMS)}^2 \left(R_{SW} + R_{L.ESR} + R_{C.ESR} \right) = (13m)^2 (0.25 + 0.5 + 0.05) = 106 \text{ μW}$$

$$P_G \approx \frac{\left(C_{GSN} + C_{GSP} \right) v_{IN}^2 + C_{GDN} \left(v_{IN} - v_D \right)^2 + C_{GDP} \left(2v_{IN} + v_D \right)^2}{t_{SW}}$$

$$= \frac{2(350p)(4)^2 + 35p(4 - 0.7)^2 + 70p \left[2(4) + 0.7 \right]^2}{1μ} = 16.9 \text{ mW}$$

7.3. Power Losses: Example

Solution (continued):

$$P_{IV} \approx \left(\frac{t_{IV}}{t_{SW}}\right)\left(v_{IN} + v_D\right)i_{L(AVG)} = \left(\frac{3n}{1\mu}\right)\left(4 + 0.7\right)0.25 = 3.52 \ mW$$

$$P_{DT} \approx 2v_D i_O t_{DT} f_{SW} = \frac{2(0.7)(0.25)(30n)}{1\mu} = 10.5 \ mW$$

$$P_{ST} \approx 4\left(\frac{v_{IN}^2}{R_{ST}}\right)t_{ST}f_{SW} = 4\left[\frac{(4)^2}{5}\right]\left(\frac{3n}{1\mu}\right) = 38.4 \ mW$$

$$\eta_C = \frac{v_O i_O}{v_O i_O + P_{R(DC)} + P_{R(AC)} + P_G + P_{IV} + P_{DT} + P_{ST}}$$

$$\approx \frac{(1.8)(0.25)}{(1.8)(0.25) + 37.5m + 106\mu + 16.9m + 3.52m + 10.5m + 38.4m} = 80.8\%$$

7.3. Boost Losses

Trace $i_{L(AVG)}$ and Δi_L and

their respective fractions.

M_{PO} conducts d_O fraction of i_L.

$$\therefore i_O = i_{L(AVG)}d_O.$$

$$P_{R(DC)} = i_{L(AVG)}^2 R_{DC} = i_{L(AVG)}^2\left(R_{LESR} + R_{SW}\right) = \left(\frac{i_O}{d_{DO}}\right)^2\left(R_{LESR} + R_{SW}\right)$$

$$P_{R(AC)} = \Delta i_{L(RMS)}^2 R_{AC} = \Delta i_{L(RMS)}^2\left(R_{L.ESR} + R_{SW} + d_{DO}R_{C.ESR}\right)$$

$$P_G = \sum C_G \Delta v_C^2 f_{SW} = \left[C_{GSN}v_O^2 + C_{GDN}\left(2v_O + v_D\right)^2 + C_{GSP}\left(v_O - v_D\right)^2 + C_{GDP}v_O^2\right]f_{SW}$$

$$P_{IV} \approx P_{IVN} \approx 0.5\Delta v_{SW}\left(i_{L(PK)-} + i_{L(PK)+}\right)\left(\frac{t_{IV}}{t_{SW}}\right) = \left(v_O + v_D\right)i_{L(AVG)}t_{IV}f_{SW} = \left(v_O + v_D\right)\left(\frac{i_O}{d_{DO}}\right)t_{IV}f_{SW}$$

$$P_{DT} \approx v_D\left(i_{L(PK)+} + i_{L(PK)-}\right)\left(\frac{t_{DT}}{t_{SW}}\right) = v_D\left(2i_{L(AVG)}\right)t_{DT}f_{SW} = 2v_D\left(\frac{i_O}{d_{DO}}\right)t_{DT}f_{SW}$$

7.3. Loss Dominance

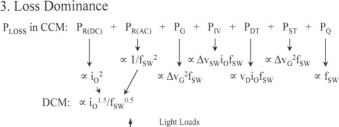

$$P_{LOSS} \text{ in CCM: } P_{R(DC)} + P_{R(AC)} + P_G + P_{IV} + P_{DT} + P_{ST} + P_Q$$

$$\propto i_O^2 \quad \propto 1/f_{SW}^2 \quad \propto \Delta v_{SW} i_O f_{SW} \quad \propto \Delta v_G^2 f_{SW}$$

$$\propto \Delta v_G^2 f_{SW} \quad \propto v_D i_O f_{SW} \quad \propto f_{SW}$$

$$\text{DCM: } \propto i_O^{1.5}/f_{SW}^{0.5}$$

i_O and f_{SW} Groupings:

$\propto i_O^2$: $P_{R(DC).CCM}$

$\propto i_O^{1.5}/f_{SW}^{0.5}$: $P_{R.DCM}$

$\propto i_O f_{SW}$: P_{IV} and P_{DT}

$\propto 1/f_{SW}^2$: $P_{R(AC).CCM}$

$\propto f_{SW}$: P_G, P_{ST}, and P_Q

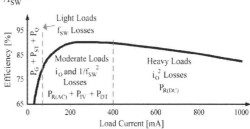

f_{SW} switching losses dominate under light loads.

i_O and $1/f_{SW}^2$ losses dominate under moderate loads.

i_O^2 conduction losses dominate under heavy loads.

7.3. Reducing Losses

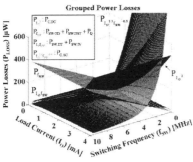

P_G, P_{ST}, and P_Q are constant over i_O.

P_G falls with less switching gates.

$P_{R(DC)}$ falls quickly when i_O falls.

P_{IV} and P_{DT} fall when i_O and f_{SW} fall.

$P_{R(AC)}$ falls quickly when f_{SW} rises.

P_{fSW} and P_{iOfSW} rise and

$P_{R.DCM}$ falls with higher f_{SW}.

∴ Raise f_{SW} until fall in $P_{R.DCM}$

balances rise in the others.

DCM is more efficient than CCM

when the load i_O is low.

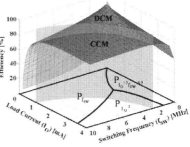

7.3. Optimum MOSFET

MOS resistance and MOS capacitance rise with longer channels L_{CH} → Use L_{MIN}.

MOS resistance falls and MOS capacitance rises with wider channels W_{CH}.

$$P_{R(MOS)} \propto R_{MOS} = \frac{v_{DS}}{i_{D(TRI)}} \approx \frac{L_{CH}}{W_{CH}K'\left(v_{GS} - v_T\right)} \propto \frac{1}{W_{CH}} \qquad P_{G(MOS)} \propto C_{MOS} = C_{OX}"W_{CH}L_{CH} \propto W_{CH}$$

∴ $P_{R(MOS)}$ falls and $P_{G(MOS)}$ rises with W_{CH} where $P_{MOS} = P_{R(MOS)} + P_{G(MOS)}$.

Optimum Width: Raise W_{CH} until rise in P_G balances reduction in P_R.

$P_{MOS(MIN)}$ when $\left. \dfrac{\partial P_{MOS}}{\partial W_{CH}} \right|_{W_{OPT}} = \left. \left(\dfrac{\partial P_{R(MOS)}}{\partial W_{CH}} + \dfrac{\partial P_{G(MOS)}}{\partial W_{CH}} \right) \right|_{W_{OPT}} = 0$

Optimize: At half the load.

At the load that yields the highest peak efficiency.

At the load that yields the highest average efficiency across load.

Or At most probable load. → This setting saves the most energy.

Note: If $R_{MOS} \ll R_{L.ESR}$, R_{MOS} hardly affects η_C ∴ Lower W_{CH} to save area.

7.3. Optimum MOSFET: Example

Example: Determine W_{OPT} for M_P in a synchronous buck dc–dc converter

in CCM when $v_D \approx 0.7$ V, $|V_{TP0}| = 0.6$ V, $K_P' = 40$ μA/V^2,

$C_{OX}" = 5$ fF/μm^2, $L \geq 0.25$ μm, $v_{IN} = 4.0$ V, $v_O = 1.8$ V, $i_O = 250$ mA,

$L_O = 22$ μH, $R_{L.ESR} = 100$ mΩ, $R_{C.ESR} = 25$ mΩ, $t_{SW} = 1$ μs, and $L_{OL} = 50$ nm.

Solution:

From previous examples, $d_E = 45\%$, $t_E = 450$ ns, $\Delta i_L = 45$ mA,

and $\Delta i_{L(RMS)} = 13$ mA.

For minimum P_{MOS}, $L_{CH} \equiv L_{MIN} = 0.25$ μm.

Gate drive v_{SG} for M_P is $v_{IN} = 4$ V.

M_P only conducts during t_E, so $R_{EQ} = d_E R_{MP}$.

∴ $R_{MP} \approx \dfrac{L_{CH}}{W_{CH}K_P'\left(v_{SG} - |V_{TP0}|\right)} = \dfrac{0.25\mu}{W_{CH}(40\mu)(4-0.6)} = \dfrac{1}{544W_{CH}}$

7.3. Optimum MOSFET: Example

Solution (continued):

$$P_{R(MP)} = \left(i_{L(AVG)}^2 + \Delta i_{L(RMS)}^2\right)d_E R_{MP} = \frac{\left[(0.25)^2 + (13m)^2\right](45\%)}{544 W_{CH}} = \frac{1}{(19.3k)W_{CH}}$$

$$C_{GSP} = C_{OX}"W_{CH}L_{CH} = \left(\frac{5f}{\mu^2}\right)W_{CH}(0.25\mu) = (1.25n)W_{CH}$$

$$C_{GDP} \approx C_{OX}"W_{CH}L_{OL} = \left(\frac{5f}{\mu^2}\right)W_{CH}(50n) = (250p)W_{CH}$$

$$P_{G(MP)} \approx \frac{C_{GSP}v_{IN}^2 + C_{GDP}\left(2v_{IN} + v_D\right)^2}{t_{SW}} = \frac{(1.25n)W_{CH}(4)^2 + (250p)W_{CH}\left[2(4) + (0.7)\right]^2}{1\mu} = \frac{W_{CH}}{25.7}$$

$$\frac{dP_{MP}}{dW_{CH}} = \frac{dP_{R(MP)}}{dW_{CH}} + \frac{dP_{G(MP)}}{dW_{CH}} = -\frac{1}{(19.3k)W_{CH}^2} + \frac{1}{25.7} \equiv 0 \quad \text{at} \ W_{CH} = 36.5 \ mm = 36.5k \ \mu m$$

M_P can incorporate 73× 500-μm, 0.25-μm gate fingers.

7.3. Other Power Considerations

Power is ultimately lost as heat.

∴ Junction Temperature $T_J \propto P_{LOSS}$.

→ If losses are great,

$T_{J(MAX)}$ is excessive.

∴ Use a heat sink or a cooling fan.

→ Additional power and/or space.

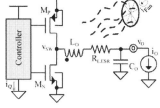

Thermal Effect: Resistances rise with temperature ∴ R_{MAX} and $P_{R(MAX)}$ at T_{MAX}.

High-Frequency Operation (for high bandwidth):

Dead time t_{DT} is significant fraction of period t_{SW}.

∴ Lose low-P_R benefits of v_{DS} while still

consuming P_G. → Diode can be more efficient at high frequency.

7.3. Other Power Considerations

Light-Load Operation: Synchronous switches can conduct negative currents.

∴ Higher conduction losses P_R → Block negative currents.

Skin Effect: i_L flows through skin at high frequency.

∴ $R_{L.ESR(HF)} > R_{L.ESR0}$.

→ Higher conduction losses P_R at high frequency.

$P_R = f(i_L)$ ∴   ↑ $v_{O(BUCK)}$ → ↓ i_O (for same P_O) ∴ ↓ $i_{L(AVG)}$ → ↓ P_R.

↑ $v_{IN(BOOST)}$ → ↓ i_{IN} (for similar P_{IN}) ∴ ↓ $i_{L(AVG)}$ → ↓ P_R.

→ Lower v_{IN}-to-v_O spreads reduce ohmic losses P_R and raise efficiency η_C.

Controller Current:

Climbs with bandwidth requirements.

Climbs with parasitic capacitance ∴ Depends on process technology.

7.3. Other Power Considerations

Buck–Boost Circuits: Lower gate-drive losses P_G

When bucking by keeping S_{GO} open.

When boosting by keeping S_I closed.

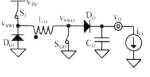

Load Power:

Lowest when v_O nears the load's headroom limit $v_{O(MIN)}$.

→ Margin for v_O's ripple and load-dump response raises load power.

MOS channel length should be high enough to sustain terminal voltages and keep short-channel conduction from leaking substantial power.

Overlap length L_{OL} is roughly 4–8× lower than L_{MIN} ∴ $C_{GD} \approx C_{GS(TRIODE)}/5$.

Input Capacitance C_{IN}:

$R_{IN.ESR}$ carries Δi_{IN} ∴ $R_{IN.ESR}$ consumes $\Delta i_{L(RMS)}$ energy.

7.4. Frequency Response

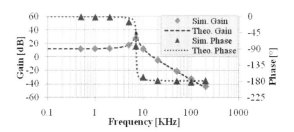

7.4. Small-Signal Analysis

Basics

Bias point (from steady-state response): Averaged signals per cycle → S_A.

Small-signal response: Determine small-signal effect on S_A → s_a.

Small-signal approximation:

Small-signal changes cause *linear* variations in S_A.

The State of the Art

State-space averaging (SSA): Average electrical equations (e.g., $L_O di_L/dt$).

Circuit averaging: Model averaged equations.

Flow graph: Display flow of averaged equations graphically.

Signal-flow graph (SFG): Average time-domain operation (i.e., waveforms)

and display flow of averaged signals graphically.

7.4. Continuous-Conduction Mode: Power-Stage Response

Non-inverting buck–boost stage incorporates all small-signal dynamics:

Switched inductor L_O, output capacitor C_O, and duty-cycled output.

∴ General case.

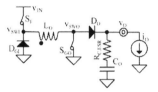

Filter:

C_O shunts v_O ∴ v_O falls with frequency → C_O pole p_C.

C_O's $R_{C.ESR}$ limits i_C ∴ Arrests effects of p_C → Left-half-plane zero LHP z_{LHP}.

L_O decouples v_O from source ∴ v_O falls with frequency → L_O pole p_L.

Together, L_O and C_O introduce a pair of complex poles p_{LC}^2 at $1/2\pi\sqrt{(L_O C_O)}$.

7.4. Continuous-Conduction Mode: Power-Stage Response

Inductor current i_L depends on voltage across inductor v_L:

$$i_L = \frac{v_L}{sL_O + R_{L.ESR}} = \frac{v_E d_E + v_D(1 - d_E)}{sL_O + R_{L.ESR}} = \frac{(v_E - v_D)d_E + v_D}{sL_O + R_{L.ESR}}$$

Two-port small-signal Norton-equivalent current (i.e., when $v_o \equiv 0$):

$v_o \equiv 0$ and v_{IN} has no feedback component in v_E or v_D ∴ $v_e \approx v_d \approx 0$.

And $\quad i_l \equiv d_e\left(\dfrac{di_L}{dd_E}\right) + \cancel{v_e}\left(\dfrac{di_L}{dv_E}\right) + \cancel{v_d}\left(\dfrac{di_L}{dv_D}\right) = d_e\left(\dfrac{di_L}{dd_E}\right) = \dfrac{d_e(V_E - V_D)}{sL_O + R_{L.ESR}}$

→ i_l is the inductor voltage per cycle $v_l = d_e(V_E - V_D)$ over inductor impedance.

∴ Pole when sL_O overwhelms $R_{L.ESR}$ at p_{LESR}.

Norton-equivalent impedance (when $d_e \equiv 0$) is Z_{LO}.

7.4. Continuous-Conduction Mode: Duty-Cycled Output

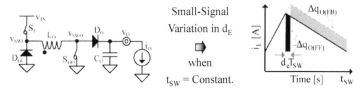

Small-Signal Variation in d_E when t_{SW} = Constant.

D_O duty-cycles (attenuates) i_L: $i_O = i_L d_{DO} = i_L(1 - d_E)$ and $i_o = i_l D_{DO} = i_l(1 - D_E)$.

Negative feedback raises d_E when v_O drops, which also lowers d_{DO}:

$$v_o' \downarrow \to d_e \uparrow \to v_l \uparrow \to i_l \uparrow \to i_{o(FB)} \uparrow \to v_o \uparrow$$
$$\to d_{do} \downarrow \qquad \to i_{o(FF)} \downarrow \to v_o \downarrow$$

Out-of-phase feed-forward path counters negative feedback.

∴ Fraction of i_l reaches v_o and right-half-plane RHP zero z_{RHP} when $i_{o(FF)} \geq i_{o(FB)}$.

Feedback Path: $i_{o(FB)} = i_l D_{DO} = i_l(T_O/T_{SW}) = i_l(1 - D_E) \equiv \Delta q_{O(FB)}/T_{SW}$.

Feed-forward Path: $i_{o(FF)} \equiv -\Delta q_{O(FF)}/T_{SW} \approx -(d_e T_{SW})i_{L(PK)}/T_{SW} = d_{do}i_{L(PK)}$.

7.4. Continuous-Conduction Mode: Signal Flow

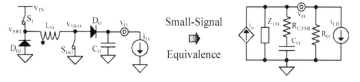

Small-Signal Equivalence

Generalized signal flow across feedback path:

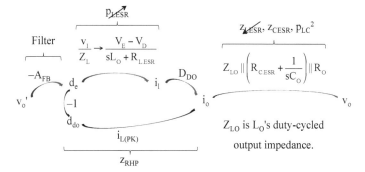

Z_{LO} is L_O's duty-cycled output impedance.

7.4. Continuous-Conduction Mode: Inductor Impedance

When not duty-cycled,

L_O connects to v_O continuously.

$\therefore Z_{LO} = Z_L = sL_O.$

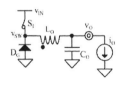

When duty-cycled with a constant frequency,

D_O duty-cycles i_l to $v_O \rightarrow i_o = i_l D_{DO} = v_o D_{DO}/Z_L \therefore Z_{EQ} = Z_L/D_{DO}$

z_{RHP} occurs when i_o reverses polarity: $i_{o(FF)} \geq i_{o(FB)} \rightarrow \Delta q_{O(FF)} \geq \Delta q_{O(FB)}$,

$i_{o(FF)} = -d_e i_{l(PK)} \geq i_{o(FB)} = v_l/Z_{FQ} = d_e(V_E - V_D)D_{DO}/(L_O 2\pi z_{RHP}).$

$\therefore$

$$z_{RHP} = \left(\frac{V_E - V_D}{2\pi i_{L(PK)} L_O} \right) \left(\frac{T_O}{T_{SW}} \right) = \frac{(V_E - V_D)D_{DO}}{2\pi i_{L(PK)} L_O}$$

L_O loads v_O a D_{DO} fraction $\rightarrow i_{ZLO} = v_o D_{DO}/Z_{EQ} = v_o D_{DO}^2/Z_L > Z_L.$

$\therefore$ Combined effect is $Z_{LO} = Z_{L.EFF} = v_o/i_{ZLO} = Z_L/D_{DO}^2 \rightarrow L_{EFF} = L_O/D_{DO}^2.$

7.4. Continuous-Conduction Mode

Example 1: Buck $\rightarrow L_O$ is not duty-cycled $\therefore$ No z_{RHP} and $Z_{LO} = sL_O.$

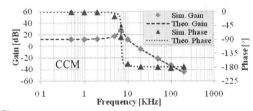

Signal-Flow Graph (SFG):

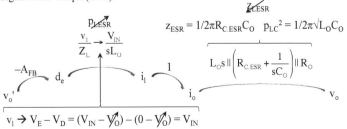

7.4. Continuous-Conduction Mode

Example 2: Boost with constant frequency.

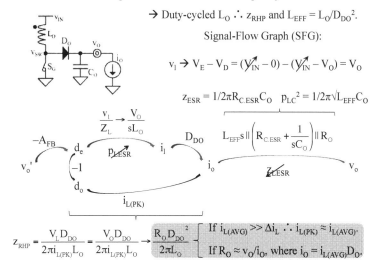

$\rightarrow$ Duty-cycled L_O $\therefore$ z_{RHP} and $L_{EFF} = L_O/D_{DO}{}^2$.

Signal-Flow Graph (SFG):

$$v_l \rightarrow V_E - V_D = (V_{IN} - 0) - (V_{IN} - V_O) = V_O$$

$$z_{ESR} = 1/2\pi R_{C.ESR}C_O \quad p_{LC}{}^2 = 1/2\pi\sqrt{L_{EFF}C_O}$$

$$z_{RHP} = \frac{V_L D_{DO}}{2\pi i_{L(PK)}L_O} = \frac{V_O D_{DO}}{2\pi i_{L(PK)}L_O} \rightarrow \frac{R_O D_{DO}{}^2}{2\pi L_O} \begin{array}{l} \text{If } i_{L(AVG)} \gg \Delta i_L \therefore i_{L(PK)} \approx i_{L(AVG)}. \\ \text{If } R_O \approx v_O/i_O, \text{ where } i_O = i_{L(AVG)}D_O. \end{array}$$

7.4. Continuous-Conduction Mode

Example 3: Non-inverting Buck–Boost with constant frequency.

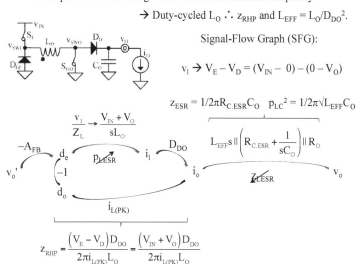

$\rightarrow$ Duty-cycled L_O $\therefore$ z_{RHP} and $L_{EFF} = L_O/D_{DO}{}^2$.

Signal-Flow Graph (SFG):

$$v_l \rightarrow V_E - V_D = (V_{IN} - 0) - (0 - V_O)$$

$$z_{ESR} = 1/2\pi R_{C.ESR}C_O \quad p_{LC}{}^2 = 1/2\pi\sqrt{L_{EFF}C_O}$$

$$z_{RHP} = \frac{(V_E - V_D)D_{DO}}{2\pi i_{L(PK)}L_O} = \frac{(V_{IN} + V_O)D_{DO}}{2\pi i_{L(PK)}L_O}$$

7.4. Discontinuous-Conduction Mode

In DCM: $\quad d_E \equiv \dfrac{t_E}{t_C} \neq \dfrac{t_E}{t_{sw}} \quad$ and $\quad D_E \equiv \dfrac{T_E}{T_C} = \dfrac{t_e}{t_c}$

L_O drains fully prior to t_{sw} → All Δq_L reaches v_O.

$\therefore \quad \Delta q_{O(FB)} = \Delta q_L > \Delta q_{O(FF)} = 0 \rightarrow$ No z_{RHP}.

And $\quad i_o = \dfrac{\Delta q_L}{T_{sw}} \approx \dfrac{i_{L(PK)} t_c}{T_{sw}} = \dfrac{i_{L(PK)}}{T_{sw}} \left(\dfrac{d_e T_C}{D_E} \right) \neq i_1 d_{DO}$

t_E and t_D *both* rise or fall proportionately $\therefore v_l = V_E t_e + V_D t_d = 0$ because $V_D < 0$.

$\rightarrow \quad i_1 = \dfrac{v_L}{sL_O} = 0 \rightarrow$ No $p_L \rightarrow L_O$ behaves like a resistor.

L_O loads i_o *only* when L_O conducts, across T_{LO}:

$v_{T(AVG)} = v_T \left(\dfrac{T_{LO}}{t_{sw}} \right) \qquad i_{T(AVG)} = \dfrac{q_T}{t_{sw}} \qquad q_T = 0.5 T_{LO} \left[\left(\dfrac{v_T}{L_O} \right) T_{LO} \right] \qquad \therefore \quad Z_{LO} \equiv \dfrac{v_{T(AVG)}}{i_{T(AVG)}} \approx \dfrac{2L_O}{T_{LO}}$

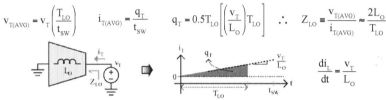

$$\dfrac{di_L}{dt} = \dfrac{v_T}{L_O}$$

7.4. Discontinuous-Conduction Mode: Signal Flow

$v_l = 0$ in DCM $\therefore$ No L_O pole, $Z_L \approx 2L_{EFF}/T_C$, and all of q_l reaches v_o $\therefore$ No z_{RHP}.

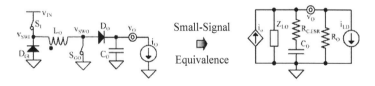

Small-Signal
➡
Equivalence

Generalized signal flow across feedback path:

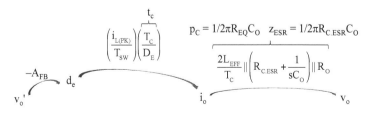

$p_C = 1/2\pi R_{EQ} C_O \qquad z_{ESR} = 1/2\pi R_{C.ESR} C_O$

$$\dfrac{2L_{EFF}}{T_C} \Big\| \left(R_{C.ESR} + \dfrac{1}{sC_O} \right) \| R_O$$

7.4. Discontinuous-Conduction Mode

Example 1: Buck

$v_l = 0$ in DCM $\therefore$ No L_O pole, $Z_L \approx 2L_O/T_C$, and all of q_l reaches v_o $\therefore$ No z_{RHP}.

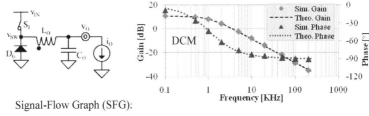

Signal-Flow Graph (SFG):

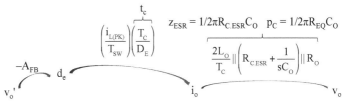

7.4. Discontinuous-Conduction Mode

Example 2: Boost $\rightarrow$ Duty-cycled L_O $\therefore$ $L_{EFF} = L_O/D_{DO}^2$.

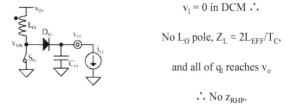

$v_l = 0$ in DCM $\therefore$

No L_O pole, $Z_L \approx 2L_{EFF}/T_C$,

and all of q_l reaches v_o

$\therefore$ No z_{RHP}.

Signal-Flow Graph (SFG):

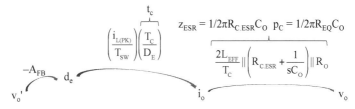

7.4. Discontinuous-Conduction Mode

Example 3: Non-inverting Buck–Boost → Duty-cycled L_O ∴ $L_{EFF} = L_O/D_{DO}{}^2$.

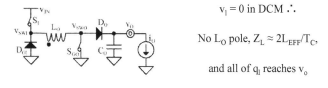

$v_l = 0$ in DCM ∴

No L_O pole, $Z_L \approx 2L_{EFF}/T_C$,

and all of q_l reaches v_o

∴ No z_{RHP}.

Signal-Flow Graph (SFG):

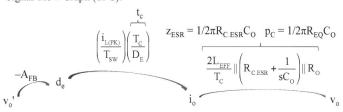

7.4. Summary

Analysis averages response over t_{SW} → Valid to f_{SW}.

R_O is not always v_o/i_o, but can be close.

$L_O C_O$ introduces complex pair of poles $p_{LC}{}^2$:

    C_O shunts v_o ∴ v_o falls with frequency → C_O Pole.

    L_O decouples v_o from source v_{IN} ∴ v_o falls with frequency → L_O Pole.

In DCM, $t_e V_E$ and $t_d V_D$ both rise with d_e.

$$\therefore \quad v_l = t_e V_E + t_d V_D = 0 \quad \text{and} \quad i_l = \frac{v_l}{L_O s} = \frac{t_e V_E + t_d V_D}{L_O s} = 0$$

→ No L_O Pole.

7.4. Summary

Duty-Cycled Output

In CCM: D_O gates i_L → $i_o = i_l D_{DO}$.

$-\Delta q_{O(FF)}$ counters $+\Delta q_{O(FB)}$ → Out-of-phase RHP zero.

In DCM, all of Δq_L reaches v_O, so $\Delta q_{O(FF)} = 0$ → No z_{RHP}.

C_O's equivalent-series resistance $R_{C.ESR}$ limits C_O's current i_{CO} to $v_O/R_{C.ESR}$:

$R_{C.ESR}$ arrests p_{CO}'s effects → In-phase LHP zero.

At $z_{ESR} \approx 1/2\pi R_{C.ESR} C_O$.

Bypass capacitor C_B shunts $R_{C.ESR}$ → Bypass pole.

At $p_B \approx 1/2\pi R_{C.ESR} C_B$.

Combined CCM response can include 2–3 poles, 1 RHP zero, and 1 LHP zero.

Combined DCM response can include 1–2 poles and 1 LHP zero.

7.5. Feedback Control

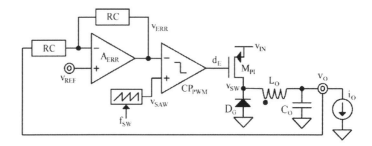

7.5. Context

Objective: Regulate v_O about v_{REF} with shunt negative feedback.

Compensation:

Ensure loop gain A_{LG} has a dominant low-frequency pole,

$\therefore A_{LG}$ reaches unity-gain frequency f_{0dB} with sufficient phase margin PM.

Challenges:

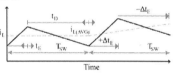

L_O's pole, C_O's pole, and a possible RHP zero.

Keep all parasitic poles above f_{0dB}.

Typical Control Method.

Loop senses v_O and modulates d_E until

v_O nears v_{REF} → Until i_L satisfies the load i_{LOAD}.

Loop processes both analog and digital information.

Typically, loop cannot respond within one cycle → Bandwidth = $f_{0dB} \le f_{SW}$.

7.5. Duty-Cycle Modulation Schemes

Fixed Frequency:

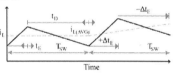

Adjust energizing time t_E.

$\therefore$ Drain time t_D changes.

Popular because switching noise is fairly predictable.

Popularly known as pulse-width modulation (PWM).

Fixed Energizing Time:

Adjust drain time t_D.

$\therefore$ Switching period t_{SW} changes.

Popular known as constant on-time control.

Fixed Drain Time:

Adjust energizing time t_E.

$\therefore$ Switching period t_{SW} changes.

Popular known as constant off-time control.

7.5. Duty-Cycle Modulation Schemes

Fixed Current Ripple:

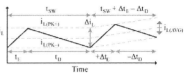

Adjust average current $i_{L(AVG)}$.

$\therefore t_E$, t_D, and t_{SW} change.

Upper peak $i_{L(PK+)}$ sets t_E and lower peak $i_{L(PK-)}$ sets t_D.

A constant current ripple Δi_L tends to produce a consistent output ripple Δv_O.

Variable Peak:

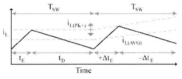

Adjust $i_{L(PK+)}$ or $i_{L(PK-)}$.

$\therefore t_E$ and t_D change.

t_{SW} is constant, but current ripple Δi_L is not $\therefore \Delta v_O$ varies with load i_{LOAD}.

Popularly known as peak-current control.

If v_O rises and falls with i_L, Δv_O, $v_{O(PK+)}$, or $v_{O(PK-)}$ can similarly set t_E and t_D.

$\rightarrow t_{SW}$ changes when Δv_O is constant or Δv_O changes when t_{SW} is constant.

7.5. Voltage Mode

Compensation Strategies

Add very low-freq. pole: $p_{LF} \ll f_{0dB}' < p_{LC}^2$, z_{RHP} $\therefore$ Low f_{0dB}'.

Add low-freq. pole and zero: $p_{LF} \ll z_{LHP}$, p_{LC}^2, $f_{0dB}'' < z_{RHP}$ $\therefore$ $f_{0dB}'' > f_{0dB}'$.

Use $R_{C.ESR}$ to save phase: $z_{ESR} \ll p_{LC}^2$, $f_{0dB}''' < z_{RHP}$ $\therefore$ High f_{0dB}'''.

But also high output ripple Δv_O.

Operate in DCM: Eliminate p_L and z_{RHP} $\therefore$ $p_C \ll f_{0dB}'''' > f_{0dB}'''$.

But output power P_O is low or Δi_L is high.

Pseudo DCM (PDCM): Short L_O (i.e., $v_1 = 0$) to emulate DCM.

$v_L \propto di_L/dt = 0$ $\therefore$ $\Delta i_L = 0$, but $i_L \neq 0$.

S_L conducts $i_{L(PK-)}$ $\rightarrow$ Lossy $\rightarrow$ Low η_C.

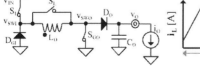
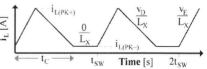

7.5. Voltage Mode: Fixed Frequency

Modulate duty cycle d_E with a constant switching period T_{SW}.

Pulse-Width Modulated Buck:

A_{ERR} senses output v_O and generates error signal v_{ERR}.

RC network establishes low-frequency pole p_{LF} and maybe a zero z_{LHP}.

CP_{PWM} pulse-width modulates power switch M_{PI} according to error v_{ERR}.

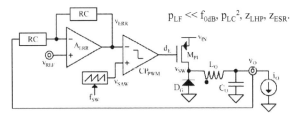

$$p_{LF} \ll f_{0dB}, \; p_{LC}^2, \; z_{LHP}, \; z_{ESR}.$$

Δv_O and therefore Δv_{ERR} are small in steady state.

$$A_{LG} = A_{RC} A_{PWM} A_{BUCK} = \left(\frac{v_{err}}{v_o}\right)\left(\frac{d_e}{v_{err}}\right)\left(\frac{v_o}{d_e}\right) \quad \left.\begin{array}{l} A_{RC0}, \; p_{LF}, \; z_{LHP} \\ A_{PWM0}, \; p_{LC}^2, \; z_{ESR} \end{array}\right.$$

7.5. Voltage Mode: Pulse-Width Modulator

v_{ERR} changes slowly across several cycles because $p_{LF} \ll f_{0dB} < f_{SW}$.

Comparator CP_{PWM} compares v_{ERR} with a sawtooth v_{SAW} clocked at f_{SW}.

Output v_{CPO} is high at the beginning of the period T_{SW} → t_E starts.

v_{CPO} falls when v_{ERR} surpasses v_{SAW} → t_E ends.

Clock f_{SW} resets v_{SAW} below v_{ERR} ∴ v_{CPO} rises → T_{SW} and t_E start.

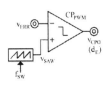 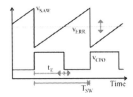

CP_{PWM}'s propagation delay $t_P \ll t_E$ and T_{SW} → No poles in A_{PWM}.

$$\frac{t_e}{v_{err}} = \frac{dt_E}{dv_{SAW}} \approx \frac{\Delta t_{E(MAX)}}{\Delta v_{SAW}} \approx \frac{T_{SW}}{V_{SAW(PP)}} \quad \therefore \quad A_{PWM} = \frac{d_e}{v_{err}} = \frac{t_e}{v_{err} T_{SW}} \approx \frac{1}{V_{SAW(PP)}}$$

7.5. Voltage Mode: Fixed Energizing Time

Constant Energizing-Time Buck:

SR flip flop decouples energizing from drain commands.

CP_{ERR} senses output v_O and adjusts drain time t_D and $v_{O(MIN)}$.

"One shot" sets energizing time T_E and $v_{O(MAX)}$.

z_{ESR} saves phase at or below p_{LC}^2 $\therefore$ $R_{C.ESR} > R_{C.ESR(MIN)} > 0$.

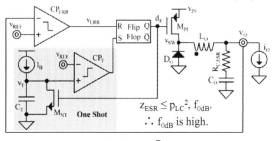

$$A_{LG} = A_{ERR}A_{BUCK} = \left(\frac{d_e}{v_o}\right)\left(\frac{v_o}{d_e}\right) \left.\right] \quad \begin{array}{l} A_{ERR0} \\ A_{PWM0}, p_{LC}^2, z_{ESR} \end{array}$$

7.5. Voltage Mode: Fixed Energizing Time

i_L's ripple Δi_L flows through C_O's $R_{C.ESR}$ and $L_{C.ESL}$ into C_O.

$\therefore \Delta v_O = v_{ESR} + v_{ESL} + v_{CO}$.

Since $R_{C.ESR} > R_{C.ESR(MIN)} > 0$, v_O rises and falls with i_L → v_O and i_L are in phase.

$\therefore v_{ESR} \gg v_{CO}, v_{ESL}$ → v_{CO} appears as slight curvature in v_O.

→ v_{ESL} appears when di_L/dt changes as small step.

$\therefore i_L$ and v_O rise across T_E.

One shot ends T_E.

i_L and v_O fall across t_D.

CP_{ERR} ends t_D when

v_O falls to v_{REF}.

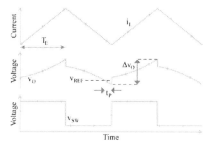

→ Propagation delay t_P extends output ripple Δv_O.

7.5. Voltage Mode: Comparator and One Shot

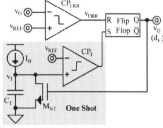

v_T is zero when v_Q is high → Across t_D.

CP_{ERR} resets v_Q → Starts "one shot" and T_E.

I_B charges C_T until

    CP_T senses v_T reaches v_{REF}.

        → CP_T ends T_E and starts t_D.

v_O falls with i_L until CP_{ERR} senses v_O drops to v_{REF}.

        → CP_{ERR} ends t_D and starts another T_E.

$\therefore$
$$T_E = C_T\left(\frac{v_{REF}}{I_B}\right) \qquad d_L = \frac{T_E}{t_{sw}} = \frac{T_E}{T_E + t_D}$$

$$\frac{t_d}{v_o} = \frac{dt_D}{dv_O} \approx \frac{dt_D}{di_L R_{C.ESR}} = \frac{L_O}{\left(v_{IN} - v_O\right)R_{C.ESR}}$$

$$A_{ERR} = \frac{d_e}{v_o} = \frac{dd_E}{dv_O} = \left(\frac{dd_E}{dt_{SW}}\right)\left(\frac{dt_{SW}}{dt_D}\right)\left(\frac{dt_D}{dv_O}\right) = \left(\frac{-T_E}{T_{SW}^2}\right)(1)\left(\frac{dt_D}{dv_O}\right)$$

7.5. Voltage Mode: Fixed Output Ripple

Keep v_O within hysteresis window v_{HYS} about reference v_{REF}.

Modulate duty cycle d_E with a nearly constant ripple Δv_O at v_{HYS}.

Hysteretic Buck:

    CP_{ERR} senses v_O.

    CP_{ERR} pulse-width modulates power switch M_{PI} according to v_O.

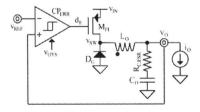

z_{ESR} saves phase at or below p_{LC}^2.

    $\therefore R_{C.ESR} > R_{C.ESR(MIN)} > 0$.

    $\therefore$ Output v_O rises and falls with i_L.

$z_{ESR} \leq p_{LC}^2$, f_{0dB} $\therefore$ f_{0dB} is high.

$$A_{LG} = A_{ERR}A_{BUCK} = \left(\frac{d_e}{v_o}\right)\left(\frac{v_o}{d_e}\right) \quad \left.\begin{array}{l} A_{ERR0} \\ A_{PWM0}, p_{LC}^2, z_{ESR} \end{array}\right.$$

7.5. Voltage Mode: Hysteretic Comparator

Hysteretic comparator CP_E compares v_{REF} with the rippling v_O.

Output v_{CPO} rises until v_{ERR} reaches upper threshold V_{TH+} → t_E ends.

Output v_{CPO} falls until v_{ERR} reaches lower threshold V_{TH-} → t_D ends.

 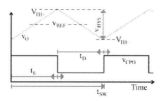

$$\frac{t_e}{v_o} = \frac{dt_E}{dv_O} \approx \frac{T_E}{\Delta v_O} \approx \frac{D_E T_{SW}}{V_{HYS}} \qquad \therefore \qquad A_{ERR} = \frac{d_e}{v_o} = \frac{t_e}{v_o t_{sw}} \approx \frac{D_E}{V_{HYS}}$$

System responds within one clock cycle $\therefore f_{0dB} \approx f_{SW}$.

7.5. Voltage Mode: Fixed Output Ripple – Noise

Switching events produce noise.

If v_{HYS} is low, switching noise can trip comparator and produce glitches.

Reduce Sensitivity:

$R_{FB}C_{FB}$ filters high-frequency noise.

C_{AC} momentarily overdrives v_{FB} to raise noise margin.

If $R_{FB} \gg Z_{CFB}$, overdrive v_{OD} is:

$$v_{OD} \approx v_{IN}\left(\frac{C_{AC}}{C_{AC} + C_{FB}}\right)$$

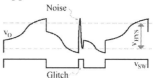 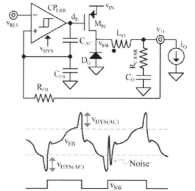

7.5. Voltage Mode: Fixed Output Ripple – Low ESR

Recall: R_{ESR} introduces z_{ESR} to recover phase lost to p_{LC}^2.

Fix: Bypass $L_O C_O$ with $R_{FF} C_{FF}$'s gain A_{FF} before loop gain A_{LG} reaches f_{0dB}.

This way, $L_O C_O$'s effects disappear from feedback signal v_{FB}.

LC-Bypassed Hysteretic Buck → Low-ESR Hysteretic Buck

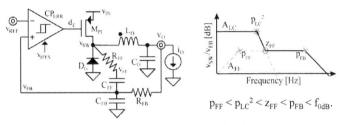

$$p_{FF} < p_{LC}^2 < z_{FF} < p_{FB} < f_{0dB}.$$

A_{FF} is low at low frequency, so $L_O C_O$'s gain A_{LC} dominates.

A_{FF} rises as C_{FF} shorts and flattens when $Z_{CFF} \leq R_{FF}$ at $p_{FF} = 1/2\pi R_{FF} C_{FF}$.

A_{FF} bypasses A_{LC} when $A_{LC} = A_{FF}$.

A_{FF} falls when parasitic capacitance C_{FB} shunts R_{FF} at $p_{FB} \approx 1/2\pi R_{FF} C_{FB}$.

7.5. Voltage Mode: Fixed Output Ripple – Low ESR

Operation:

$R_{FB} C_{FB}$ filters high-frequency noise.

R_{FF} overdrives v_{FB}, so C_{AC} is not needed.

Near f_{0dB}, $A_{FF} > A_{LC}$.

$\therefore \Delta v_{FB} \approx v_{HYS} > \Delta v_O$.

→ Δv_O is low and v_{FB} is less sensitive to noise in v_O.

$v_{FF(AVG)} = v_{SW(AVG)} = v_{O(AVG)}$, so

$$\frac{dv_{FB}}{dt}\bigg|_{Rise} = \frac{i_C}{C_{FF}} \approx \frac{v_{IN} - v_{O(AVG)}}{R_{FF} C_{FF}} \approx \frac{v_E}{R_{FF} C_{FF}} \propto \frac{di_L^+}{dt} \qquad \frac{dv_{FB}}{dt}\bigg|_{Fall} = \frac{i_C}{C_{FF}} \approx \frac{-v_{O(AVG)}}{R_{FF} C_{FF}} \approx \frac{v_D}{R_{FF} C_{FF}} \propto \frac{di_L^-}{dt}$$

$\therefore v_{FB}$ rises and falls with i_L (i.e., preserves d_E) without $R_{C.ESR}$.

Loop responds quickly to v_{FB} variations.

$R_{FB} C_{FB}$ delays v_O-to-v_{FB} translations → Slows load-dump response slightly.

7.5. Voltage Mode: Notes on Fixed Output Ripple

No component of a duty-cycled v_O rises and falls with i_L → Hysteretic is not easy.

How fast v_{FB} reaches thresholds sets t_E and t_D ∴ $f_{SW} = f(v_{HYS}, di_L/dt, R_{FF}, C_{FB})$.

CP_E's propagation delay t_p extends v_{FB}'s ripple Δv_{FB}.

∴ Δv_{FB} is slightly greater than CP_E's v_{HYS} and effective $v_{HYS}' > v_{HYS}$.

Feature: Loop reacts within one cycle → $f_{0dB} \geq f_{SW}$ → Fast (limited by t_p).

Drawback: $f_{SW} \neq$ Clock → Not well defined → Less suppressible.

Other names for hysteretic buck:

Self-oscillating, free-running,

bang-bang, bi-stable, two-state,

sliding-mode, and ripple dc–dc converter.

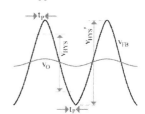

7.5. Current Mode

Concept: Regulate i_L above f_{0dB} to perceive L_O's i_L as current source below f_{0dB}.

Feature: Eliminating small-signal dynamics in i_L removes L_O's pole p_L.

Loops: Outer loop regulates v_O up to outer loop's bandwidth f_{0dB}.

Inner loop regulates i_L up to inner loop's bandwidth $f_{I.0dB}$.

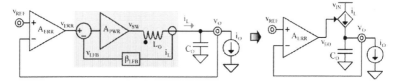

Feature: z_{ESR} can be high ∴ $R_{C.ESR}$ and therefore Δv_O can be low.

Requirements: Since $f_{I.0dB}$ is a pole in system's loop gain A_{LG},

∴ C_O's pole $p_C < f_{0dB} < f_{I.0dB} < f_{SW}$.

Inner loop should be stable.

7.5. Current Loop

Inductor current i_L depends on the voltage v_L across inductor L_O.

v_{IN} does not carry feedback signals → v_{in} in v_E and v_D disappears.

L_O may not energize to v_O (like in boost), but always drains to v_O.

$$\therefore \quad i_L = \frac{v_L}{sL_O + R_{L.ESR}} = \frac{v_E d_E + v_D d_D}{sL_O + R_{L.ESR}} \quad \text{and} \quad i_l = d_e\left(\frac{di_L}{dd_E}\right) - v_o\left(\frac{di_L}{dv_O}\right)$$

$$d_e = -d_d \qquad v_o = i_l\,[R_O\|(1/sC_O + R_{C.ESR})]$$

$$i_l = \frac{d_e\left(V_E - V_D\right) - v_o D_O}{sL_O + R_{L.ESR}} = \frac{d_e\left(V_E - V_D\right)}{sL_O + R_{L.ESR} + \left[R_O \,\|\, \left(\dfrac{1}{sC_O} + R_{C.ESR}\right)\right]D_O}$$

$\therefore i_l$ is inductor voltage per cycle $v_l = d_e(V_E - V_D)$ over duty-cycled impedance.

7.5. Current Loop

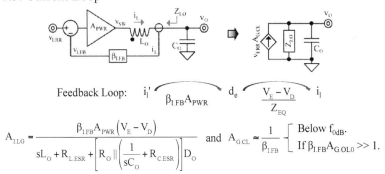

Feedback Loop: $\quad i_l' \xrightarrow{\beta_{LFB}A_{PWR}} d_e \xrightarrow{\dfrac{V_E - V_D}{Z_{EQ}}} i_l$

$$A_{LLG} = \frac{\beta_{LFB}A_{PWR}\left(V_E - V_D\right)}{sL_O + R_{L.ESR} + \left[R_O \,\|\, \left(\dfrac{1}{sC_O} + R_{C.ESR}\right)\right]D_O} \quad \text{and} \quad A_{G.CL} \approx \frac{1}{\beta_{LFB}} \begin{cases} \text{Below } f_{0dB}. \\ \text{If } \beta_{LFB}A_{G.OL0} \gg 1. \end{cases}$$

C_O shorts R_O → z_{CO}, $R_{C.ESR}$ limits i_C → p_{CESR}, and L_O overwhelms ESR's → p_{LESR}.

$\therefore$ Loop gain A_{LLG} drops to f_{0dB} at -20 dB/decade → Stable.

$$Z_{LO} = \frac{v_o}{-i_L} = \frac{-i_L\beta_{LFB}A_{PWR} - i_L L_O s}{-i_L} = \beta_{LFB}A_{PWR} + L_O s \begin{cases} \beta_{LFB}A_{PWR} \text{ at low frequency} \to R_L. \\ L_O s \text{ at high frequency} \to L_O. \end{cases}$$

7.5. Current Loop

Since $Z_{LO} = \beta_{I.FB}A_{PWR} + L_Os$.

$Z_{LO} \approx \beta_{I.FB}A_{PWR}$ at low frequency $\therefore p_C \approx 1/2\pi(\beta_{I.FB}A_{PWR}\|R_O)C_O$.

$Z_{LO} \approx L_Os$ at high frequency $\therefore v_o$ falls with a decoupling pole.

When $L_Os \geq \beta_{I.FB}A_{PWR}$ $\rightarrow$ $p_L \approx \beta_{I.FB}A_{PWR}/2\pi L_O$.

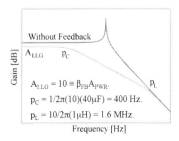 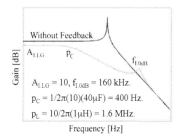

$$p_{LC}{}^2 = 1/2\pi(1\mu H)^{1/2}(40\mu F)^{1/2} = 25\ kHz$$

Past loop's BW $f_{I.0dB}$, feedback fades $\therefore A_{ILG}$ peaks near $f_{I.0dB}$.

7.5. Current Loop

Validation:

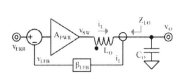

$$\frac{v_O}{v_{ERR}} = \left(\frac{i_L}{v_{ERR}}\right)\left(\frac{v_O}{i_L}\right) = \left(\frac{i_L}{v_{ERR}}\right)\left(\frac{1}{C_Os}\right)$$

$$i_L = \frac{v_{SW}}{Z_{LC}} = \frac{(v_{ERR} - i_L\beta_{I.FB})A_{PWR}}{L_Os + \dfrac{1}{C_Os}}$$

$\therefore$

$$\frac{v_O}{v_{ERR}} = \frac{A_{PWR}}{L_Os + \dfrac{1}{C_Os} + \beta_{I.FB}A_{PWR}}\left(\frac{1}{C_Os}\right) = \frac{A_{PWR}}{L_OC_Os^2 + 1 + \beta_{I.FB}A_{PWR}C_Os}$$

At low frequency, s^2 term is negligible $\therefore p_C \approx 1/2\pi\beta_{I.FB}A_{PWR}C_O$.

At high frequency, s^0 is negligible $\therefore p_L \approx \beta_{I.FB}A_{PWR}/2\pi L_O$.

7.5. Average Current Mode

Regulate duty cycle d_E with a constant switching period T_{SW}.

Regulate L_O's average current $i_{L(AVG)}$.

Average Current-Mode Buck:

A_{ERR} senses output v_O and generates error signal v_{ERR}.

A_I's RC network averages inductor current i_L to $v_{I(AVG)}$ with a pole p_I.

CP_{PWM} pulse-width modulates power switch M_{PI} according to $v_{I(AVG)}$.

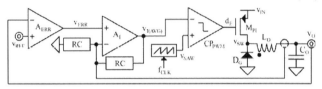

$f_{0dB} < f_{I.0dB} < f_{SW}.$ $p_C < f_{0dB} < f_{I.0dB}, p_L.$ p_I slows $f_{I.0dB}$ ∴ f_{0dB} is low.

$$A_{LG} = A_{ERR}A_{G.CL}A_{BUCK} = \left(\frac{v_{err}}{v_o}\right)\left(\frac{i_1}{v_{err}}\right)\left(\frac{v_o}{i_1}\right)\left.\begin{array}{l} A_{ERR0}, 1/\beta_{I.FB0}, f_{I.0dB} \\ R_O, p_C, p_L, z_{ESR} \end{array}\right.$$

7.5. Average Current Mode

Closed-Loop Gain:

$$\frac{i_1}{v_{err}} \approx \frac{1}{\beta_{I.FB}} = \frac{1}{R_{EQ}}$$

Waveforms:

Δv_O and Δv_{ERR} are small in steady state.

A_{ERR}'s v_{ERR} adjusts $v_{I(AVG)}$ → Sets $i_{L(AVG)}$.

A_I's and RC's $v_{I(AVG)}$ adjusts t_E.

f_{CLK} ends t_D → Sets T_{SW}.

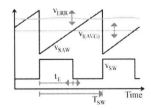

7.5. Peak Current Mode

Regulate duty cycle d_E with a constant switching period T_{SW}.

Regulate L_O's positive peak current $i_{L(PK+)}$.

Peak Current-Mode Buck:

A_{ERR} senses output v_O and generates error signal v_{ERR}.

SR flip flop decouples energizing from drain commands.

CP_I regulates $i_{L(PK+)}$ and f_{CLK} sets $i_{L(PK-)}$.

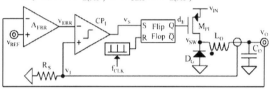

$f_{0dB} < f_{I.0dB} < f_{SW}.$ $p_C < f_{0dB} < f_{I.0dB}, p_L.$ No pole slows $f_{I.0dB}$ ∴ f_{0dB} is higher.

$$A_{LG} = A_{ERR} A_{G.CL} A_{BUCK} = \left(\frac{v_{err}}{v_o}\right)\left(\frac{i_l}{v_{err}}\right)\left(\frac{v_o}{i_l}\right) \quad \Big] \quad \begin{array}{l} A_{ERR0}, 1/\beta_{I.FB0}, f_{I.0dB} \\ R_O, p_C, p_L, z_{ESR} \end{array}$$

7.5. Peak Current Mode

Since $v_I = i_L R_S$, v_I rises and falls with i.

∴ $v_{I(PK+)} = i_{L(PK+)} R_S$ and $v_{I(PK-)} = i_{L(PK-)} R_S.$

Operation:

A_{ERR}'s v_{ERR} adjusts $v_{I(PK+)}$ → Sets $i_{L(PK+)}$.

i_L's v_I into CP_I sets flip flop

and adjusts t_E → $v_{ERR} \approx v_{I(PK+)} = i_{L(PK+)} R_S.$

f_{CLK} resets flip flop and ends t_D → Sets T_{SW}.

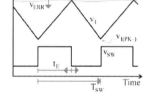

Closed-Loop Gain: Since T_{SW} is constant, $\Delta t_E = t_e = -\Delta t_D = -t_d$ ∴

$$i_{l(pk+)} = \left(\frac{V_E}{L_O}\right)t_e \qquad \text{and} \qquad i_{l(pk-)} = \left(\frac{V_D}{L_O}\right)t_d = -\left(\frac{V_D}{L_O}\right)t_e = -i_{l(pk+)}\left(\frac{V_D}{V_E}\right)$$

∴

$$i_l = 0.5\left(i_{l(pk+)} + i_{l(pk-)}\right) = 0.5 i_{l(pk+)}\left(1 - \frac{V_D}{V_E}\right) \rightarrow \frac{i_l}{v_{err}} = \left(\frac{i_{l(pk+)}}{v_{err}}\right)\left(\frac{i_l}{i_{l(pk+)}}\right) \approx \left(\frac{1}{R_S}\right)\left[0.5\left(1 - \frac{V_D}{V_E}\right)\right]$$

7.5. Peak Current Mode: Sub-Harmonic Oscillations

Load dumps to v_{IN} or v_O can vary di_L/dt enough to produce an imbalance Δi_0 in L_O.

Under peak-current control with a constant period T_{SW},

t_E variations cause equal, but opposite changes in $t_D \rightarrow \Delta t_E = -\Delta t_D$.

Δi_0 varies t_E, which changes t_D to produce another imbalance Δi_1 $\therefore$

Energize Slope   Drain Slope   Buck: $v_E = v_{IN} - v_O$, $v_D = -v_O$, $d_E = v_O/v_{IN}$.

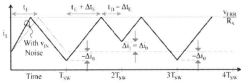

$$\Delta i_0 \overset{\displaystyle -\frac{L_O}{v_E}}{} \Delta t_E \overset{\displaystyle -1}{} \Delta t_D \overset{\displaystyle \frac{v_D}{L_O}}{} \Delta i_1 = \Delta i_0 \left(\frac{v_D}{v_E}\right) = \Delta i_0 \left(\frac{-v_O}{v_{IN} - v_O}\right) = -\Delta i_0 \left(\frac{d_E}{1-d_E}\right)$$

T_{SW} = Constant

$\therefore$ When $d_E = 50\% \rightarrow v_O = 0.5 v_{IN} \rightarrow \Delta i_1 = -\Delta i_0$.

$\rightarrow$ Each cycle reproduces an opposing imbalance that sustains oscillations.

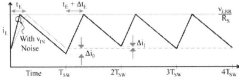

Boost: $v_E = v_{IN}$, $v_D = v_{IN} - v_O$, and $1 - d_E = v_{IN}/v_O$ $\rightarrow$ Same Δi_1 and issues at $d_E = 50\%$.

7.5. Peak Current Mode: Sub-Harmonic Oscillations

When $d_E < 50\% \rightarrow v_O < 0.5 v_{IN} \rightarrow |\Delta i_1| < |\Delta i_0|$.

$\therefore$ Imbalance diminishes across cycles $\rightarrow$ Oscillations die.

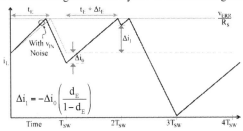

When $d_E > 50\% \rightarrow v_O > 0.5 v_{IN} \rightarrow |\Delta i_1| > |\Delta i_0|$.

$\therefore$ Imbalance grows across cycles $\rightarrow$ Oscillations grow.

$$\Delta i_1 = -\Delta i_0 \left(\frac{d_E}{1-d_E}\right)$$

7.5. Peak Current Mode: Slope Compensation

Fix: Reduce Δi_0-to-Δt_E gain translation with an opposing slope in $i_{L(PK)}$.

Slope Compensation: Add $v_D/2L_O$ slope to $i_{L(PK)}$ $\rightarrow$ To v_{ERR}/R_S.

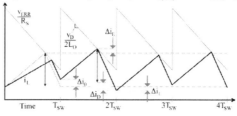

$i_{L(PK)}$ slope projects Δt_E.

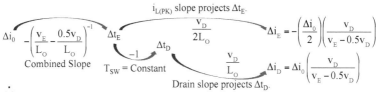

$$\Delta i_0 \quad -\left(\frac{v_E}{L_O} - \frac{0.5v_D}{L_O}\right)^{-1} \Delta t_E$$

$$\frac{v_D}{2L_O} \qquad \Delta i_E = -\left(\frac{\Delta i_0}{2}\right)\left(\frac{v_D}{v_E - 0.5v_D}\right)$$

Combined Slope $\qquad \Delta t_D$

$T_{SW} = \text{Constant}$ $\qquad -1 \qquad \frac{v_D}{L_O} \qquad \Delta i_D = \Delta i_0\left(\frac{v_D}{v_E - 0.5v_D}\right)$

Drain slope projects Δt_D.

$$\therefore$$

$$\Delta i_1 = \Delta i_E + \Delta i_D = \left(\frac{\Delta i_0}{2}\right)\left(\frac{v_D}{v_E - 0.5v_D}\right) = \Delta i_0\left(\frac{-d_E}{2 - d_E}\right) \rightarrow |\Delta i_1| < |\Delta i_0| \text{ because } 2 - d_E > 1.$$

$$\therefore \text{ Imbalance diminishes.}$$

7.5. Peak Current Mode: Slope Compensation

Dampen sub-harmonic oscillations with slope compensation.

Slope-Compensated Peak Current-Mode Buck:

A_{ERR} senses output v_O and generates error signal v_{ERR}.

SR flip flop decouples energizing from drain commands.

Summing comparator CP_I adds slope to v_{ERR}.

CP_I regulates $i_{L(PK+)}$ and f_{CLK} sets $i_{L(PK-)}$.

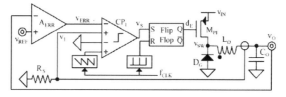

Slope compensation in a buck converter is only needed when $d_E \geq 50\%$.

7.5. Hysteretic Current Mode

A hysteretic (relaxation) oscillator sets a constant current ripple Δi_L.

The voltage loop adjusts L_O's average current $i_{L(AVG)}$.

Hysteretic Current-Mode Buck:

A_{ERR} senses output v_O and generates error signal v_{ERR}.

Hysteretic comparator CP_I sets Δi_L and adjusts $i_{L(AVG)}$.

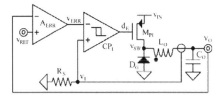

$$p_C < f_{0dB} < p_{LBW}, \; p_L < f_{OSC} = f_{SW}.$$

$$A_{LG} = A_{ERR} A_{OSC} A_{BUCK} = \left(\frac{v_{err}}{v_o}\right)\left(\frac{i_{l(avg)}}{v_{err}}\right)\left(\frac{v_o}{i_l}\right) \quad\left]\begin{array}{l} A_{ERR0}, A_{OSC0}, p_{LBW} \\ R_O, p_C, p_L, z_{ESR} \end{array}\right.$$

7.5. Hysteretic Current Mode: Hysteretic Oscillator

Hysteretic comparator CP_I compares rippling $i_L R_S$ with slow-moving v_{ERR}.

i_L rises until $i_L R_S$ reaches upper threshold $v_{ERR} + 0.5 V_{HYS}$ → t_E ends.

i_L falls until $i_L R_S$ reaches lower threshold $v_{ERR} - 0.5 V_{HYS}$ → t_D ends.

∴ $\quad \Delta i_L R_S \approx V_{HYS} \quad$ and $\quad i_{L(AVG)} R_S \approx v_{ERR}.$

$$\rightarrow \Delta i_L \approx \frac{V_{HYS}}{R_S} \qquad \rightarrow A_{OSC0} = \frac{i_{L(AVG)}}{v_{ERR}} = \frac{i_{l(avg)}}{v_{err}} \approx \frac{1}{R_S}$$

CP_I responds to v_{ERR} within one clock cycle.

Except, i_L's di_L/dt slews and delays the response,

like a pole would → Bandwidth limited.

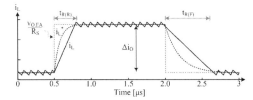

7.5. Hysteretic Current Mode: Hysteretic Oscillator

RC Bandwidth Model: $R_{EQ}C_{EQ}$ time-constant models delay.

Time required for i_L to slew to its target depends on load dump Δi_O:

$$t_L = \frac{\Delta i_{L(AVG)}}{di_L/dt} = \Delta i_{L(AVG)}\left(\frac{L_O}{v_L}\right) = \Delta i_O\left(\frac{L_O}{v_L}\right)$$

$R_{EQ}C_{EQ}$ requires four time constants to reach 98% of its target:

$$t_{RC} = R_{EQ}C_{EQ}\ln\left(\frac{1}{1-0.98}\right) = 4R_{EQ}C_{EQ} \equiv \frac{4}{2\pi p_{LBW}}$$

$R_{EQ}C_{EQ}$ pole models the oscillator's bandwidth p_{LBW}.

Since rising time t_L^+ differs from falling time t_L^-,

p_{LBW} reflects the average $\rightarrow t_{L(AVG)} = 0.5(t_L^+ + t_L^-)$.

$$\therefore \quad p_{LBW} \approx \left(\frac{4}{2\pi}\right)\left(\frac{1}{t_{L(AVG)}}\right) = \left(\frac{4}{2\pi}\right)\left(\frac{1}{\Delta i_O}\right)\left(\frac{v_E + v_D}{2L_O}\right)$$

Bandwidth changes with Δi_O and p_{LBW} is an RC approximation of average.

7.5. Digital Control

Replace analog front end with an analog-to-digital converter (ADC).

Use digital-signal processor (DSP) to adjust d_E according to v_O's error.

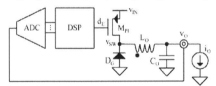

Feature: DSP can program modes, process multiple outputs, and

compensate response with less steady-state quiescent power.

Drawbacks: DSP occupies substantial silicon area.

Switching gates require considerable gate-drive power.

DSP requires many clock cycles to process an output.

$\rightarrow f_{0dB} \le f_{SW} \ll f_{CLK}$ $\therefore$ Slow load-dump response.

For a faster response, DSP should only adjust the loop variables

of an analog front end.

7.5. Summary and Conclusions

Control Objective: Establish dominant low-frequency pole.

Control Scheme

Modulate duty cycle d_E with fixed f_{SW}, t_E, t_{DE}, or Δv_O.

Adding a dominant pole slows loop response → Current mode is often faster.

Voltage Mode

z_{ESR} saves phase, but requires $R_{C.ESR}$ → Output ripple Δv_O is usually high.

DCM and PDCM exclude p_L and z_{RHP} → No compensation → Can be fast.

Pulse-width modulating (PWM) i_L fixes switching frequency f_{SW},

but system responds after several switching cycles → $f_{0dB} \ll f_{SW}$.

Hysteretic control fixes output ripple Δv_O or Δv_{FB}.

Can respond within one switching cycle → $f_{0dB} \approx f_{SW}$.

No need for $R_{C.ESR}$ when $R_{FF}C_{FF}$ bypasses L_OC_O (and delays response).

7.5. Summary and Conclusions

Voltage Mode Hysteretic (continued)

f_{SW} depends on v_{IN}, v_O, L_O or R_{FF}, and C_O → Less systemic.

Voltage-mode hysteretic control is straightforward only for bucks.

Current Mode

Current loop regulates i_L ∴ L_O behaves like a current source up to $f_{I.0dB}$.

→ Bandwidth requirement is $f_{0dB} \leq f_{I.0dB} \leq f_{SW}$.

L_O and C_O's complex poles p_{LC}^2 split ∴ p_C can be dominant and f_{0dB} high.

No need for z_{ESR} → No need for $R_{C.ESR}$ → Output ripple Δv_O can be low.

Must sense inductor current i_L → Higher power losses.

Peak-current control requires slope compensation when $d_E > 50\%$.

Peak and hysteretic are faster than average current.

Digital Control: Flexible, but also often slow and area intensive.

Chapter 8. Switched-Inductor Systems

8.1. Integration

8.2. Useful Circuits

8.3. Current Sensing

8.4. Boost Converters

8.5. Single-Inductor Multiple-Output Supplies

8.1. Integrated Circuit

Typical Design Sequence

Select process technology.

Select package.

Design system (i.e., architecture).

Determine block-level specifications.

Design die floor plan.

Design transistor-level circuits (i.e., blocks).

Design block layouts according to the floor plan.

Assemble top-level layout.

Extract top-level schematic from layout and simulate.

Submit IC design for fabrication (i.e., "tape-out" design).

Test and evaluate IC in the laboratory.

Iterate another design to fix possible bugs and complications.

8.1. Process Technology

Electric field intensifies with a shorter L_{MIN} $\therefore$ $|V_{GS(MAX)}|$ and $|V_{DS(MAX)}|$ drop.

Threshold $|V_{TH0}|$ is adjusted $\rightarrow$ V_{TH0} is independent of L_{MIN}.

T_{OX} falls with L_{MIN} $\therefore$ $C_{OX}"$ and K' rise.

L_{MIN}	0.5 μm N/P-MOS	0.35 μm N/P-MOS	0.18 μm N/P-MOS
$\|V_{GS(MAX)}\|$ $\|V_{DS(MAX)}\|$	4.5 V	3.3 V	1.8 V
$\|V_{TH0}\|$	0.86/0.8 V	0.5/0.6 V	0.65/0.58 V
T_{OX}	151 Å	74 Å	45 Å
$C_{OX}"$	2.3 fF/μm^2	4.5 fF/μm^2	7.7 fF/μm^2
$K' = \mu_{N/P}C_{OX}"$	47/12.5 μA/V^2	89/33 μA/V^2	135/35 μA/V^2

Since R_{MOS}, C_G, and g_m depend on L_{MIN} and $C_{OX}"$,

conduction, gate-drive, and quiescent losses and efficiency vary with process node.

8.1. Process Technology

Conduction Losses P_R

Rise in $C_{OX}"$ partially offsets drop in $|V_{GS(MAX)}|$ $\therefore$ P_R falls with L_{MIN}/W_{OPT}.

$$P_R \propto R_{MOS} \propto \frac{L_{MIN}}{C_{OX}"W_{OPT}\left|V_{GS(MAX)} - V_{TH0}\right|} \propto \frac{L_{MIN}}{W_{OPT}}$$

Gate-Drive Losses P_G

Rise in $C_{OX}"$ offsets drop in L_{MIN} $\therefore$ P_G falls with $W_{OPT}L_{MIN}{}^2$.

$$P_G \propto C_G V_{DS(MAX)}{}^2 \propto C_{OX}"W_{OPT}L_{MIN} V_{DS(MAX)}{}^2 \propto W_{OPT} L_{MIN}{}^2$$

Quiescent Losses P_Q

For same f_{0dB}, i_Q falls with $L_{MIN}{}^2$ $\therefore$ $P_{Q(BW)}$ falls with $L_{MIN}{}^3$.

$$f_{0dB} \propto \frac{g_{m(MOS)}}{C_{PAR}} \propto \frac{\sqrt{i_{Q(BW)}}}{C_{OX}"} \qquad i_Q \propto C_{OX}"^2 \propto L_{MIN}{}^2 \qquad P_{Q(BW)} = i_Q v_{IN} \propto L_{MIN}{}^2 V_{DS(MAX)} \propto L_{MIN}{}^3$$

And for slow bias circuits, $P_{Q(B)}$ falls with L_{MIN}.

$$P_{Q(B)} = i_{Q(B)} v_{IN} \propto V_{DS(MAX)} \propto L_{MIN}$$

8.1. Process Technology

Optimum Width W_{OPT}

Fall in P_R should balance rise in P_G $\therefore$ W_{OPT} climbs with fall in $\sqrt{L_{MIN}}$.

$$\frac{dP_R}{dL_{MIN}} \propto \frac{1}{C_{OX}" W_{OPT} \left| V_{GS(MAX)} - V_{TH0} \right|} \equiv \frac{dP_G}{dL_{MIN}} \propto C_{OX}" W_{OPT} V_{DS(MAX)}{}^2$$

$$W_{OPT} \propto \frac{1}{\sqrt{C_{OX}"^2 \left| V_{GS(MAX)} - V_{TH0} \right| V_{DS(MAX)}{}^2}} \propto \frac{1}{\sqrt{\left| V_{GS(MAX)} - V_{TH0} \right|}}$$

$\therefore$ P_R and P_G fall with $L_{MIN}{}^{1.5}$.

$$P_R \propto \frac{L_{MIN}}{W_{OPT}} \propto L_{MIN}{}^{1.5}$$

$$P_G \propto W_{OPT} L_{MIN}{}^2 \propto L_{MIN}{}^{1.5}$$

And efficiency improves

with reductions in L_{MIN}.

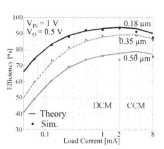

8.1. Package

Considerations

Number of pins: Consider application.

Package material: Consider package stress on die, ambient and

junction temperatures T_A and T_J, etc. (e.g., ceramic, plastic, etc.).

Type: Consider space requirements (e.g., small-outline IC SOIC,

shrink small-outline package SSOP, quad-flat no leads QFN, etc.).

Size: Consider die area.

Heat transfer: Consider power dissipation and heat flow

(e.g., power-padded package, heat sinks, heat pipes,

fan on the printed-circuit board PCB).

8.1. Package: Heat

Power switches and other circuits generate heat when they dissipate power.

∴ Junction temperature $T_J <$ Ambient temperature T_A.

∴ T_J rises with power consumption $P_{IC} \rightarrow T_J \propto P_{IC}$.

A plastic package melts at roughly 170° C ∴ T_J should be less than 150° C.

Typical Specification: $T_{A(MAX)}$ is 125° C ∴ T_J is higher.

Convention: T_A refers to temperature at the edge of the package.

Heat Flow:

Thermogram

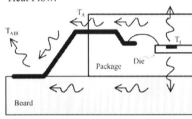

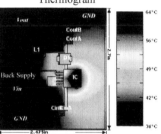

8.1. Package: Thermal Model

$T_{AB} \equiv \Delta T_{AB} =$ Power $P_X \times$ Thermal Resistance $\theta_{AB} \rightarrow V_{AB} = I_X R_{AB}$.

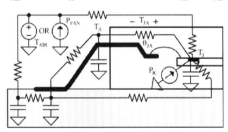

$T_{JA} = P_{IC}\theta_{JA}$ ∴ $T_J = T_A + T_{JA} = T_A + P_{IC}\theta_{JA}$.

Typical thermal resistances and capacitances (i.e., thermal time constants):

$\theta_{JA} \approx 30\text{–}300$ °C/W, $C_J \approx 1.2\text{–}200$ mJ/°C, and $C_A \approx 1\text{–}20$ J/°C

Assuming $T_{AIR} \equiv T_A$ in θ_{JA} measurements is practical.

For widest temperature range, keep P_{IC} and θ_{JA} low.

8.1. Die: Floor Plan for Noise

Categorize into

Sensitive blocks: Bias, v_{REF}, feedback amplifier, etc.

Noisy (switching) sensitive blocks: Feedback comparator.

Noise generators: High-current drivers, power switches, DSP, etc.

Quiet insensitive blocks: Protection, trim, monitors, etc.

Separate sensitive, noisy sensitive, and noisy signals, blocks, pads, and pins.

Place quiet insensitive blocks between them as noise buffers.

Separate noise regions and isolate with deep N- and P-type guard rings

to collect and block lateral substrate current.

Use ground and supply metal and diffusion planes and lines to shunt noise.

Separate analog from power grounds and supplies.

Star ("Kelvin")-connect supplies on the board (if possible), pin, or pad.

Sprinkle substrate contacts throughout the die to suppress ground bounce.

8.1. Die: Floor Plan for Power and Matching

Use multiple pads, bond wires, and pins (if possible) for high-current paths.

Place power blocks near their corresponding high-current pads.

Select pad–pin combinations with short bond-wire lengths for high-current paths.

Shorten high-current paths and at-speed signals to lower R and RC delays.

Place electrostatic-discharge (ESD) protection circuits next to pads.

Guard-ring ESD circuits to collect stray ESD carriers.

Separate and star-connect low- and high-current paths to lower IR drops.

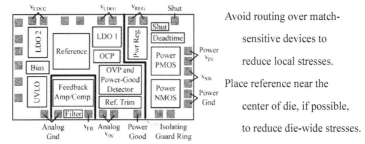

Avoid routing over match-sensitive devices to reduce local stresses.

Place reference near the center of die, if possible, to reduce die-wide stresses.

8.1. Off-Chip Components

Discrete inductors typically outperform

(i.e., lower $R_{L.ESR}$ and higher L_O)

on-chip inductors by orders

of magnitude.

One in-package inductor achieves

SiP footprint objectives.

Practicable nH–µH inductances

are possible with

MEMS-based magnetic cores.

One or two in-package flip-chip capacitors

achieve SiP footprint objectives.

Tiny Off-Chip Inductors

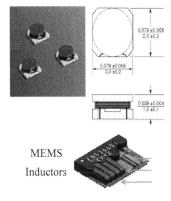

MEMS Inductors

Flip-Chip Capacitors

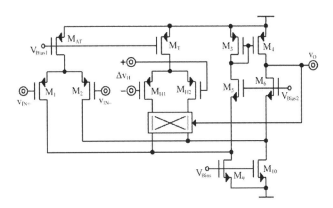

8.2. Useful Circuits

8.2. Startup

Problem: v_O starts at zero, feedback loop maxes i_L to raise v_O to target.

→ Sudden inrush of current can damage components in power path.

Option 1: Limit i_L to $i_{L(MAX)}$ with over-current protection (OCP).

→ OCP engages until v_O reaches target, so

Drawback: v_O is not well-controlled.

Option 2: Start the reference v_{REF} at zero and raise slowly to its final state.

→ v_O rises slowly to target.

Digital: DAC generates v_{REF} and counter and clock raise v_{REF}.

→ Generates switching noise and occupies substantial silicon area.

Analog: Short v_{REF} to ground and slew to target.

→ Noise-free and compact.

Drawback: Requires dedicated or buffered (degraded) v_{REF}.

8.2. Startup

Option 3: Bypass feedback amplifier's or comparator's M_{REF} with M_{SLOW}.

Regulate v_O to ramping v_{SLOW} until v_{SLOW} surpasses v_{REF}.

Operation:

v_{FB} starts at zero ∴ M_{REF} is off and M_{SLOW}–M_{FB} regulates v_{FB} to v_{SLOW}.

When v_{SLOW} surpasses v_{REF}, M_{SLOW} shuts ∴ M_{REF}–M_{FB} regulates v_{FB} to v_{REF}.

Features: Fast, accurate, and small silicon area.

Design Notes:

M_{SLOW} need not match M_{REF}–M_{FB} well.

→ M_{SLOW} can be small and off to side.

M_{SLOW}'s C_D slows circuit

∴ Feed i_{REF} and i_{FB} into current

buffers (into low-impedance nodes).

If $I_S = K_S v_{REF}$, $t_{START} = C_S \left(\dfrac{v_{REF}}{I_S} \right) = \dfrac{C_S}{K_S} \neq f(v_{REF})$.

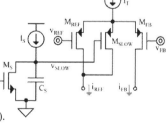

8.2. Load-Dump Compensation

Concept: Centering the combined load-dump variation $2\Delta v_{LD(MAX)}$ about v_{REF}

can cut the total variation in half: From $2\Delta v_{LD(MAX)}$ to $\Delta v_{LD(MAX)}$.

How: Incorporate, center, and tune a load-induced variation.

$$v_{REF}' = v_{REF} + 0.5\Delta v_{LD(MAX)} - i_O R_{EQ} \quad \text{where} \quad i_{O(MAX)} R_{EQ} \equiv \Delta v_{LD(MAX)}.$$

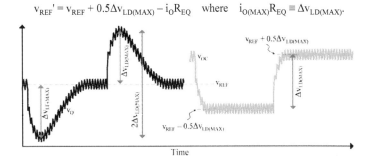

Notes: Actual response to load-dump $\Delta v_{LD(MAX)}$ remains unchanged.

Amounts to intentional (and tuned) load-regulation effect: $v_O \propto -i_O R_{EQ}$.

8.2. Load-Dump Compensation

Implementation:

Raise target by $0.5\Delta v_{LD(MAX)}$ to $v_{REF} + 0.5\Delta v_{LD(MAX)}$.

Sense i_O via i_L.

Translate to voltage v_I with R_S.

Subtract v_I from target with a summing amplifier or comparator.

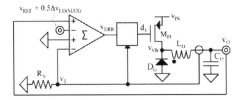

Note that sensing i_L requires a circuit that dissipates power.

8.2. Comparators: Hysteresis

Noise produces uncertainty in transition and jitter at the output.

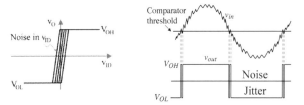

Hysteresis in the comparator suppresses noise jitter.

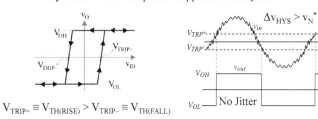

$$V_{TRIP+} \equiv V_{TH(RISE)} > V_{TRIP-} \equiv V_{TH(FALL)}$$

8.2. Hysteretic Comparators: Current-Induced Hysteresis

i_H and state of v_O produce an offset that v_{ID} must overcome to trip the comparator.

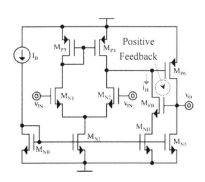

When v_{IN+} rises towards v_{IN-},

v_O is initially low,

$\therefore$ M_{FB} is off and i_H is 0, so

v_O rises when i_2 overcomes i_1.

When v_{IN+} falls towards v_{IN-},

v_O is initially high,

$\therefore$ M_{FB} is on and $i_H > 0$, so

v_O falls when i_1 overcomes $i_2 + i_H$.

Hysteresis is asymmetrical: $V_{TH+} + V_{TH-} \neq 0$.

8.2. Hysteretic Comparators: Hysteretic Load

When v_{I1} rises towards v_{I2},

v_{O1} is initially high,

$\therefore$ M_{P3}–M_{P6} is off and v_{O1} falls

when i_1 overcomes $i_2(S_5/S_4)$.

When v_{I1} falls towards v_{I2},

v_{O2} is initially high,

$\therefore$ M_{P4}–M_{P5} is off and v_{O2} falls

when i_2 overcomes $i_1(S_6/S_3)$.

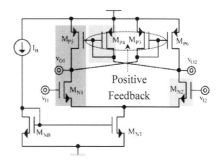

Since i_1 and i_2 must overcome $i_{2,1}(S_{5,6}/S_{4,3})$,

i_1 and i_2 must surpass $0.5I_T$ by some margin to induce a transition.

Note S_6/S_3 and S_5/S_4 set the symmetry of the hysteresis.

8.2. Hysteretic Comparators: Voltage-Induced Hysteresis

Δv_H produces an offset that v_{ID} must overcome to transition v_O.

Summing comparator adds offset Δv_H when v_O is low

and subtracts offset Δv_H when v_O is high $\therefore$ $V_{TRIP+} = \left| V_{TRIP-} \right| = \Delta v_H \left(\dfrac{g_{mH1,2}}{g_{m1,2}} \right)$.

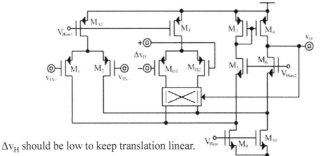

Δv_H should be low to keep translation linear.

M_{H1}–M_{H2} should match M_1–M_2.

Hysteresis is symmetrical.

8.2. Ramp Generator

Clock-Synchronized Ramp:

Current source I_R slews C_R and ramps v_R.

Clock f_{CLK} ends ramp and resets v_R.

Inverter INV_R and M_F restart ramp.

Diode D_R offsets ramp.

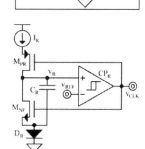

Ramp-Generating Clock:

I_R ramps v_R and D_R offsets ramp.

Comparator CP_R ends ramp and resets v_R

when v_R surpasses V_{TH+}.

After CP_R's propagation delay t_p,

CP$_R$ restarts ramp → t_p should be long enough for M_{NF} to reset v_R.

8.2. Gate Driver

Small inverters cannot drive large gates quickly.

∴ Build drive with chain of increasingly sized inverters:

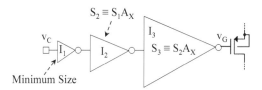

Minimum propagation delay $t_{P(MIN)}$ results when

successive gain A_X is "*e*", which in practice relaxes to 5.

Each inverter loses shoot-through power P_{ST}.

→ Power losses rise with more inverters in the link.

∴ Balance t_p and P_{ST}.

→ 3 to 5 stages is a typical balance.

8.2. Dead Time

Risk: Adjacent switches can short supplies.

Fix: Engage power switches only after adjacent switches shut.

Implementation:

Sense adjacent gate signals.

RC or inverter chain delay adjacent gate signals → t_{DEAD}.

NOR engages NMOSFETs only when other gate signals are low.

NAND engages PMOSFETs only when other gate signals are high.

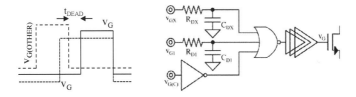

8.3. Current Sensing

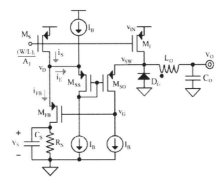

8.3. Current Sensing

Purpose:

Current-mode control.   Over-current protection.

Load-dump compensation.

Power modes: Adjust to load current.

Current-mode capacitor and inductor multipliers.

Important Features:

No additional conduction losses P_R in the power path.

No additional quiescent power P_Q.

Monitors i_L continuously.

All on chip.

Linear.

Accurate.

8.3. Series Resistances

Sense Resistor R_S: Monitor R_S's voltage $i_L R_S$.

+ Simple.

+ Accurate, if R_S is off chip.

+ Senses i_L continuously.

− R_S can vary 50–200% on chip.

− Additional P_R.   − Extra pin, if on chip.   − v_R is small ∴ Additional P_Q.

Switch's R_{DS}: Monitor R_{DS}'s voltage $i_L{}^+ R_{DS}$.

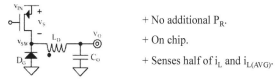

+ No additional P_R.

+ On chip.

+ Senses half of i_L and $i_{L(AVG)}$.

− R_{DS} varies 50–200% across process and temperature ∴ Inaccurate.

− v_{DS} is small and discontinuous ∴ Additional P_Q.

8.3. Inductor's Resistance

Averaged (Filtered) Difference: Monitor $R_{L.ESR}$'s voltage $i_L R_{L.ESR}$.

→ $R_F C_F$ averages (low-pass-filters) v_{SW}.

∴ $v_S = v_{SW(AVG)} - v_O \approx v_{RL.ESR} = i_{L(AVG)} R_{L.ESR}$.

But only when $v_{CF} \approx 0$ and $v_{LO} \approx v_{RL.ESR}$.

→ $Z_{CF} \ll R_F$ and $Z_{LO} \ll R_{L.ESR}$ → $\dfrac{1}{2\pi R_F C_F} \ll \dfrac{R_{L.ESR}}{2\pi L_O}$

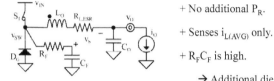

+ No additional P_R.

+ Senses $i_{L(AVG)}$ only.

+ $R_F C_F$ is high.

→ Additional die or board area.

− $R_{L.ESR}$ drifts with frequency (skin effect), temperature, and process → 50–200%.

− v_{ESR} is small ∴ Additional P_Q.

8.3. Inductor's Resistance

Matched R_F–C_F Filter: Monitor $R_{L.ESR}$'s voltage $i_L R_{L.ESR}$.

If time constants match ∴ $R_F C_F = \dfrac{L_O}{R_{L.ESR}}$.

v_L across $sL_O + R_{L.ESR}$ produces in i_L what v_L across $R_F + 1/sC_F$ does in v_S.

$$v_S = \frac{v_L}{R_F + \dfrac{1}{C_F s}}\left(\frac{1}{C_F s}\right) = \frac{v_L}{R_F C_F s + 1} = \frac{v_L}{\left(\dfrac{L_O}{R_{L.ESR}}\right)s + 1} = \frac{v_L R_{L.ESR}}{L_O s + R_{L.ESR}} = i_L R_{L.ESR}$$

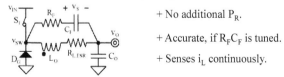

+ No additional P_R.

+ Accurate, if $R_F C_F$ is tuned.

+ Senses i_L continuously.

+ $R_F C_F$ is moderately high → On chip, but with additional die area.

− Requires tuning or trimming.

− v_{ESR} is small ∴ Additional P_Q.

8.3. Inductor's Resistance

Matched G_M–C_F Filter: Same as before, but with programmable gain.

If time constants match $\therefore$ $R_F C_F = \dfrac{L_O}{R_{L.ESR}}$.

$$v_S = \frac{v_L G_M R_F}{R_F C_F s + 1} = \frac{v_L G_M R_F}{\left(\dfrac{L_O}{R_{L.ESR}}\right)s + 1} = \frac{v_L G_M R_F R_{L.ESR}}{L_O s + R_{L.ESR}} = i_L G_M R_F R_{L.ESR}$$

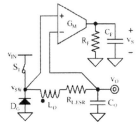

Tune: Inject i_{ac} into v_{SW} and adjust R_F

to match i_{AC}'s and v_{SW}'s phases.

Calibrate Gain: Inject I_{DC} into v_{SW} and

adjust G_M to desired gain.

+ Higher v_S.

– G_M's ICMR spans v_{SW}'s range. ⎤
                                        ⎬ Additional P_Q.
– v_L is small.   ⎦

8.3. Mirroring Sense FET

$v_{SG.S} = v_{SG.I}$ and Q_S–Q_P ensures $v_{SD.S} \approx v_{SD.I}$ $\therefore$ $i_S = \dfrac{i_L^+}{A_I}$.

M_S samples i_L^+, Q_S current-buffers i_S, and

R_S–C_S translates and holds average $\therefore$ $v_S = \dfrac{i_{L(AVG)} R_S}{A_I}$.

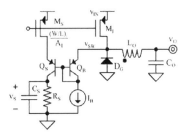

+ No additional losses

in power path.

+ On chip and lower P_Q.

+ Senses $i_{L(AVG)}$ with C_S and

half of i_L without C_S.

– $v_{SD.S} \approx v_{SD.I}$ when $i_S \approx I_B$, but not exactly otherwise $\rightarrow$ Nonlinear.

$\therefore$ $v_{SD.S}$ falls when i_O rises, so i_S is a nonlinear reflection of i_O.

– Nonlinear, mirror mismatch, and resistor tolerance $\therefore$ ±50% $\rightarrow$ Inaccurate.

8.3. Regulated Sense-FET Mirror

Negative-feedback loop regulates M_S's v_D and i_S.

v_G is the only high-resistance node

$\therefore$ One dominant low-frequency pole at v_G $\rightarrow$ Loop is stable.

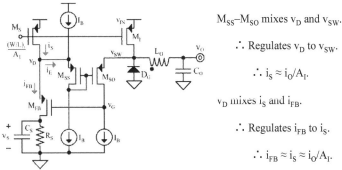

M_{SS}–M_{SO} mixes v_D and v_{SW}.

$\therefore$ Regulates v_D to v_{SW}.

$\therefore$ $i_S \approx i_O/A_I$.

v_D mixes i_S and i_{FB}.

$\therefore$ Regulates i_{FB} to i_S.

$\therefore$ $i_{FB} \approx i_S \approx i_O/A_I$.

Same as unregulated sense FET,

but without nonlinearity (i.e., ±30%) and with feedback delay (i.e., slower).

8.3. Comparison

		P_R	P_Q	Monitor	On Chip	Accuracy	Cost
	R_S	Yes	Yes	i_L	Yes	R_S	1 Pin
	R_{DS}	No	Yes	½ i_L & $i_{L(AVG)}$	Yes	R_{DS}	
$R_{L.ESR}$	R–C Filter	No	Yes	$i_{L(AVG)}$	Yes	$R_{L.ESR}$	Area
	Matched Filter	No	Yes	i_L	Yes	Tuned	Area, Tune
	G_M–C Filter	No	Yes	i_L	Yes	Tuned	Area, Tune
MOS Mirror	Unregulated	No	Lower	½ i_L & $i_{L(AVG)}$	Yes	±50%	
	Regulated	No	Lower	½ i_L & $i_{L(AVG)}$	Yes	±30%	Delay

R_{DS}, MOS mirror, and regulated MOS mirror are popular

because their accuracy-to-cost tradeoff is usually more favorable.

8.4. Boost Converters

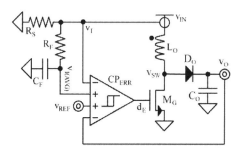

8.4. Hysteretic Current-Mode Boost

A hysteretic (relaxation) oscillator sets a constant current ripple Δi_L.

The voltage loop adjusts L_O's average current $i_{L(AVG)}$.

Operation:

A_{ERR} senses output v_O and generates error signal v_{ERR}.

Hysteretic comparator CP_I sets Δi_L and adjusts $i_{L(AVG)}$.

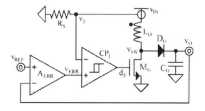

Current loop shifts L_O's p_L to high frequency.

$\therefore$ C_O's p_C dominates $\rightarrow$ $p_C \ll f_{0dB} < p_L$, z_{RHP} $\rightarrow$ Fast.

8.4. Hysteretic Current-Mode Boost

Reduce A_{ERR} to 1 → v_O feeds directly into CP_{ERR}.

Reduce $A_{LG.I0}$ to ensure $A_{LG.V0} \gg A_{LG.I0}$ → $v_I - v_{I(AVG)}$ feeds into CP_{ERR}.

Operation:

At low frequency, $v_I - v_{I(AVG)}$ is low → Current loop gain $A_{LG.I0}$ is low.

∴ Voltage loop adjusts $i_{L(AVG)}$ to regulate v_O to v_{REF}.

As C_F shunts, $v_I - v_{I(AVG)}$ rises with frequency → $A_{LG.I}$ climbs.

$A_{LG.I}$ should surpass outer loop gain $A_{LG.V}$ before reaching f_{0dB}.

∴ CP_{ERR} ripples i_L about $i_{L(AVG)}$ to hysteretic limits.

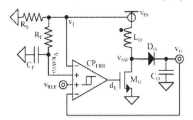

If $R_F \gg R_S$,

$A_{LG.I}$ climbs past $1/2\pi R_F C_F$.

If $1/2\pi R_F C_F$ is low,

$v_{I(AVG)} \approx i_{L(AVG)} R_S$.

8.4. Voltage-Mode Non-inverting Buck–Boost

For low gate-drive losses P_{GD}: Replace diodes with synchronized MOSFETs,

and open M_{NBST} when bucking and close M_{PBCK} when boosting.

CP_{BCK}, CP_{BST}, and v_{TRI} pulse-width-modulate (PWM) switches.

Buck: v_{ERR} is low ∴ CP_{BST} opens M_{NBST} and CP_{BCK} switches L_O.

Boost: v_{ERR} is high ∴ CP_{BCK} closes M_{PBCK} and CP_{BST} switches L_O.

Buck–Boost: v_{ERR} is mid-range ∴ CP_{BCK} and CP_{BST} energize L_O from v_{IN} to 0.

CP_{BST} drains L_O to v_O first, and then CP_{BCK} drains L_O from 0.

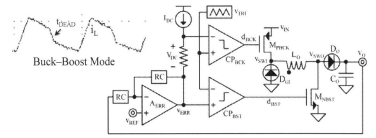

Buck–Boost Mode

8.5. Single-Inductor Multiple-Output Supplies

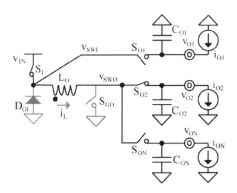

8.5. Market

Emerging applications are small and highly functional → Highly integrated.

Functions: DSPs → Programmable 0.5–1.8-V supplies.

PAs → Dynamic 3-V supplies.

ADCs and DACs → Noise-free 1.8-V supplies.

∴ Diverse v_O–i_O profiles require supplies with multiple outputs.

Battery operation requires high efficiency → Switched-inductor system.

Except power inductors are bulky ∴ Use only one inductor.

Single-inductor multiple-output (SIMO) supplies:

Extrapolate from basic converters.

→ Duty-cycle (i.e., time-multiplex) inductor between outputs.

8.5. Power Stages: Buck- and Boost-Derived Systems

Switched inductor (to v_{SWO}) implements a current source.

Output switches S_{O1}, S_{O2}...S_{ON} distribute current to outputs v_{O1}, v_{O2}...v_{ON}.

Buck SIMO

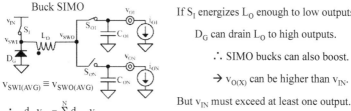

If S_I energizes L_O enough to low outputs,

D_G can drain L_O to high outputs.

$\therefore$ SIMO bucks can also boost.

$\rightarrow$ $v_{O(X)}$ can be higher than v_{IN}.

But v_{IN} must exceed at least one output.

$v_{SWI(AVG)} \equiv v_{SWO(AVG)}$

$$\therefore \quad d_{IN}v_{IN} = \sum_{K=1}^{N} d_{O(K)}v_{O(K)}$$

D_G can energize L_O to low outputs,

if D_O drains L_O enough to high outputs.

$\therefore$ SIMO boosts can also buck.

$\rightarrow$ $v_{O(X)}$ can be lower than v_{IN}.

But at least one output must exceed v_{IN}.

Boost SIMO

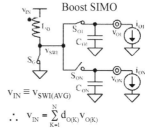

$v_{IN} \equiv v_{SWI(AVG)}$

$$\therefore \quad v_{IN} = \sum_{K=1}^{N} d_{O(K)}v_{O(K)}$$

8.5. Power Stages: Buck–Boost-Derived Systems

Switched inductor (to v_{SWO}) implements a negative current source.

Output switches S_{O1}, S_{O2}...S_{ON} distribute current to outputs v_{O1}, v_{O2}...v_{ON}.

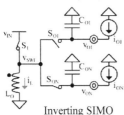

Inverting SIMO

Since all outputs are below ground,

L_O can always drain,

$\rightarrow$ $|v_{O(X)}| \geq \leq v_{IN}$.

$0 \equiv v_{SWI(AVG)}$ $\therefore$ $0 = d_{IN}v_{IN} + \sum_{K=1}^{N} d_{O(K)}v_{O(K)}$

Since all outputs are above ground,

L_O can always drain,

$\rightarrow$ $v_{O(X)} \geq \leq v_{IN}$.

$v_{SWI(AVG)} \equiv v_{SWI(AVG)}$.

$$\therefore \quad d_{IN}v_{IN} = \sum_{K=1}^{N} d_{O(K)}v_{O(K)}$$

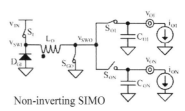

Non-inverting SIMO

8.5. Power Stages: Complementary Outputs

Non-inverting systems can also invert, and vice versa.

How: Tap into L_O's inverting terminal → Duty-cycle v_{IN}.

If S_I energizes L_O enough to ground or low outputs,

L_O can drain from negative outputs.

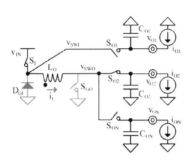

Buck SIMO: With D_{GI}, not S_{GO}.

Boost SIMO: With S_{GO}, not D_{GI}.

Non-inverting

buck–boost SIMO:

With D_{GI} and S_{GO}.

8.5. Power Stages: Charge-Pumped Outputs

How: A switching node v_{SW} initializes a flying capacitor C_F.

C_F then "flies" with v_{SW}.

A rectifier D_{CP}–C_{CP} then detects and holds peak voltage.

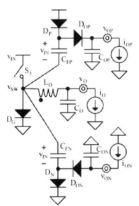

Positive Voltage:

When v_{SW} falls, D_G–D_P recharges C_{FP} to v_{IN}.

When v_{SW} rises, D_{OP}–C_{OP} holds peak $2v_{IN}$.

Negative Voltage:

When v_{SW} rises, S_I–D_N recharges C_{FN} to v_{IN}.

When v_{SW} falls, D_{ON}–C_{ON} holds peak $-v_{IN}$.

→ Replace diodes with MOSFETs to reduce losses.

→ Charge-pumped outputs are unregulated.

→ $C_{FP/N}$ and $C_{OP/N}$ occupy board or silicon area.

8.5. Dedicated Energizing Events: Energy Flow

One energizing event per output within each operating period t_O.

∴ Multiple cycles per period t_O.

One energize/drain sequence per output $v_{O(K)}$.

∴ Regulate each output → One feedback mixer per output.

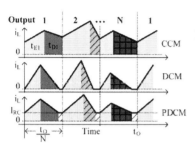

Cross-Regulation Effects:

Loop over-reactions to individual load

dumps offset L_O's i_L for other outputs.

∴ L_O over-/under-supplies other outputs.

→ Other loops react and further offset i_L.

Switching Events: t_E and t_D per v_O ∴ 2N.

Time buffer between sequences reduces cross-regulation effects.

∴ Discontinuous-conduction modes DCM and PDCM are less sensitive.

8.5. Dedicated Energizing Events: Feedback Control

PWM Current Mode:

Shared current loop turns L_O into a current source.

∴ L_O's p_L shifts to high frequency and p_C is dominant.

Time-multiplex individual error signals $v_{ERR(K)}$ into the loop with v_{CLK}.

Each error amplifier $A_{ERR(K)}$ adjusts each $t_{E(K)}-t_{D(K)}$ sequence to regulate $v_{O(K)}$.

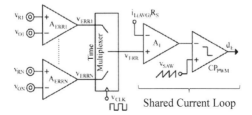

Shared Current Loop

8.5. Dedicated Energizing Events: Feedback Control

Hysteretic Current Mode:

Share one current sensor and corresponding $R_F C_F$ filter.

The hysteretic current loop is an oscillator that turns L_O to a current source.

Time-multiplex individual loop commands into power switches with v_{CLK}.

Each comparator $CP_{ERR(K)}$ adjusts each $t_{E(K)}$–$t_{D(K)}$ sequence to regulate $v_{O(K)}$.

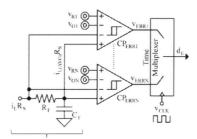

Shared Current Sensor

8.5. One Energizing Event: Energy Flow

One energizing event for all outputs within each operating period t_O.

→ Collective demand sets L_O's energizing time t_E.

→ Individual demand sets what fraction of L_O's i_L reaches each output.

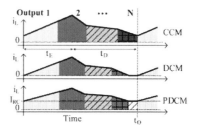

No time buffer between outputs, not even in DCM or PDCM.

∴ Considerable cross-regulation effects.

Switching Events: t_E plus one transition per v_O ∴ $1 + N$ → Less gate-drive losses.

8.5. One Energizing Event: Feedback Control

Approach:

Determine L_O's energizing time t_E from the demand of all outputs.

Distribute L_O's i_L according to the needs of each output.

Distribute i_L:

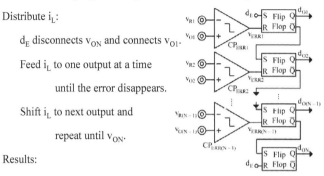

d_E disconnects v_{ON} and connects v_{O1}.

Feed i_L to one output at a time

until the error disappears.

Shift i_L to next output and

repeat until v_{ON}.

Results:

Each comparator $CP_{ERR(K)}$ regulates $v_{O(K)}$ to $v_{R(K)}$ up to $v_{O(N-1)}$.

i_L connects to $v_{O(N)}$ for what remains of the operating period t_O.

8.5. One Energizing Event: Feedback Control

Set t_E: Share the current loop that turns L_O into a current source.

Mix all outputs and their references.

Use the compounded error v_{ERR} of all outputs to set L_O's i_L.

$\therefore$ Since all errors up to $v_{O(N-1)}$ are low,

setting t_E regulates v_{ON} to v_{RN}.

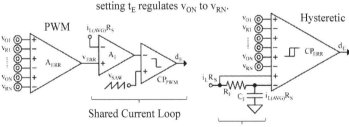

Notes on Hysteretic:

At low frequency, $i_L - i_{L(AVG)} = 0$ $\therefore$ $v_{RN} - v_{ON} \approx 0$.

Near f_{SW}, voltage loop gains are low and $i_L - i_{L(AVG)} \approx i_L$ $\therefore$ $\Delta i_L \approx CP_{ERR}$'s v_{HYS}.

Final Notes on Design

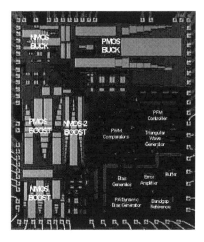

Too many factors can spoil performance, so risk only when necessary.

A bad layout or a poorly packaged die can spoil a good circuit,

　　so consider all vertical issues: from devices to application.

Good designers balance optimism with pragmatism by

　　challenging convention while catering to worst-case possibilities.

The simplest circuit is usually the fastest and most reliable solution.

The simulator is good for tweaking and validating a design,

　　not for conceptualizing circuits,

　　　　so simulate *only* when you *believe* you know what to expect.

Meaningful innovation ultimately results from intuitive and

　　insightful understanding of related technologies.

…The END…

Thanks for your interest,

and best wishes.

www.Rincon-Mora.com

Printed in Poland
by Amazon Fulfillment
Poland Sp. z o.o., Wrocław